DB2 Database Design and Administration, Version 2

Robert Heydt and Diane Heydt

WILEY

JOHN WILEY & SONS

New York   Chichester   Brisbane   Toronto   Singapore

Trademark

IBM is a registered trademark of International Business Machines Corporation, as are IMS/VS, CICS/VS, TSO/E, DB2, and RACF.

Library of Congress Cataloging-in-Publication Data:

Heydt, Robert.
   DB2 database design and administration : version 2 / Robert Heydt
and Diane Heydt.
     p. cm.
   Bibliography: p.
   ISBN 0-471-62051-3
   1. Data base management.   2. IBM Database 2 (Computer system)
I. Heydt, Diane.   II. Title.   III. Title: DB two database design and
administration.

  QA76.9.D3H49   1989
 005.75'65—dc19   88-26795
                                            CIP

Printed in the United States of America

10 9 8 7 6 5 4 3 2 1

Alyssa Lauren
and
Brenton Alexander,
the joy and perspective
in our lives

Preface

This book is intended for readers with a minimum of one year's experience with DB2. If you have never created a table or compiled and executed a DB2 program, do not read this book. On the other hand, if you will be designing DB2 tables, developing a DB2 system, managing a DB2 project, or establishing a DB2 application environment (test, production, information center, etc.), this book will save you both time and money.

At this writing, there is absolutely no doubt that DB2 is a very strategic product for IBM and the data processing community. DB2 is a very young product experiencing an evolution of design and performance. Its future will have far-reaching ramifications for all levels of users.

Distinguished from other database management systems (DBMS), DB2 did not evolve until the (relational) data model upon which it was based had matured and been precisely defined.

The relational approach was itself a response to the need for data independence, integration of flat files into data bases, access by multiple user types in multiple online sessions, ability to share data, and networks of remote data bases.

The resulting relational model provides simplicity, uniformity, completeness, data independence, and data integrity and security. Because DB2 data models are so predictable and readily modified, more prototyping of applications will occur, increasing the interaction of users and reducing development timeframes.

Until relational DBMSs became a reality, data base products were capable only of rapid retrieval of small pieces of detail information. In contrast, relational functions return results that may consist of many rows of detail. Consequently, considerably more data is being manipulated. The administrative impact of dramatically more extensive data manipulation will be felt throughout the data processing community.

Until a few years ago, distributed processing was considered nothing more than a mainframe-to-mainframe environment with a daily download to some other machine. Distributed processing within DB2 is expected to enable table joins across DB2 systems and possibly to allow personal computer tables to tie into multiple DB2 systems. The potential for distributed processing with such capabilities is tremendous.

DB2 Database Design and Administration is a complete presentation by the authors intended to apply theoretical discussion of Database 2 (DB2) concepts to the practical presentation of database design as it directly impacts performance and the realization of system objectives. Administrative issues, including naming conventions, job descriptions, delegation, and operations considerations are thoroughly discussed.

This text intends to identify the often precarious balance between design and performance in a way which will not only enlighten the reader, but will also provide a framework within which that same balance can be best achieved and maintained.

Incorporated throughout the text are comprehensive illustrations of the mechanics required to effectively address performance requirements as well as problem detection, resolution, and prevention.

Topics will evolve far beyond the typical "how to" SQL approach into a fully integrated analysis that seeks to identify all the issues before attempting to solve them, thereby reducing the risk of design obsolescence.

Procedures for automation of DBA functions have the potential to reduce staffing requirements in many DB2 installations. Furthermore, use of such procedures may also eliminate the need to purchase additional software to administer the DBA environment.

References to functional enhancements and/or differences announced with the release by IBM of DB2 Version 2 (released in October, 1988) are included for consideration.

This book will expose and exploit standard facilities within the DB2 product, currently underutilized in most DB2 installations, in ways that will turn even a DB2 novice into a productive analyst (i.e., DB2 catalog tables are presented as a potential data dictionary and design tool).

Specifically, we will present DB2 application environments, conceptual modeling, data definition language, data control language, and application design and administrative issues—all from an administrative perspective. DB2 commands, DSN commands, utilities, recovery, and security considerations are included.

DB2 Database Design and Administration is intended for all data processing professionals from application programmers to data administrators and database administrators with a minimum understanding of DB2/SQL. Additionally, those creating or working within a DB2 environment will find this writing invaluable for establishing or understanding the administration of DB2.

The text is presented in order of progression through the development of a DB2 application. While the overall objective is to integrate all topics, it is the authors' intent to deliver each chapter in a format that may be used subsequently as an independent reference.

■ FIGURE SYNTAX

In order to present design and administration of DB2, it is necessary to discuss the SQL language as well as the DB2 Commands and Utilities. Instead of the line-and-arrow-method that is used to present the SQL language syntax in most DB2 technical manuals, the authors opted for the more conventional upper case/lower case and bracket method prevalent throughout the data processing industry. In any event, instructions are not covered in minute detail (how to use an instruction can be found in a manual). Rather, the purpose of presenting these instructions is to distinguish what the instructions do and their related impact.

A typical example for a statement is shown in Figure P–1.

Uppercase words must be coded exactly as shown. Lowercase words are values that the invoker of the statement supplies. The OR sign, |, separates mutually exclusive elements. Brackets, [ ], enclose optional elements. Underscores identify default values for parameters that are omitted when coding a statement. Braces, {}, enclose elements for which one value must be coded.

In Figure P–1

CREATE TABLESPACE tablespace-name

is the only required parameter. Note that *tablespace-name* must be entered by the invoker of this statement. The following defaults would be taken within the example if the related parameters were not coded:

FIGURE P–1
STATEMENT SYNTAX

```
CREATE TABLESPACE tablespace-name
    [IN data-base-name]
    [USING
          VCAT catname |
          STOGROUP [stogroup-name | SYSDEFLT]
                    [PRIQTY integer]
                    [SECQTY integer]
                    [ERASE YES | NO]
    ]
    [FREEPAGE integer | PCTFREE integer]
    [BUFFERPOOL bufferpool]
    [SEGSIZE page-int]
    [LOCKSIZE PAGE | TABLESPACE | ANY ]
          TABLE]
    [CLOSE YES | NO]
    [DSETPASS password]
```

```
STOGROUP SYSDEFLT
ERASE NO
CLOSE YES
LOCKSIZE ANY
```

In some cases, defaults are not shown within the figure, but are discussed within the statement's description. For instance, the default for BUFFER-POOL is BPO, generally accepted knowledge at this level of discussion.

A comprehensive description follows each statement figure. The descriptions will cover design tradeoffs and considerations, administrative issues (environment, security, naming convention impact), operational suggestions, performance recommendations, and DB2 Version 2.1 differences.

■ ACKNOWLEDGMENTS

The authors would like to acknowledge the contribution made by Security Pacific Business Credit (in particular, Joseph Callilillo and Joseph Varvaro) toward the creation and verification of several of the procedures and statements included in the text. Use of such resources has significantly advanced the integrity and timeliness of this book.

Special thanks are also extended to family and friends for their invaluable support and assistance in enabling the efforts of the authors to be realized.

Edison, New Jersey   *Robert Heydt*
October 1988   *Diane Heydt*

Contents

The program, subroutines, and SQL examples contained in this publication are available in source code on diskette (IBM, 5-1/4 inch, PC-DOS 9 sector double-sided) from the authors. These disks are NOT copy protected in any way and are offered only as a convenience for programmers who do not wish to key these routines themselves. To order, send $39.95 in U.S. funds, checks, money orders, Visa, or Master Card. If you are using a credit card, include your card number, expiration date, and signature. For personal checks, allow two weeks for processing.

Send all orders to:
  Computing & Software Services
  6 Traci Lane
  Edison, NJ 08817
  Attn: Book division

- -

Please send me ＿＿ copies of DB2 Administration Routines
I am enclosing a check or money order for $39.95 for each copy
(Shipping & handling IS included).

Enclosed $＿＿＿＿＿＿ Visa ＿＿ Master Card ＿＿

Please charge my credit card number ＿＿＿＿＿＿＿＿＿＿＿＿＿＿

Signature (Order invalid unless signed)

_____

Name (please print)

_____

Expiration Date ＿＿＿＿＿＿＿＿＿＿＿＿＿＿＿＿＿＿＿

Company

_____

Address

_____

City ＿＿＿＿＿＿＿＿＿＿＿＿＿＿＿ State ＿＿＿＿＿ Zip ＿＿＿
Prices and Terms Subject to Change Without Notice

Introduction

Database 2 (DB2) is the relational data base management system (DBMS) offered by IBM for MVS environments. DB2 supports simultaneous accesses to data from CICS, IMS DC, and TSO foreground and background. Such access may be achieved by applications written in COBOL, PL/I, Assembler, or Fortran through use of DB2's user interface language, **Structured Query Language** (SQL).[1]

DB2 as a data base management system is based on concepts of the relational data model. Introduced by Dr. Edgar Codd in 1970, relational technology is derived from the application of mathematical principles to data base management. Codd's work remains as the foundation of all relational development.

Relational theory draws most of its import from its distinction between user views of data and the physical storage representation of the same. While most nonrelational data base management systems require some knowledge and manipulation of data based on physical storage concepts, relational theory presents data for manipulation in the form of table sets without limitations based on storage considerations. In fact, manipulation of relational table structures (composed of rows and columns) itself produces result tables, which in turn may be the object of further manipulation. This data independence and the consistency of table handling mean that access strategies will be transparent to the user and insulated from many physical storage modifications.

DB2 is divided into two major service categories: Database services and System service. **Database services** basically manage user data, essentially through SQL requests. **System services**, in contrast, deal with more internal functions such as DB2 commands, statistics, virtual storage, recovery processes, and attachment and startup/shutdown functions.

---

[1] *Sequel* is the accepted pronunciation of the acronym.

As previously stated, DB2 represents data to the user in table form. Data definition, manipulation, access, and control is managed by SQL through one of its three component languages: Data Definition Language (DDL), Data Manipulation Language (DML), and Data Control Language (DCL).

Data Definition Language (DDL) defines all DB2 objects.

Data Manipulation Language (DML), as its name implies, is used to retrieve, update, insert, and delete any data stored within DB2 tables with a somewhat free-form language that may be executed interactively or as embedded code within a program. A powerful component of SQL, DML operates on entire sets of table rows at a time, unlike most other high-level languages.

Data Control Language (DCL) explicitly extends privileges to potential users of DB2 objects through the two primary commands, GRANT and REVOKE. This is in contrast to implicit privileges obtained by users without the use of DCL, most commonly in cases where ownership of a DB2 object has been established or administrative authority applies.[2]

SQL is a high-level, nonprocedural language consisting of commands, keywords, and parameters. Because SQL is structured in a format consistent with the English language, it provides a framework within which both end users and programmers may develop a narrow specification of data requirements. SQL applies strictly to data base management without regard to elements of program control. Consequently, its strongest impact is to free application development languages from the burden of data base structure.

DB2 in interactive mode (**DB2I**) provides programmers and some users with the capability not only to debug SQL statements and execute DB2 utilities, but also to install DB2 itself.

The **Data Extract facility** (DXT) allows data to be extracted from IMS, VSAM, SQL/DS, or sequential storage structures in a format suitable for load processing into DB2 tables. DXT is not included as part of the basic DB2 installation, but is available at an additional charge.

The **Query Management Facility** (QMF) assists end users in interactive report design and generation through two alternative methods: SQL and **Query By Example** (QBE). Reporting may range from default format to highly tailored presentations at the user's request. The report capabilities of QMF may serve as an integral part of design review, application debugging, or special request processing—all with minimal interaction between the programmer and user.

Comprehensive storage of data definitions and access authorization for all DB2 objects is maintained in special DB2 tables collectively called the **DB2 catalog**. The catalog is controlled by DB2 and contains information that may be accessed by any authorized user as if it were any common DB2 table. As such, its potential as a resource or even a quasi-data dictionary is unlimited.

---

[2] This topic will be thoroughly discussed in Chapter 11 of this book.

■ HISTORY

Unlike other data base management systems, DB2 (and its predecessors) did not evolve until the data model upon which it was based (i.e., the relational data model) had matured and been precisely defined. Translation of Codd's relational theory into a functional data model has developed through research and prototyping of relational languages and data base systems in a way that embodies the principles of Codd's model.

Significant among language prototypes, Structured English Query Language (SEQUEL) was introduced by IBM in 1974 and revised in 1976. With the definition of a relational language prototype known as SQL, IBM research produced a compatible data base prototype, which became operational in 1977. This prototype, dubbed **System R**, was so well accepted that it spawned several efforts by IBM aimed at incorporating SQL into a line of relational products. Thus, SQL/DS for VM operating systems (1982) and DB2 for MVS environments (1983) remain today the most popular mainframe applications of relational DBMS theory.

Introduction of Codd's relational theory (and DB2 in particular) was in total harmony with economic and technical shifts in the data processing environment. Once the primary target of cost control measures, hardware expenses were rapidly being exceeded by the costs of employing computer personnel trained to use the hardware. User groups were downgrading software requests to levels thought to be achievable by technical staff in a reasonable timeframe, rather than to levels that addressed true user requirements. Demand was strong for a data base management system that would raise programmer productivity to levels that would satisfy real user needs, as well as allow users to interact directly with the system, both in terms of application development and real time information requests. Consequently, a DBMS architecture had to incorporate access to data in several forms, across several environments, by multiple users. This implied a simplicity in a design model that could be employed by programmers and users alike, reduce lead time for application development, and handle high-volume data processing with security and integrity as well as acceptable performance through the entire time frame from system origin to the realization of system growth potential. The DBMS must also offer increased participation by the user in development phases as well as provide capability for formatted report generation and problem analysis of existing applications.

The relational approach was itself a response to the need for data independence, integration of flat files into data bases, simultaneous access by multiple user types in multiple online sessions, ability to share data, and networks of remote data bases. The resulting relational model provides simplicity, uniformity, completeness, data independence, and data integrity and security.[3] It is obvious that there exists a strong compatibility between the

[3] This historical perspective is presented by C. J. Date in *Relational Database: Selected Writings.*

objectives demanded in a new DBMS based on the changing technical and economic environment and those designed into the relational data model, SQL/DS (which executes under a VM operating system), and its successor, DB2.

■ FUTURE OF DB2

At this point there is absolutely no doubt that DB2 is a very strategic product for IBM and the data processing community. Its future will have far-reaching ramifications for all levels of users. DB2 shows great promise for promotion of Codd's relational model, a model that may grow to accommodate new data types and access path selection criteria. Because DB2 data models are so predictable and readily modified, more prototyping of applications will occur, increasing the interaction of users and reducing development timeframes. Nevertheless, DB2 is a very young product still experiencing an evolution of design and performance. Other DBMS products have been available since the early 1970s, leaving data processing professionals with preconceived notions about the nature of mature data base structures and processing.

The area of most concern about DB2 at this writing is the excessive Input/Output (I/O) that will be necessary to support **referential integrity**. For an employee-to-department (one-to-many) relationship, DB2 Version 2 will likely be satisfactory. However, an association of projects-to-employees (many-to-many) will require the use of a junction table that with current hardware will result in inordinate I/O. With the projected utilization of VSAM LINEAR data sets and Expanded Storage Management (ESM),[4] however, the wait for data retrieval will be more acceptable.

There are also discrepancies that need to be rectified between Codd's relational data model and its representation by DB2. According to Dr. Codd, IBM's DB2 needs to improve its support of domains and updatability; however, it still outranks any other product on the market in its application of the relational model.[5]

To the seasoned data base user of conventional structures, the most obvious missing element of DB2 is the data dictionary capability. If the user examines DB2 functionality rather than similarity to previous DBMSs, however, he or she will recognize the data dictionary capacity of DB2. Dictionaries are traditionally employed as a control mechanism and/or a development tool. As a control mechanism, the current DB2 catalog structure is capable of supporting over 95% of the control requirements of an installation. The LABEL ON and COMMENT ON facilities, in conjunction with the tables that manage PLAN information, can answer all control related questions except "Which

[4] New IBM software products.
[5] E. F. Codd, The Relational Institute, 1986.

programs use what columns?"[6] If history repeats itself, other vendors will develop dictionaries to compete with those announced by IBM. Even more likely is the possibility that installations will find it faster and more economical to develop their own dictionaries by augmenting the DB2 catalogs with private tables.

Until relational DBMSs became a reality, data base products had only to be concerned with rapid retrieval of small pieces of detail information. In contrast, relational built-in functions return results information that may consist of many rows of detail. Consequently, considerably more data is being manipulated. In order to support this tremendous amount of item retrieval in a timely fashion, extensive data buffers are required. The buffers serve two purposes. First, they allow one I/O request to return multiple pages of details. Second, once data is returned it may stay resident long enough to avoid additional read operations. Even when browsing details, the issue is not that DB2 requires more I/O, but rather the point at which the actual I/O is performed. With the exception of single table unordered retrieval, all I/O is completed prior to a program's first FETCH request! Given a poorly coded program/query that retrieves too many rows, it is no surprise that a user may pray for a response when depressing the ENTER key on a keyboard.

The authors had anticipated an announcement for a "back end" data base machine that would support enormous amounts of memory such that complete data bases/tables could remain resident in huge buffer pools. The IBM 3090-600E series (or better) and 370/ESA architecture is a step in that direction. Figure 1–1 illustrates the virtual addressability of MVS (16 million bytes), MVS/XA (2 billion bytes), and MVS/ESA (16 trillion bytes). However, the current maximum real memory size is still constrained to 256 Megabytes by 3090E architecture.

As ESA is exploited by DB2 with the utilization of ESM and LINEAR data sets, the I/O problems inherent in DB2 will diminish. The initial I/O delays will disappear as tables become more memory resident. With respect to the issue of referential integrity in the relational model as reflected by DB2 implementation, it may well be that IBM was wise to delay support of referential integrity until announcing an operating system architecture that could support the associated processing. The resulting I/O under MVS/XA may be unacceptable.

An interesting phenomenon has been occurring in the personal computer world: Let's call it the "faster and smaller" syndrome. A person may have a PC on his/her desk that has the processing speed of some presently used mainframes (4 to 5 mips). There is an insatiable need for data to be used within word processors and spread sheet programs that execute on these machines. Accustomed to their PCs' processing speed, people wanting this data cannot understand why it takes so long for it to be transferred to their

6 See Chapter 2 for a description of DB2 catalog tables functioning as a quasi-data dictionary.

FIGURE 1–1
OPERATING SYSTEM ADDRESSABILITY

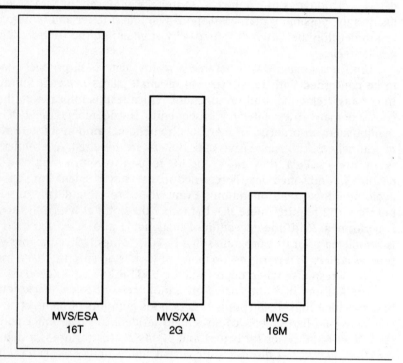

| MVS/ESA | MVS/XA | MVS |
| 16T | 2G | 16M |

PC from a mainframe that is only a few hundred feet away. Because of economy of scale, IBM will be able to satisfy this requirement very quickly. The problem has been that, until a few years ago, distributed processing was considered nothing more than a mainframe-to-mainframe environment with a daily download to some other machine. With the current endless appetite for data at the PC level, however, distributed processing is being redefined.

Distributed processing is expected to enable table joins across DB2 systems and, possibly, to tie personal computer tables into the multiple DB2 systems. System architecture to facilitate such processing would require a universal language (such as C Language for the PC) for use by mainframes and personal computers alike. The potential for distributed processing with such capabilities is tremendous.

With data stored within SQL-type tables, it will become advantageous to JOIN data from tables located at different nodes (i.e., mainframes) as well as those on mini- and microcomputer systems. The demand for high-speed telecommunications will be unrelenting. DB2 distributed processing (R-STAR) will finally become a reality.

Another future requirement will be greater portability. SQL must become portable across the spectrum of machines, ranging from mainframes to personal computer systems, together with an application language (which should also be portable) to interface with SQL. As just discussed, that language will probably be C Language. Currently, C Language compilers are available for mainframe, micro-, and minicomputers. On the other hand, DB2 or SQL/DS is available only for mainframes, with a subset of SQL planned for PCs (minis) as a part of OS/2 Extended Edition. At this time there is no SQL type of DBMS planned for the System 3X series. Moreover, System 3X series machines have a difficult time talking with one another, as well as with mainframes and minis. For these reasons you may expect an announcement of the replacement for this level of processors that will include a SQL type of DBMS with communication compatibility with other processors.

Development is the final area to be viewed through the authors' crystal ball. There is a need to create tools for rapid application development that are portable and transparent to both the operating system and teleprocessing access method. We have pointed out the need for a portable language because, even though applications can be developed very quickly with high-level languages, development still isn't fast enough. Just as languages utilize libraries of common system routines, swift application development will necessitate a collection of standardized application procedures. Given such a collection, only nonstandard application processes would require custom coding. **Cross System Product** (CSP) is an initial effort at adopting a common repository for predefined application processes. Much work must be done in this area to facilitate control and migration of source statements and object code.

Many batch applications are operating system and hardware transparent. However, when it comes to interfacing with a terminal, things become a bit clouded. Again, Cross System Product (CSP) is an attempt at progress in this direction. CSP will generate the necessary terminal interfaces for either TSO or CICS, but not for IMS-DC. In addition to the technical issues, screen functions must be standardized. Windowing within TSO is implemented differently than for most PC packages. It doesn't exist at all for CICS. We don't expect a generalized TP access method specifically for DB2. Rather, an add-on feature will be offered to interface with **Graphics Display Device Manager** (GDDM). In turn, GDDM, in one form or another, will be available throughout some of IBM's product line.

■ APPLICATION ENVIRONMENTS

DB2 exists as a subsystem in an MVS environment with up to three other subsystems: **IMS, CICS,** and **TSO.** DB2 is connected to these subsystems by their respective **call attachment facilities.** The TSO attachment facility is required to run TSO or batch applications that access DB2 data, to use DB2 interactive panels supplied with DB2, or to bind application programs. TSO access may be batch (via the terminal monitor program, TMP) or online from a TSO terminal but may not access any IMS data bases. The DSN subcommand processor used in conjunction with TSO transfers commands to DB2 for processing. However, because it can establish a connection to DB2 only when DB2 is running, it may not be used to start DB2 itself. ISPF panels provided with DB2 offer an interactive way to invoke the performance of SQL commands (SPUFI processing), program preparation, DB2 commands, utilities, and help facilities. The IMS and CICS attachment facilities translate the requests for DB2 data from IMS/VS and CICS applications, respectively. DB2 is able to support IMS and CICS application DB2 data requests because its data base recovery capabilities function in concert with those of IMS and CICS. With the exception of the actual coding of DB2 data base access requests, most other indications of the connection to IMS/VS or CICS by DB2 are generally transparent to the application coder. Both the IMS/VS and CICS master console operators are able to monitor and control several DB2 functions. DB2 applications accessing IMS or CICS communications facilities must be <u>online</u> and may access IMS data bases as well as other DB2 tables. DB2 is capable of sharing its data bases concurrently with multiple CICS and/or IMS address spaces and/or TSO sessions because of its security mechanism. Additionally, one IMS subsystem may concurrently access more than one DB2 subsystem while one CICS address space may access only one DB2 subsystem.

■ DB2 OBJECTS

Something is classified as a DB2 object if it is defined in the DB2 catalog and can be manipulated by a SQL statement.

The most encompassing object of DB2 is the **data base**; all components related to the data base pertain to it exclusively. At the same time, a data base is not a physical object. Rather, it is an entry in the DB2 catalog that administratively connects and controls tablespaces. In this sense, a data base can be considered the administrative overview of the relation. The data base is the smallest unit referenced by a START or STOP request, so it is clear that there are operational ramifications for the groupings within the data base.

Each data base is, in turn, divided into space components for tables and indices. Space components are collections of physical storage blocks, or pages, used as the unit of transfer for I/O operations.

Tablespaces contains one or more[7] DB2 **tables** within its physical storage representation. Tables are the DB2 objects that contain data in the format of rows and columns. Within a given table, all rows contain the same columns, although the actual content may differ or be NULL. Tables may

---

[7] Usually one for performance purposes (i.e., locking at the tablespace level will lock <u>all</u> tables within the tablespace, not just the one desired).

not extend beyond one tablespace. In this way, tablespaces are the unit of recovery and reorganization in DB2. A tablespace may be divided into multiple **partitions** if its size would otherwise be unwieldy for such operations. Partitions are also utilized to vary device types and to speed processing activity. The partitions may then be independently reorganized or recovered.

An **indexspace** must contain only one **index**, which must be self-contained within the indexspace. Indices contain pointers (known as Row IDs or RIDs) to data within DB2 tables, based on the values of the data. A table may have multiple indices. An index may be created at any time after the creation of the table to which it corresponds. Indices are defined for a table to ensure uniqueness among rows, increase performance for data access, designate data clustering during table population, or specify partitions based on key ranges for a very large table. However, the user is not able to specify to DB2 when a particular index should be used (although he is responsible for creation and deletion). The EXPLAIN command may be issued during the BIND of a plan or via SPUFI to disclose to the user the index that DB2 intends to invoke for a given SQL request. A tablespace must be related to a data base with all its corresponding indices. Since there can be only one index per indexspace, DB2 automatically allocates the indexspace when the index is created. As with tablespaces, indexspaces (including partitions) may be recovered and reorganized separately. Indices are defined for a table to ensure uniqueness, increase performance for data access, designate data sequence (clustering) during table population, or to specify partitions based on key ranges for a very large table.

Each space (table or index) is resident on a physical storage device defined to be part of a **stogroup**. A stogroup is simply a collection of direct access storage device (DASD) of the same device type. Storage is extended automatically as necessary within the stogroup for a DB2 table or index; no explicit request is made by the user. VSAM ESDS datasets are used to store all spaces within the stogroup, even indexspaces. Unlike other constraints, a stogroup may contain spaces that will be controlled by several different data bases. Further, a data base does not necessarily have to specify one stogroup. In this way, different device types can be chosen for different spaces as appropriate for their anticipated access. For example, an indexspace may be resident in a stogroup using a faster device type than its corresponding tablespace, or different stogroups may be specified to reduce DASD contention.

A **view** is an alternative method of presenting data to a user without actually requiring storage space. It may contain subsets of tables or joins between them and, as such, may encompass more than one data base.[8]

Bufferpools are areas of temporary storage in memory for pages of tables or indices invoked by DB2 access requests. DB2 retrieves the page of

[8] Please refer to the discussion of views later in this chapter within the *Security* and *Why Use DB2* sections.

data containing the requested row into a buffer if it does not already exist in a buffer.[9]

Locks enable concurrency—simultaneous access to the same data from multiple users. Locks accomplish concurrency by preventing data errors such as lost updates and thereby increase the integrity of the data.[10]

■ CONTINUOUS OPERATION

DB2 allows several functions to occur as long as it is running. These include the creation and dropping of tables; retrieval of data; insertion, deletion, and update of rows within a table; the addition of columns to a table; and the granting and revoking of privileges to accomplish the preceding functions.

Twenty-four hour operation is possible because maintenance functions can be performed concurrently with the preceding functions. Tables may be reorganized, image copied, or recovered at any time.

■ SECURITY

DB2 employs three major security mechanisms to control the authorization and integrity of data access within a given application: a DB2 subsystem of **privilege authorization**, a sophisticated **transaction tracking and locking mechanism**, and a less tangible feature in the **view**. All three mechanisms, however, are inextricably intertwined with the **authorization identifier** (AUTHID) used to access DB2. AUTHID is the method of establishing the legitimacy of one's access to the subsystem that connects to DB2. Since DB2 must be attached to at least one subsystem (IMS/VS DC, CICS/VS, or TSO/E) in order to execute, entry authorization checking is performed at the subsystem level, independent of DB2. Consequently, a user who is capable of gaining access to the subsystem connected to DB2 will automatically have his authorization ID passed to DB2 for further processing. It is at this point that DB2 employs its internal controls.

The DB2 subsystem of privilege authorization consists of the provision of specific system capabilities against a specific number of levels of system resources. In order to execute a request against DB2 data, a user must be authorized with the capability, or privilege, to perform the requested action. Privileges may be issued at the table, plan, data base, user, or system level.

---

[9] DB2 does not retrieve data that already exists in a buffer, allowing efficiency in I/O processing. It is up to the application to maximize the benefit of this efficiency.

[10] Please refer to the section on *Security* in this chapter for a more complete discussion of the lock mechanism.

They may be extended to a specific user individually or on a group basis, depending upon the level of intended authorization of the user.[11]

Briefly, privileges are extended by means of the **GRANT** command and taken away by the **REVOKE** command. GRANT enables one user to provide a privilege to another user; thus, the system administrator is the ultimate point of origin of all privileges. REVOKE disables the privileges previously extended to a user via a GRANT command. Moreover, REVOKE acts with a **cascading effect** to revoke any privileges that have been extended to another user exclusively by the user whose authorization is being revoked. Therefore, it is important that a user be aware of the origin of his particular authority. Any revoked privilege may be reinstated by issuance of another GRANT command by an authorized user.

DB2 provides a mechanism for transaction tracking and locking which ensures recovery and data integrity in a concurrent environment. Because DB2 is subordinate to the subsystems to which it connects, DB2 is subject to subsystem transaction management controls in order to bring a transaction to completion. Transaction status is impacted by the COMMIT and ROLLBACK statements. COMMIT indicates that all phases of the transaction have terminated appropriately and that the associated updates should be permanently incorporated into the system. On the other hand, ROLLBACK indicates an error in some phase, which should cause the "backing out" of any updates associated with the unsuccessful transaction.

The IMS/VS Resource Lock Manager (IRLM), as the locking feature of DB2's security mechanism, manages all requests for locks and controls access to DB2 and IMS data bases. As such, it guarantees that the data manipulated by one user will be in a predictable state, unmolested by another user who may be concurrently trying to access it. The lock will remain in effect until the invoked transaction has been committed by DB2.

Locks will be established on a first-come, first-serve basis in **share** or **exclusive** mode, depending upon the nature of the data request. The requests are analyzed for compatibility with one another before the locks are established. Basically, an update request requires an exclusive lock on a resource and must wait until all other locks are released by other users, even if they are only share locks (i.e., read only). A share lock may be acquired only if there does not already exist an exclusive lock against the resource. In other words, exclusive locking is just that—incompatible with any other type of lock request—whereas shared locking may peacefully coexist with other share lock requests. Of course, lock requests may go into prolonged wait states, particularly in the case of a deadlock where two transactions are tying up each other's resources in such a way that a COMMIT of either transaction (and thus, release of a lock) will never be achieved. In such a prolonged wait

---

11 For example, the system administrator at the highest level of authorization has many privileges extended to his or her AUTHID on a group basis.

state, DB2 will designate one transaction to proceed (i.e., succeed in obtaining the lock required) and all others to fail, either by automatic ROLLBACK or by requesting the user to issue a ROLLBACK. A **SQLCODE** will be issued to indicate the deadlock situation.

Locks may be employed at the page, table, or tablespace level. For this reason, it is usually advisable to allocate only one table to a tablespace. Otherwise, inadvertent locking of unrelated tables may occur.

DB2 provides the concept of the view to effectively limit table access to the record level, if necessary. A DB2 view is an alternative presentation of tables to the user in a way in which sensitive data may be excluded from the specific user's access. No actual storage is used by the alternate data representation; the view is processed at the time of request based on information stored in the DB2 catalog. Additionally, a view may encompass data across multiple tables without the awareness of the user.

In this approach, DB2 enables security administrators to restrict access to data inappropriate for a user painlessly and without totally denying access to associated data that may not be restricted. This is all possible within the current framework of DB2 without proliferation of additional tables. Remember, however, that a view does relate to an underlying table that physically exists. Care should be used in allowing the user to possess update privileges against the view. Use of the "WITH CHECK OPTION" clause of the view definition will ensure that all requests for update or insertion of rows into a view are compatible with the view definition itself.

■ WHY USE DB2?

Perhaps the feature of DB2 that makes it preferable to a multitude of other data base management systems is its appeal to the end user whose business requirements have been progressively compromised in recent history. A nonprocedural language, DB2 code states the problem—not the procedure required to resolve it. Moreover, it operates in terms of sets that are specifically defined for the data relation in question. There are no hidden relationships built into the structure to intimidate the user. Therefore, DB2 is adaptable to a wide range of skill levels. Since projections are for more rapid growth in the number of casual online users than in all other categories, the appeal to users with a broader range of skill levels is more significant. This, in turn, promises to further education and productivity in its use.

DB2 operates within a table structure that is the same data model for users and technical developers. Since tables most closely exhibit the qualities of flat files, logical data structure is simpler. There are three advantages to this. First, this data model brings users closer to development sooner than would be the case in other data models. Application understanding during development is increased as well as monitored <u>throughout</u> the <u>design process</u>, rather than at the end, when design errors brought on by misinterpretation of user requests represent costly if not formidable modifications. Second, the data model built around a table concept is more easily reduced for distribution to all skill levels involved in the application development than might otherwise be the case. Design can be done in phases and modified for additional requirements or error detection through normalization techniques. Third, normal form lends more stability to the design model by reducing redundancy.[12] These considerations taken together will stimulate the utilization of <u>system</u> <u>prototyping</u>—the development of high-level models within a small timeframe to bring the user immediate feedback as to the progress of the application under development. Such prototyping is significant in that it introduces feedback at a point where corrections make more sense and are simpler to implement.

The independence of logical data representation from physical data representation enables modification to data base structure without a corresponding change to the program accessing it. Access strategies such as index utilization are automatically incorporated as appropriate into the execution of a program through a feature called **automatic rebind**. This feature is capable of evaluating the access data available to it and modifying the **access path strategy** (determined by the BIND process) of the program in question. This type of automatic access adjustment is possible due to the noninterpretive nature of DB2. That is to say that DB2 uses a compilation approach to data requests: Requests are converted from SQL commands and parameters to the executable code of the language in which the program is written. Performance is enhanced since the interpretation of commands is not left until execution time.

An advantage of the independence of physical data from logical design is the possibility of adding a new table within an existing data base (or column to an existing table) without interfering with the work of current users of the system. This is especially appropriate for applications where a large number of relationships exist, or where several relationships may initially be unidentified or subject to change.

Performance of DB2 as a data base management system has been much maligned. Controversy usually centers on the use of DB2 as an information center and the associated conflict with other planned activities. It is certainly acknowledged that there will be conflicts of this type whenever spontaneous and planned activities must compete for the same resources. However, we should not lose sight of the fact that DB2 at least allows us the flexibility to choose between spontaneous and planned activities—something not available in other DBMSs. Further, there is not necessarily a need to run both types of activities at the same time. Control mechanisms exist to enable scheduling of the events.

The high-level nature of the relational language incorporates semantics

12 However, third normal form optimizes update at the expense of retrieval and may require some adjustment on that basis.

to tell the system what the user is trying to accomplish. This is an advantage over a nonrelational system, which cannot always detect when the user is in error. After compilation, a tailored code is produced that captures the user's intent.

The pathlength of instruction execution is likely to be less for a compilation approach DBMS such as DB2 than for an interpretive one. This is because the access strategy is chosen, execution authorization checked, and machine code generated from most SQL instructions before execution takes place. This reduction in runtime is not at the expense of flexibility; remember that a change of access strategy prompted by a change of physical data representation is incorporated by automatic rebind.

Beyond pathlength, the actual number of I/O operations may be reduced by being rendered more effective by the access strategy choices of the system. Optimization may be greater when performed by the system rather than by the programmer because the system has more information generally available to it. The system optimizer is aware of how data is actually clustered, the table size, index selectivity, and complexity of the requested access, among many other items. Because DB2 is constantly reviewing this information, up-to-date strategies are reflected before any execution takes place. The process of adjusting these access strategies within DB2 is itself a trivial matter, as already discussed in automatic rebind. Hierarchic structures, in contrast, force the programmer to choose an access path by anticipation of factors, usually when initially coding a program. Furthermore, every DB2 JOIN or UNION request is itself a relationship; this cannot be extended to hierarchic linkage of relationships. This is not to say that nonrelational systems will not have tailored code that succeeds in more impressive performance. There is ample evidence to demonstrate that data forming a natural hierarchy that is anticipated to be stable for all applications is much better served, to date, by a hierarchic data structure.

This is true particularly if a given application needs access to only one data record, or at least one record at a time. Further, in an environment where resource constraints and performance tuning are more significant than flexibility of design, hierarchic data structures are, again, the appropriate choice at this writing. However, with the addition of new applications, especially those that change the logical structure of the data model, performance is often substantially degraded by lack of flexibility.

Flexibility is significantly reduced in a hierarchic structure due to the use of parent-child links to represent the user view of data. To a significant degree, logical relationships are represented by the physical structure itself. Nonrelational links, insofar as they are both physical and logical, are rendered more static than relational foreign key usage. Relational data structures represent all relationships between data values strictly by the values themselves—it's that simple. All equivalent data values for the same column represent the same relationship. Further, relational data values are not directional as are parent-child links; the relationship is consistent when taken from either direction. Each operation performed on a relational table occurs in terms of table rows and columns identified by the values they contain, not on implicit relationships and dependencies as in hierarchic systems. For each new link that must be added to a hierarchic structure to represent a user view, a new access path will be created. Again, given the physical nature of links, such design modification becomes extremely complex. Links add complexity but not power to hierarchic structures; there is nothing that may be represented in a hierarchic structure that cannot be paralleled by relational representation. In fact, a hierarchic link is capable of representing only a one-to-many relationship, whereas relational design may represent many-to-many relationships.

All this flexibility is certainly not without cost, at least at the moment. There is currently a lack of support in DB2 for foreign key constraints. That is, there is no mechanism to guarantee that all occurrences of a foreign key column reference will be modified (or deleted) to correspond to a modification in the key itself, and vice versa. However, it is expected that a future release of DB2 will incorporate corrections for this shortcoming. In any case, flexibility may be well worth the price of monitoring foreign keys within the application.

The level at which data manipulation occurs between hierarchic and relational data models also contributes to the relative complexity of each. Relational models, DB2 models in particular, provide only one way to express most data manipulation requests. A manipulative expression is actually a definition of the set of data values requested—direct support for relational theory, which states that all data values are acted upon in sets. As previously discussed, relational model relationships are always represented by the values of the data within the table structures. Because all relationships are represented in a similar manner (i.e., field data values), data manipulation requests of the relationships are similar in format. Since there is only subtle latitude in the way in which data requests may be formed, communication is more effective (one request per set rather than one request per element), and there is a lower incidence of decision error regarding the request. Further, the result of each table set operation is itself a table that may, in turn, be used as input to another set level operation. The functionality of DB2 Data Manipulation Language (DML) is maximized since it accomplishes retrieval without branching. Hierarchic data manipulation occurs on an element-by-element basis, thereby making direct representation of a relationship too complex to support in most instances. Retrieval occurs within a procedure rather than simply a statement.

The fact that DB2 Data Manipulation Language (DML) uses nonembedded commands and parameters makes its intent obvious to the optimizer, which may in turn dynamically determine access strategy using information it has available to it at all times. Data clustering may be achieved through judicious use of the REORG utility.

DB2, in its user orientation, reduces dramatically the amount of development and maintenance time required to achieve functionality. Clearly, the tradeoff between performance of hierarchic structures and usability of relational models becomes the issue.

DB2 provides sophisticated security capabilities which effectively limit table access to the row and column level and provides both a basis for transaction recovery or concurrent execution and authorization specific to an individual user. Finally, a major feature offered within the security framework is the concept of a view. A DB2 view provides a simplistic presentation to multiple users based on variable sets of criteria without use of actual storage.

■ REFERENCES

C. J. Date, *Relational Database: Selected Writings* (Reading, MA: Addison-Wesley, 1986).

C. J. Date, *A Guide to DB2*, (Reading, MA: Addison-Wesley, 1984).

Sam Kahn, "An Overview of Three Relational Data Base Products," *IBM Systems Journal*, Vol. 23, No.2 (1984), p. 100.

Goren Sandberg, IBM Sweden, *IBM Database 2 Relational Concepts* (Santa Teresa, CA: International Systems Center, 1983).

Richard Hale Shaw, "SQL: An Emerging Database Standard for PC's," *PC Magazine* (May 17, 1988), p. 275.

CHAPTER 2

Conceptual Model

As relational data base systems begin to penetrate the marketplace, the need for sound design methodology becomes critical. In a data processing environment historically saturated with theory that is rarely translated into promised performance, such methodology will likely determine the extent to which potential implementation of relational concepts will be realized and sustained.

The relational design methodology offered in the following text transforms a user view of system requirements into a **conceptual model**. The derivation of a conceptual model addresses the dynamic nature of system requirements through <u>data</u> <u>independence</u>, the separation of logical from physical design considerations. It is precisely this separation which exploits the flexibility and, therefore, the stability of relational theory.

The conceptual model ultimately derived reconciles two familiar design approaches, entity modeling and normalization, into a **composite logical design**. The composite logical design (CLD) will be mapped to the physical DBMS of implementation. The mapping process translates the optimized ("reconciled") relations into data access paths. These data access paths will enable the required operational performance levels to be achieved within the physical constraints of the DBMS. Note that the authors are not declaring that physical considerations are insignificant but that they are more effectively addressed after the independent logical design has been derived. The logical design may then function as an interface between data structures and the physical processes that manipulate them. In fact, the logical design has validity for the physical requirements of both relational and hierarchical DBMSs. Further, the design methodology as presented in this book recognizes the complementary nature of the top-down approach of the entity model and the bottom-up approach of normalization. Please refer to Figure 2–1 for a schematic representation of this concept.

The composite logical design (CLD) produced from such a union yields the best of both worlds: Higher-level user requirements (**process orientation**) are refined by a more detailed **data orientation**. Result: greater

FIGURE 2–1
MODELING PROCESS FLOW

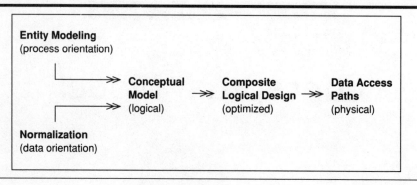

flexibility and ease of implementation than would have resulted from either approach taken in isolation. Performance is improved in terms of <u>user satisfaction</u> and <u>physical</u> <u>processing</u>.

Too often, the business needs of a system under development are sacrificed for the physical aspects of system implementation. Do not underestimate the importance of user satisfaction in the design process. Management (and ultimately, users) must be thoroughly convinced of and sincerely sympathetic toward the merits of the design methodology with respect to the cost and time horizons at issue. This commitment must be maintained through the implementation phase of the design in order for its potential to be realized and manifested to the user. Therefore, a carefully thought out entity model is critical to the high-level orientation necessary for an understanding of the objectives of the design at all levels. Further, a high-level design presentation gives management and user groups what they may need most: an immediate deliverable to hold in their hands, as well as a feeling of participation in, rather than alienation from, the design process. Psychological comfort aside, the high-level presentation will dramatically reduce the probability of serious design flaws, since all subsequent commitment to a deficient model will serve only to multiply errors in exponential fashion.

■ THE ENTITY MODEL: A SYNTHETIC APPROACH

Entity modeling is the synthesis of a detailed logical data structure from a high-level external user view of application system requirements. This synthetic approach has as its basic modeling unit the **entity**; simply, any discernible object, tangible or conceptual, about which information is to be stored and retrieved.

Books, publishers, and *orders* may all qualify as entities.

FIGURE 2–2a
SIMPLISTIC PROCESS ORIENTATION

Authors write books	(1 – M) and (M – 1)
Books have titles	(1 – 1)
Books have subjects	(1 – M)
Books have prices	(1 – M)
Books have publishers	(1 – 1)
Publishers publish books	(1 – M)
Publishers are located in cities	(M – M)
Publishers have names	(1 – 1)
Publishers distribute books based upon orders	(M – M)
Orders involve quantities	(1 – M)
Orders involve publishers	(1 – M)
Orders involve books	(1 – M)

The user view identifies and classifies all system entities by processing volume, frequency, type, definition, and usage within the given system requirements. This user view drives the process orientation of the entity model. The actual data structures associated with an entity are classified at a later stage of model development during normalization; thus, the distinction between process and data orientation (comparatively depicted in Figure 2–2a and Figure 2–2b[1]).

---

[1] Note that "M" in Figure 2–2 stands for the generally accepted relationship characterization of *Many* (i.e., many-to-many, many-to-one). Similarly, "1" represents the *one* side of a design relationship.

FIGURE 2–2b
SIMPLISTIC DATA ORIENTATION

Books have authors
titles
subjects
prices
Publishers have names
cities
orders
Orders have quantities
publishers
books

Do not become overwhelmed with this classification scheme as it unfolds. Alas, into every data base designer's life a little theory must fall. Initially, accept the design methodology as it progresses at a theoretical level; do not become lost in detail. Once presented, the theory will be illustrated by simplistic, but not unrealistic, examples. Further, do not assume that all entities will lend themselves to classification in black and white terms. Some overlap of identification may occur—justifiably, given the user view originating it. We are attempting to derive a model based on system requirements, not modify system requirements based on a design model!

The entity model derived must address all corresponding data items, inherent data relationships between the data items, and the required access paths serving the data relationships. In order to portray the integration of entity relationships, the entities themselves must be classified into subtypes to function as building blocks in the relationships; these subtypes may be labeled kernel, association, and characteristic.[2]

As the name implies, a **kernel** entity is the focal point of information storage and retrieval, having an <u>independent</u> <u>existence</u> <u>and</u> <u>primary</u> <u>key</u> from which other entity types draw their significance.

Books and Publishers could both represent kernel entities.

An **association** represents a <u>many-to-many</u> relationship among two or more other entities.

Orders qualifies as an association between the Book and Publisher entities (i.e., many books are distributed by many publishers based upon orders).

A **characteristic** is an entity whose sole purpose is to <u>describe or qualify another entity</u>. It is required due to the existence of multivalued properties (e.g., size, color), which are not supported in relational data base methodology. (Recall that repeating groups, as often stored within a COBOL "occurs" table structure, are not allowed in a relational data base in order to preserve the "one value at any given intersection of data rows and columns.") A characteristic has no existence of its own; the removal of the entities which it describes will force its elimination from the conceptual model.

City is a characteristic that qualifies the Publisher entity.

All three entity subtypes are clearly entities in their own right. They may participate in other associations and have properties as described in text which follows. They are differentiated by <u>decreasing</u> <u>levels</u> <u>of</u> <u>independence</u> <u>of</u> <u>existence</u>; a kernel entity (e.g., *Book* or *Publisher*) is not dependent on any other entity type and is a prerequisite for the existence of either an

---

[2] This classification has been proposed by C. J. Date in Appendix B of his book, *A Guide to DB2*.

association or characteristic entity although the converse is not true. This differentiation is necessary to identify the participation of different entity subtypes in several kinds of relationships throughout the entity model. The concept of independence of existence will be important for the introduction of foreign keys later.

In addition to its independent classification, each entity may act to designate another entity or exist as a property of another entity, to portray realistic user requirements. A **designation** is nothing more than a <u>many-to-one</u> (or one-to-one) relationship between two entities. Although similar in concept to an association, a <u>designation</u> is <u>not</u> <u>itself</u> <u>an</u> <u>entity</u>—any properties that would be associated with it are essentially attributable to the entity being designated.

> *Author* is designated by the entity *Book*.
> *Book* is designated by the entity *Author*.

A designation draws its significance from its relation type. The designation of a many-to-one relationship between entities is crucial to the representation of an association within an entity model. Remember the basic premise of a relational data base—there is one and only one value at any given intersection of a row and column. Consequently, in any proposed entity model of a relational system, <u>every</u> <u>many-to-many</u> <u>entity</u> <u>relationship</u> <u>(association)</u> <u>must</u> <u>be</u> <u>resolved</u> <u>by</u> <u>some</u> <u>link</u> <u>(two</u> <u>or</u> <u>more</u> <u>designations)</u> into multiple many-to-one relationships. This link (see Figure 2–3) will be tied to the base table of the entity on the "one" side of the relationship (i.e., the entity being designated).

A **property** is simply a <u>fact</u> <u>about</u> <u>an</u> <u>entity</u> that can serve to identify the entity, reference a related entity, or stand alone. At any given time, there may be only <u>one</u> <u>value</u> for a property.

> *Quantity* is a property of the *Order* entity, which is itself an association between the *Book* and *Publisher* entities.

FIGURE 2–3
BASIC ENTITY RELATIONSHIPS

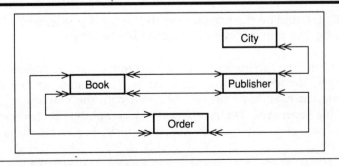

Title, *Subject*, *Price*, and *Publishing* Date are all properties of the *Book* entity.
Name of Publisher is a property of the *Publisher* entity.

The synthetic design approach, given the preceding terminology, proceeds as a top-down entity model derivation that identifies all kernel entities and the associations and designations that connect the various entities. The preceding relationships are then qualified by property and characteristic entities.

The entity model to be derived is somewhat complicated by the concept that associations and characteristics are themselves entities and may participate in other associations or have properties and characteristics of their own. Hence, a more complex web of entity relationships will develop than might initially have been implied. Again, we are reminded of the process orientation of the synthetic approach. The real world seldom respects the simplicity so desirable in data base design. The point to be made is that the entity model will address the reality of the situation: (1) at a high level where interaction with the user is still possible, and (2) at a low level where all meaningful relationships will have been identified.

How does this impressive classification of entity types translate into a practical design model? Let's reconsider the basic element of an entity: **its presence is consistently discernible by some unique qualifier**. This identifying aspect (one or more fields that make up the **primary key**) of the entity is subject to the following properties.[3]

1. Uniqueness. There will never simultaneously exist two distinct records having the same primary key. A unique index must be established to enforce uniqueness, and consequently referential integrity, <u>before</u> the load of any data.
2. Minimality. No primary key (or portion of one if multiple fields make up the key) may be dropped without violating the preceding uniqueness property.
3. Entity Integrity. Given the uniqueness property, no primary key may be NULL.

BOOK_ID could be the primary key of the *book* entity, while PUBL_ID could be the primary key of the *publisher* entity.

Kernel entities, the nuclei of the design model, are identified via their primary keys. However, associations exist as relationships among different entities, relationships that must be associated with the primary keys of the entities being connected. The association is accomplished by **foreign keys**, similar in concept to the primary keys to which they relate. In fact, they

---

[3] The DB2 "COMMENT ON" facility should be used to preserve documentation in DB2 catalog tables.

must denote the same type of aspect or quality about the entity in order to ensure that they will identify the intended object entity.[4] The only difference is that foreign keys are physically removed from the tables that they must reference and in which they must reside as data fields in a different relation. Foreign keys must have: Referential Integrity—the value of every foreign key specified must match the primary key to which it relates, or be NULL.

> ORDR.BOOK_ID, ORDR.PUBL_ID could be a combined key acting as a foreign key to uniquely identify the *Order* entity.
> (Note the relationship to the primary key of the *Book* and *Publisher* entities of the two columns comprising the foreign key—the respective column definitions must match both physically and logically for this association to occur.)

Foreign keys are subject to the following constraints:[5]

1. NULLs are not allowed if the definition of the foreign key is such that they are not appropriate. (Some foreign key definitions may allow nonunique keys.)

2. An index should be defined (although it may not be unique) if efficient for the type of processing anticipated (i.e., if frequent JOINS are anticipated). Otherwise, the overhead of maintaining indices may not be justified.[6]

3. DB2 authorization mechanisms should be used to restrict online access and thus prevent violations of the rules for the foreign key in question.[7]

4. Usage constraints should be adhered to by maintenance programs, and such maintenance should be restricted to one foreign key maintained per maintenance program (i.e., no multiple points of maintenance).

5. Even if DB2 Version 2 referential integrity is utilized, full integrity is still an application function. See the Table Creation section of the Data Definition Language (DDL) chapter for more information.

6. A user utility program should periodically check the integrity of the foreign keys as specified. This would be an excellent Query Management Facility (QMF) application.

---

[4] This point relates to the relational concept of **domain**—pools of values from which entities draw their values. Of primary consequence is the notion that two or more entities that draw their respective values from the same domain are likely to be good candidates for association. Otherwise, associative relationships will probably not be required and more than likely will have no significance if represented.

[5] As implemented in DB2 Version 2.

[6] Refer to the concluding section of this chapter, which deals with considerations applicable to index utilization. Note that use of foreign key indices in DB2 Version 2 for enforcement of referential integrity will greatly enhance performance of the function. Such an index is automatically used if available.

[7] Refer to discussions of DB2 security issues and referential integrity in the Security chapter of this book.

Using the discernible element as established via primary and foreign keys, the data base design is derived through iterations of the following.

1. Represent each kernel entity as a base table and identify its primary key.

    ```
    BOOK_TABL (primary key BOOK_ID)
    PUBL_TABL (primary key PUBL_ID)
    ```

2. Represent each association among entities as a base table and identify the foreign keys that will connect the participants in the association (correspondence to the primary key). Identify the primary key of this table—probably the composite of the foreign keys.

    Establish the action to occur in response to a delete request for the entity described by the primary key to which the foreign key is associated.[8]

    Cascade: Delete all matching associations.

    Restricted: Delete base table entities only where no associations exist.

    Nullified: Delete base table entities after setting the foreign key of the association to NULL (assuming, of course, that NULL is an appropriate value established for the foreign key).

    Establish the action to occur in response to an update request for the entity described by the primary key to which the foreign key is associated.

    Cascade: Update the foreign key for all matching associations.

    Restricted: Update base table entities only where no associations exist.

    Nullified: Update base table entities after setting the foreign key of the association to NULL (assuming, of course, that NULL is an appropriate value established for the foreign key).

    Note the impact of independence of existence, or lack of it, on foreign key processing.

    ```
    ORDR_TABL (primary key
    BOOK_ID, PUBL_ID)
    as a foreign key to
    BOOK_TABL.BOOK_ID,
    PUBL_TABL.PUBL_ID

    NULLs not allowed

    Delete of BOOK_TABL.BOOK_ID    CASCADES

    Delete of PUBL_TABL.PUBL_ID    CASCADES

    Update of BOOK_TABL.BOOK_ID    CASCADES

    Update of PUBL_TABL.PUBL_ID    CASCADES
    ```

---

[8] Note that the following terminology is compatible with delete and update key constraints implemented by the referential integrity feature in DB2 Version 2.

3.   Represent each characteristic as a base table and identify the foreign key that will tie the entity being described to the description (correspondence to the primary key). Identify the primary key of this table—probably the composite of the foreign key and a property that would establish uniqueness within the entity described.

```
    CITY_TABL (primary key
    CITY_NAME,PUBL_ID)
as a foreign key to
    PUBL_TABL.PUBL_ID
```

4.   Represent each designation (not already represented as a characteristic) as a foreign key pointing to the base table that contains the entity being designated.

```
    AUTH
as a foreign key of
    BOOK_TABL.AUTH
```

5.   Represent each property as a field within the base table representing the entity most immediately described by that property.

```
    ORDR_QTY
    field of
    ORDR_TABL

    SUBJ
    field of
    BOOK_TABL

    PRC
    field of
    BOOK_TABL

    PUBL_DATE
    field of
    BOOK_TABL

    TITL
    field of
    BOOK_TABL

    NAME
    field of
    PUBL_TABL
```

Consequently, all three entity subtypes will map into their own respective base tables. Designations and properties, although not entities, will map into fields (or columns) within the related base table. See Figure 2–4 for an illustration of the relationships just discussed.

FIGURE 2–4
BASIC ENTITY RELATIONSHIPS: REFINED

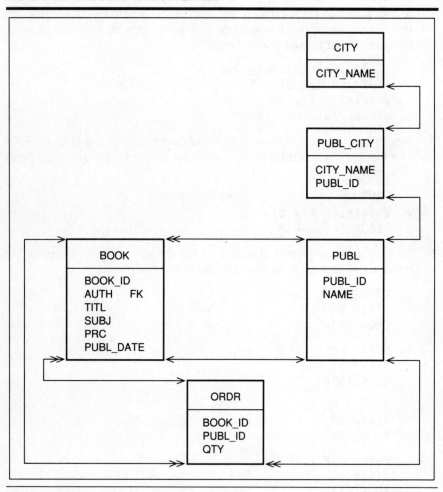

To summarize, the entity model is derived by the application of several rules to the following phases.

1. Selection of the basic system entities (data groups) that require data collection—identify the aspect providing uniqueness (i.e., key).
2. Identify interrelationships between entities.
3. Convert interrelationships into a logical data structure chart for subsequent refinement by normalizing relationships into a composite logical design (as illustrated in the next two sections of this chapter):

a. Each data group is drawn as a box and identified within the box (with the primary key, optionally).

b. Lines are drawn between boxes to represent the interrelationships between the data groups (access paths).

c. One end of the access path denotes dependency (i.e., an arrow head) where the detail group, or child, resides. The other end of the access path represents the parent in the relationship. Thus, the access path is directional from one to many, irrespective of actual data flow.

d. Link data groups are introduced to eliminate all many-to-many relationships.

4. Validate the logical data structure chart against the user view. Any direct access to a data value that is not already part of the primary key for that data group must be highlighted as a potential for a serial scan of the data base. If so required, this data value must be segregated into its own data group to facilitate its direct access. This segregation may be accomplished by establishing an additional primary key in a new data group, or by definition of an **alternate key** composed of the fields requiring direct access.[9]

As demonstrated, the graphic representation of an application in an entity relationship model is quite straightforward, albeit tedious. All data groups participating in relationships are reduced to one-to-many access paths via link data groups as required.

Note that any detail group may relate to the same parent in multiple ways, and may have several different parent data groups. A parent may be the parent of several different types of data groups, although not to another data group of the same type. A detail generally cannot exist without at least one parent data group, while a parent data group can certainly exist without any detail group occurrences.

We now have the process. What we must pursue is the data composition (i.e., data structures to be manipulated) of the process.

■ NORMALIZATION: THE ANALYTIC APPROACH

Application of the synthetic approach has enabled the derivation of an entity model based on the user view of system requirements. This process-oriented model will next be refined through normalization.

The outline of normalization as presented here has been expanded to include the functions of data collection and analysis. Although not generally included as part of normalization methodology, the authors feel that these preliminary phases must be exposed in order to convey the comprehensive

---

[9] Refer to the Data Definition Language chapter for more information on alternate keys.

normalization (analytical design) approach. Otherwise, the designer may be left with a lack of continuity as the methodology makes the transition from entity to data elements. Moreover, it is exactly this continuity that we are seeking to express.

Once identified and classified, data interrelationships will be progressively optimized through normalization to resolve ambiguity, eliminate redundancy, and clearly separate distinct data items into appropriate data groups (i.e., data relations). This data orientation will focus on the logical data relationships themselves, regardless of physical ordering of the fields—a crucial assumption to the analytical approach (to be elaborated upon later).

Data collection is the first phase actually involved in supplying data elements to the normalization process. There is no mystique surrounding it; quite simply, all data elements that could conceivably be stored within a given entity should be recorded and qualified with functional descriptions and storage characteristics. Such data elements are assigned **domains** that reflect the pool of values from which a given data element may draw. The data values within a domain are considered atomic, or the smallest divisible unit that may represent the domain within an entity. See Table 2–1 for an example.

Once a domain has been associated with a data element and a corresponding entity, we are in a position to apply the "brown bag" approach to the data elements. Specifically, the functional descriptions and storage considerations previously recorded should be used to classify the data elements in a way that will help eliminate redundancies in subsequent steps. Each class (e.g., AMT, DATE, PCT, NAME, etc.) is user defined, implicitly or explicitly, within the entity model. The domains that fall into a given class are thrown into a brown bag (figuratively or literally, at your discretion) for that class. The contents of each bag may then be scrutinized to see if any previously undetected duplication or overlap exists. Overlap or duplication may be due to the application of different naming conventions across a user group or to weaknesses in the entity model design, among other causes. The publisher of the order entity, for instance, could be equivalent to the publisher of the book and publisher entities. Our original entity model may then require some restructuring to accommodate the elimination of redundancies. Now we have demonstrated the import of thoughtful characterization of the data elements as they are associated with an entity: class similarities went into the brown bag and out came redundancy! Not too shabby for an understated brown bag. Note that the brown bag could be replaced with a good data dictionary and its element reports.

Redundancy dealt with, at least at a basic level, the next task to address is that of naming conventions. Domains of data may be accessed through a multitude of relationships within our entity model. Further, it may be necessary to maintain these domains in the future (e.g., increase the length of a field), and it would be desirable to be able to use existing DB2 facilities such

Table 2–1
SAMPLE DATA COLLECTION

List of Data Elements	Description	Domain
Publisher	Book Publisher	
Publ_Id	ID number of Publ	0001–9999
Name	Name of Publ	30 char abbrev
City	City where Publ is located	30 char abbrev
Book	Book Published	
Book_Id	ID number of Book	000001–999999
Author	Author of Book	30 char abbrev
Publ	Publisher of Book	0001–9999
Title	Title of Book	30 char abbrev
Edition	Edition of Book	01–99
Subject	Subject area of Book	30 char abbrev from list
Price	Price of Book	000.01–999.99
Discount	Price discount percent	000.00–100.00
Publ_Date	Date of publication	yyyy/mm/dd
Order	Order info for Book(s) from Publ(s)	
Qty	Qty of Books ordered	000000–999999
Book	Book ordered	000001–999999
Publ	Publ of Book ordered	0001–9999

as catalog table scans to extract all common domains.[10] Consequently, users, designers, and technicians should be able to assign data classes to derive the relationship of data elements by domain. Given the class associations of domains already tested in the brown bag procedure, then, we can generate meaningful naming conventions and maintain design continuity.

Similar in concept to our brown bag approach, data classification proceeds from the functional descriptions, storage considerations, and domains first identified and recorded during data collection. Data classification involves the assignment of naming levels (high-order to low-order) to fields that will ultimately form a column in the table form of the relationship. This high-to-low order of assignment is somewhat analogous to the domains that make up a composite primary key of an entity. The highest order of naming will function as the prefix of the column name, the second level is subordinate to the prefix, and so on until the suffix of the column name has been assigned.

---

[10] For example, SQL could easily be utilized to locate a column name string in the SYSIBM.SYSCOLUMNS DB2 catalog table with a command such as **... WHERE NAME is LIKE '%AMT' ...** to locate all columns (within a specified table) whose name ends with AMT.

The high-order qualifier is most appropriately designated as the entity ID or table name. This qualifier addresses the function or identity of the table of the domain (e.g., PUBL, BOOK, ORDR).

The second-order qualifier should serve as a descriptor of the high-order qualifier to which it is subordinate (e.g., DSTR, TITL, SUBJ, AUTH).

The third-order (and any lower) qualifier lends further description to the high-order qualifier in decreasing levels of significance from the qualifiers to which it is subordinate. Class descriptions are appropriate at this level of qualification (e.g., AMT, PCT, NAME, ID, DATE, CITY).

Possible domain names may result as follows:

PUBL_DSTR_ID
PUBL_DSTR_NAME
PUBL_DSTR_DATE
PUBL_DSTR_CITY
PUBL_CITY_NAME
PUBL_CITY_ID
CITY_PUBL_NAME
BOOK_DSTR_PRC
BOOK_DSTR_ID
BOOK_DSTR_GROS_AMT
BOOK_DSTR_DISC_PCT
BOOK_TITL_NAME
BOOK_SUBJ_NAME
BOOK_AUTH_NAME
BOOK_PUBL_DATE
ORDR_BOOK_ID
ORDR_PUBL_ID
ORDR_DSTR_QTY

It may be more efficient to consolidate like-named qualifiers (such as START, BEGIN) and to shorten the length of each qualifier to three or four positions. Regardless, the major thrust of establishing naming conventions has been delivered.

To summarize the preceding data analysis, redundancy increases the risk of error. The more domains to be maintained, the higher the likelihood that a failure to do so will occur. It is also far simpler and more cost-effective to change a process than a data structure—with regard to design complexity, less is more! Using the analytical approach at this point, we can examine our entity model (shown in Figure 2–5) as it will become involved in the normalization process.

The main objective of normalization is to produce a clean design through which one fact will be presented in one place (not unlike the synthetic

FIGURE 2–5
DATA ANALYSIS INPUT TO NORMALIZATION

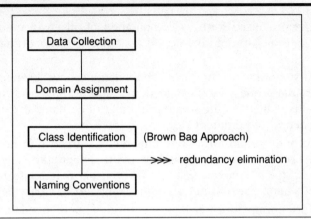

approach). Further, each fact will relate to the entire key (or entity as identified by the primary key) and nothing else in the table but the entire key.[11]
Thus, each table will relate to one key entity type only—facilitating understanding, use, and potential modification.

Through normalization, we are striving to reach a state where **functional dependency** is reduced to its simplest form, **primary key to field**.
No other functional dependencies will exist within the same table, and this
relationship will hold for all fields within the table. In essence, for each distinct key value there will be only one distinct field value for any given field
type (i.e., column). All column names will be unique and the ordering of
the rows insignificant.

If this is not valid, then hidden relationships exist, and they must be
extracted before further normalization is possible.

The process of normalization itself proceeds from first to fourth normal
form,[12] with **redundancy decreasing as normal form is increasing**.
Obviously, we are involved in a tradeoff of increasing restrictions versus
increasing benefits to be derived from normalized states. Note that the relationships established as a result of our entity approach fulfill the requirements
for first normal form (1NF).

First normal form is present in all relational tables by virtue of their
definition: At each row and column intersection there will be one atomic
value, not a range of values. Therefore, it is simply a matter of promoting
the level of normalization relating to a given key-entity type by ensuring that

---

[11] Or as Date puts it in Appendix B of his book, *A Guide to DB2*, "the key, the whole key, and
nothing but the key."

[12] Actually, six normal forms are possible, but it is rarely necessary to exceed four forms in
normalization design methodology for relational data bases.

subsequent normal forms are equivalent to the prior form plus an additional condition that will further reduce redundancy.

1. (UNF) Unnormalized form: a combination of all environmental data, without identification of primary keys and possibly containing repeating groups.
2. (1NF) First normal form: UNF, and relations have been established with minimal primary keys assigned and all repeating groups removed. (Minimal is defined as the smallest number of domains that will satisfy the uniqueness requirement.)
3. (2NF) Second normal form: 1NF plus removal of all non-key domains that are not functionally dependent upon the primary key taken in its entirety (i.e., removal of all non-key fields that relate to and are dependent upon part but not all of the compound primary key).
4. (3NF) Third normal form: 2NF plus removal of interdependencies among non-key domains (i.e., all non-key domains are totally functionally dependent on the primary key but mutually independent of each other).
5. (4NF) Fourth normal form: 3NF plus identical keys combined.

The preceding progression will be achieved by iteration of two basic rules.

1. If there is a partial dependency of a field to a compound primary key, eliminate that field and create a second table where the field has as its primary key the portion of the original compound primary key upon which it was dependent.

Key (field A, field B) → field C, field D

where field C is dependent only upon field B becomes

$$\text{Key (field A, field B)} \rightarrow \text{field D}$$
$$\text{Key (field B)} \rightarrow \text{field C}$$

2. If there is a dependency among fields other than in the form of simple functional dependency (i.e., fields dependent on each other rather than on the primary key alone), eliminate the field dependent on a field other than the key. Create a second table where the dependent field has as its primary key the non-key field upon which it was dependent.

$$\text{Key (field X)} \rightarrow \text{field A} \rightarrow \text{field B}$$

becomes

$$\text{Key (field X)} \rightarrow \text{field A}$$
$$\text{Key (field A)} \rightarrow \text{field B}$$

To reiterate, the preceding normalization procedure is a process complementary to that of the entity modeling approach. While normalization succeeds in breaking down larger tables into smaller, less redundant tables, it does nothing to indicate how to arrive at the resulting tables themselves. For this purpose the entity model is essential.

The data orientation of normalization has, however, enabled us to resolve several major physical design issues that tend to degrade ultimate physical data structures and thus data manipulation. Normalization has expanded upon the high-level entity model to specify exactly which domains are related, which domains are distinct from one another, and where duplication or overlap of domains may exist.

■ COMPOSITE LOGICAL DESIGN

Composite Logical Design (CLD) provides the simplest possible method for achieving compatibility between the entity model and fourth normal form representation of the entities identified.

It is derived from the comparison of a logical data structure (drawn from the 4NF model) and a systems process structure (the entity model previously obtained) to produce a compromise design model, which in its ideal form reflects the benefits of both approaches and the disadvantages of neither.

Normalization does not produce a chart as output of its design methodology. The logical data model chart of fourth normal form must be derived in a manner that will yield a grid consistent with that produced from the entity model. It must

1. Represent each relation as a data group.
2. Assign each composite key and compound key as a detail data group of those relations to which they refer as part of the key.
3. Assign each foreign key as a detail data group of the relation that has that foreign key as its primary key.

Once schematically represented by a logical data model chart, the fourth normal form model can be compared with the entity model. The two models may now be reconciled to each other by iterations of the following processes.

1. Match link entity model data groups to 4NF compound key relations and resolve differences. This may require the repetition of 4NF relational groups.
2. Review the user view of system requirements to drop/create data groups that are currently mutually exclusive between the two models.
3. Resolve access paths.
4. Validate the CLD against the user view to ensure consistency between the two.

Given the resulting composite logical design, the data base designer may translate the model to the physical DBMS of implementation, tempering it with any obvious performance considerations relevant to the DBMS itself. Note that the logical design phase has become a transition point for the physical representation of the system requirements. Subsequent chapters will deal with the physical representation of the conceptual model within the constraints of the DB2 environment.

■ CONCLUDING DESIGN CONSIDERATIONS

Whenever additional criteria exist that force uniqueness of certain field combinations within a given base table, the same tactic used to enforce such uniqueness among primary keys may be applied. Specifically, define the field combination as an **alternate key** and create a unique index over it in the same way you would create the unique index of a primary key. While NULL values will be allowable, only one set will be introduced.

For all primary keys relating to kernel entities, avoid the definition of a composite (multiple field) key. Introduce a combined field to represent the two original fields, which will then exist as properties of the entity being identified.

When naming the data fields in the physical DBMS, try to maintain consistency within a domain of values. All fields derived from the same domain should carry the same name (i.e., reflect the domain relationship) across base tables. This technique is especially efficient for future maintenance where identifications such as those enabled by the SQL "LIKE %" clause will be desirable.

Do not normalize relationships beyond the point where redundancy has been eliminated. Otherwise, inefficiencies such as machine processing excesses are likely. Furthermore, certain data manipulations may be prevented altogether (i.e., update of a JOIN where the data fields have been normalized into separate base tables but whose retrieval must be performed to execute an update function).

As previously stated, reduction of redundancy through increased normalization levels is a tradeoff between update efficiency (where reduced redundancy is preferable) and retrieval (where redundancy may be desirable). If retrieval is more applicable to a relation than update, decreasing the level of normalization in a thoughtful manner may be more efficient and acceptable within the conceptual model. Careful documentation of all such normalization reversals is necessary because of potential changes of circumstance rendering them inappropriate unless they are self-explanatory.

NULL values should be carefully evaluated for fields likely to participate in built-in functions (e.g., AVG) and where presence in the sense of a count is necessary to produce the intended result. NULLs do not participate in most built-in functions.

Do not overload keys with meanings that are sensitive to circumstance. The most common violation of this guideline occurs in a design where multiple ranges of values are meant to reflect different domains.[13]

In contrast to overload of keys, do not arbitrarily designate additional fields to act as indicators for the existence of some requirement within another field when the field itself is indicative of such a requirement. For example, a design model may have defined two columns:

`BOOK_PUBL_DATE_IND` and `BOOK_PUBL_DATE`

The indicator column may be intended to detect the conditions where books have been published and where they have not. Such an indicator column is probably redundant with the contents of the BOOK_PUBL_DATE column itself; BOOK_PUBL_DATE could be interrogated directly to determine whether a nonzero value is present. If zero should happen to be considered a valid published date, then the user could define the column as capable of containing NULLs and assign NULLs as the default value, meaning no date has been established.

---

[13] For example, do not use PUBL_ID values 0001–4999 to reflect domestic publishers and PUBL_ID values 5000–99999 to reflect international publishers. It will be difficult to change these designations later, as they do not reflect the different entities they represent. Further, do not assume that this type of informational segregation is intuitively obvious to designers who will subsequently examine such a model.

CHAPTER 3

Logical Model

The purpose of a **logical model** is to refine the normalized Conceptual Model (Composite Logic Design) and <u>map</u> it <u>to the</u> <u>physical</u> <u>DBMS</u> of implementation. In short, it is time to "get physical. " During this mapping process, conflicts between design and DB2 rules must be resolved, performance tradeoffs must be evaluated, and additional relationships that may emerge must be considered.

As mentioned during the presentation of the conceptual model, logical modeling seeks to represent the entities of the conceptual model as components of physical tables. Associations between entities (many-to-many relationships) will be segregated into distinct junction tables; elements will become columns within tables. Design considerations such as referential integrity, column attributes, and the physical sequence of tables must be finalized. Of great significance is the finalization of access paths among the derived tables, which will in turn determine index requirements.

System analysis was performed in conjunction with the data analysis of the conceptual model, resulting in the definition of processing requirements. Now is the time to test the outputs of such data and systems analyses by subjecting a hypothetical transaction to a "walk through" of the logical model. Are all required fields defined and data relationships identified? Are element names and/or column names meaningful? Will data retrieval meet or exceed established response time objectives?

We touched on the fact that additional relationships might surface. Within the book order case study in the conceptual model derivation, we neglected the fact that both internal and external sales representatives may be used. Some customers may be serviced by more than one salesrep of each *type*, so a customer-to-salesrep relationship must be satisfied within our logical model. As shown in Figure 3–1, three methods of representation could be considered.

A sales representative (SRP) table would exist that contains the salesperson's name, type (i.e., internal or external), and other applicable information. The representation depicted in Method 1 would require repeated access to the SRP table to establish the type of salesrep relationship in force. Method

FIGURE 3–1
CUSTOMER-SALESREP RELATIONSHIP

	Primary Key		
1	CUST_NO	CUST_SRP_NO	
2	CUST_NO	CUST_SRP_NO	CUST_SRP_TYP_CD
3	CUST_NO	CUST_INT_SRP_NO	CUST_EXT_SRP_NO

2 presents an update anomaly in that it requires the addition of a column (CUST_SRP_TYP_CD) to carry data that could be inferred from existing columns. Method 3 was chosen and implemented with both internal and external SRP_NO columns, defined to allow NULLs, as a means of reflecting the type of salesrep relationship in force. Note that in the preceding example, Method 1 represents the highest level of both normalization and resource consumption. It is appropriate to reiterate that the conceptual model derived as input to the logical modeling process is not cast in concrete; it must be tempered by the constraints of the physical DBMS of implementation.

Further, recall that the maximum number of rows per page within a DB2 table is 127. A row length of less than 24 bytes will never allow a page to be fully utilized. Therefore, Methods 1 and 2 would require twice as many pages as Method 3 to represent the same information.

Referential integrity, even though supported in Version 2, may still be an application responsibility to be considered in logical modeling. In the following example of accounts and monthly account balances (Figure 3–2), how do we ensure that the correct number of monthly balance rows will exist for each account?

Since each BALANCES row consists of over 30 columns, the DB2 size limitation of 300 columns per row together with the concept of fourth nor-

FIGURE 3–2

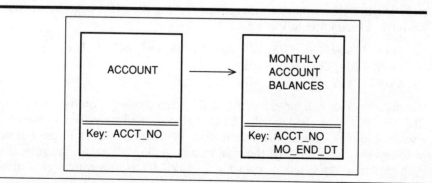

mal form will dictate that a distinct row be utilized for each month of data. Therefore, the primary key required to uniquely identify the MONTHLY ACCOUNT BALANCES rows will be a composite of an account number and a date column. Account number in the composite key of MONTHLY ACCOUNT BALANCES will also act as a foreign key to the ACCOUNT table. While referential integrity can guarantee that a MONTHLY ACCOUNT BALANCE row may not exist if its account number is not a unique primary key in the related ACCOUNT table, it will still be the <u>application's</u> responsibility to ensure that the number of monthly rows (dates) being stored is correct.

Column attributes such as NULL, variable length, and data type should be resolved as the next phase of logical modeling. The logical model may have identified elements as being variable in size. However, is it physically efficient to store and process a column with a variable character definition? For example, asset location may be a maximum of 40 and a minimum of 10 characters. If the assets are very mobile (e.g., ships, trucks, railroad cars), then the constant fluctuation in column length may result in excessive page overflow of the related rows.

Numeric data can also present unexpected overflow. For example, which of the following should a percent item be stored as?

```
DECIMAL(5,2)
DECIMAL(5,4)
DECIMAL(5,0)
```

To the average coder, there won't appear to be any significant difference in storage definition until a SQLCODE-802 (arithmetic overflow) is received. Such an error condition will occur when column or arithmetic functions calculate an intermediate result that forces the precision of the final result to exceed the permissible maximum for the numeric data type in use. The culprit in this case is the scale of the intermediate result. Decimal processing permits a maximum precision of 15 digits. DB2 will not convert numeric data types if the precision limit is exceeded. (Decimal values will not be changed to single or double precision.) To illustrate, consider a case requiring the summation of a daily interest value that must be derived from the current available amount and interest percentage columns (i.e., CHK_CUR_AVL_AMT and CUS_INT_PCT columns, respectively). Using the SUM column function we might execute the following:

```
SELECT SUM(CHK_CUR_AVL_AMT * CUS_INT_PCT / 366)
FROM TDDA_CHK,TDDA_CUS
WHERE........
```

Division by 366 will produce the daily interest rate. Unfortunately, the CUS_INT_PCT column, defined as DECIMAL(5,4), had a precision of five and a scale of four — causing the intermediate DIVIDE calculation to use a scale of **fourteen**. Consequently, the final result overflowed. In this instance, the problem can be remedied by replacing the DIVIDE function with a calculation of MULTIPLY BY .00272322, which changes the scale to 12. This situation is not unique to DB2; a COBOL compute statement would encounter the same problem.

Beyond column attributes, the physical placement of columns must be considered. There are two simple rules to follow.

1. Columns with varying lengths (NULL or VARCHAR) should be positioned at the end of a row.

2. Frequently referenced columns should be at the beginning of the row.

Both rules are intended to reduce processing time. See the DDL CREATE TABLE statement in Chapter 4 for a detailed explanation.

■ NAMING CONVENTIONS

The implementation of naming standards that began during the development of the conceptual model will be extended to all DB2 objects that are created using DDL. In order to use the DB2 catalogs as a control dictionary, a strict naming convention must be enforced. The query in Figure 3–3 would be

FIGURE 3–3
TYPICAL DB2 CATALOG QUERY

```
--
--
--   TOTAL SPACE AND SPACE USED FOR EACH TS
--
   SELECT TS.DBNAME, TS.NAME, TB.CARD,
       TB.RECLENGTH, TB.NPAGES, TS.NACTIVE,
       TS.SPACE
   FROM SYSIBM.SYSTABLES
           TB,SYSIBM.SYSTABLESPACE TS
   WHERE TS.DBNAME LIKE 'AU%' -- IDX1 (TS)
   AND TS.CREATOR = 'TSOIDxx' -- NO IDX
   AND TB.TYPE = 'T'          -- NO IDX
   AND (TB.NAME LIKE 'TDDA%'--IDX2 (TB)
   OR TB.NAME LIKE 'TMAS%')--IDX2 (TB)
   AND TS.CREATOR = TB.CREATOR
      -- IDX1 (TB)
   AND TS.NAME = TB.TSNAME -- IDX2 (TS)
      --IDX2 (TB)
    ORDER BY TS.DBNAME, TS.NAME;
```

very difficult to run if data bases and tables did not adhere to a common naming convention.

Recommended naming conventions for DB2 objects that may be utilized in multi-division and multi-application environments are listed below. Additionally, the authors recommend that full use be made of the COMMENT ON (254 character maximum) and LABEL ON (30 character maximum) statements to enable the DB2 catalogs to function as a quasi-dictionary for control purposes. COMMENT and LABEL may be used in conjunction with COLUMN and TABLE names. Optionally (and on an individual basis), LABEL may be used in place of original column and table names produced by a DCLGEN, or in page headings on QMF reports. The COMMENT ON statement is an excellent method of documenting design decisions and table/column modifications. Design documentation will be discussed in more detail later in this chapter.

COLUMN names may have a maximum of 18 characters.

ttt_xxxxxxxxxxxxxx

Where t = Three-letter table acronym

_ = Underscore delimiter

x = Descriptive name using standard abbreviations. The last qualifier must be its data class (DT, ID, CD, BAL, etc.).

TABLE names may have a maximum of 18 characters but should be limited to 9 characters, including the underscore delimiter. This will ensure that the member produced as output from a DECLARE TABLE operation (DCLGEN) will have the same name as its respective DB2 table (minus the underscore delimiter). This will minimize the confusion involved in matching tables to DCLGEN output. Such naming standards will also facilitate the use of a common TSO CLIST to control table creation and execution of a DCLGEN. See the "Generating Utility Control Statements" section of the **DB2 Utilities** chapter or "DSN Subcommand Execution" section of the **DB2 DSN Subcommand** chapter. Suggested table naming conventions follow:

Tsss_xxx

Where T = The letter T to identify the object as a DB2 table.

s = Three-letter system identifier (e.g., ABL)

_ = Underscore delimiter

x = One- to four-character table acronym

SYNONYM names may have a maximum of 18 characters. As in the case of table names, synonym names should be limited to 9 characters, including the underscore delimiter. All other conventions similarly apply. Except for the owner (AUTHID/creator), the synonym must be the same as its affiliated base table. Recall that fully qualified TABLE, VIEW, and SYNONYM names (i.e., AUTHID.tabnam) must be unique within a DB2 system. This will eliminate program code changes and control the total number of synonyms. Unless absolutely necessary, never allow one AUTHID to have more than one synonym (i.e., different names) for the same base table. The loss of control could be devastating.

TABLESPACE names may have a maximum of 8 characters. (Note that there will be only one table per TABLESPACE.)

T$xxxnnn

Where T$ = The characters T$ to identify this as a tablespace object
      x = One- to three-character table acronym
      n = Three-character sequence

VIEW names may have a maximum of 18 characters. As with table names they will be limited to 9 characters, including one underscore delimiter. This will ensure that the DCLGEN output member name is the same as the view name

Vsss_xxxx

Where V = The letter V to identify the object as a DB2 VIEW
      s = Three-letter system identifier (e.g., ABL)
      _ = Underscore delimiter
      x = One- to four-letter VIEW acronym

DATA BASE names may have a maximum of 8 characters. To avoid DB2 catalog contention, it is strongly recommended that each developer have his or her own data base.

Desssnnn

Where D = One letter to relate the data base to a division
      e = One-character environment identifier (P = production, T = test, V = volume, etc.)
      s = Three-letter application/system identifier
      n = Up to three characters for sequence or owner

If the installation standard in production environments dictates the allocation of one data base per tablespace, then the last three characters in the data base name (i.e., "nnn") must be selected to allow functionally related data bases to be sequentially referenced. The START/STOP DB commands allow the use of generic (wildcard) data base names to facilitate daily operations and recovery procedures.

STOGROUPs may have a maximum of 8 characters. The authors recommend a different STOGROUP allocation for each test environment within an application. In production, however, it may be best to define your own VSAM ESDS datasets; then, STOGROUPs would not be required.

Edddiiii

Where E = One character to identify the environment (P = production, T = test, V = volume, etc.)

d = Three numbers to identify the division account

i = One- to four-character identifier determined by data administration. This identifier is best used to relate volume serial numbers.

PLAN names may have a maximum of 8 characters and must be unique within a DB2 subsystem. Unlike tablespaces and tables, <u>plan</u> <u>names</u> <u>are</u> <u>never</u> <u>qualified</u> <u>and</u> <u>must</u> <u>therefore</u> <u>be</u> <u>unique.</u>

Asssnnnv

or

Assspppp

Where A = One letter to relate a PLAN to a division

s = Three-character application/system identifier

n = Three-character sequence; in a test environment, this should relate to a developer's TSOID

v = One character for version control

p = Four characters to relate PLANs to a specific program or driver program.

Data Base Request Module (DBRM) names should be the same as the name of the program that generated them. DBRM creation and use is not protected by DB2 security mechanisms, and DBRM names are recorded within DB2 catalogs for REBIND purposes only. In order to use the DB2 catalog tables collectively as a control dictionary, DBRM names must match the names of their respective programs.

■ THE DB2 CATALOG TABLES AS A DESIGN TOOL

When using naming conventions such as those just presented, it is possible to utilize the DB2 catalog tables as a development tool. By using the TABLE, COLUMN, COMMENT ON, and LABEL ON facilities; entities, properties (elements), and their respective relationships may be derived and reported from information stored as columns within the catalog tables. Utilization of

DB2 catalog tables essentially eliminates the need to introduce and maintain a redundancy of information in user datasets. DB2 will automatically update its catalog tables as an integral part of its processing. Any information not provided may be user supplied within the same tables.

To exploit the DB2 catalog tables during application development, all application-related *table* entries should be defined within one DB2 data base. Because information about the tables will be retrieved from columns within the SYSIBM.SYSTABLES and SYSIBM.SYSCOLUMNS DB2 catalog tables and not the actual application tables being created, your data base will also serve to reduce DB2 catalog contention during the development process.

As already suggested, create a separate table within the data base for each entity defined, with its properties included as column names. Related descriptions for the entities and properties must be entered with COMMENT ON statements for storage within the DB2 catalog tables.

At this point SQL Processor Using File Input (SPUFI) or Query Management Facility (QMF) may be utilized to produce data analysis reports from the information that DB2 has extracted from the CREATE TABLE statements and stored within its catalog tables. Examples of queries to produce data reports are shown in Figure 3–4.

FIGURE 3–4
DB2 CATALOG REPORT QUERIES

```
--
--   List all entities and properties
--
   SELECT C.NAME,TBNAME,LENGTH,COLTYPE
     ,C.REMARKS ,T.REMARKS
    FROM SYSIBM.SYSCOLUMNS C
     ,SYSIBM.SYSTABLES T
   WHERE TBNAME = C.NAME
    AND DBNAME = 'devdb001'
   ORDER BY 2,1;
--
--   List all properties (element)
--     (detect redundancies)
--
   SELECT NAME,TBNAME,LENGTH
     ,SCALE,REMARKS
    FROM SYSIBM.SYSCOLUMNS
   WHERE NAME LIKE'%_AMT'
   ORDER BY 1;
```

The second query will detect duplicate data elements in the model if the data class is the last qualifier of the data names.[1]

As access paths are determined, indices may be added. Queries of SYSIBM.SYSKEYS and SYSIBM.SYSINDEXPART catalog tables will reveal key column sequence (properties, elements) and the actual access path (index) sequence.

After all this data is faithfully entered into the design definitions, how do we migrate it into our physical implementation? Two alternatives for

[1] Please refer to the section on *Normalization: The Analytic Approach,* in the **Conceptual Model** chapter for further explanation of naming standards and data name class assignment.

FIGURE 3–5
TABLE DEFINITION QUERY

```
SELECT NAME, COLTYPE||'('||LENGTH||')'
   'NOT NULL', COLNO
 FROM SYSIBM.SYSCOLUMNS
 WHERE TBNAME = 'some_tab'
  AND NULLS = 'Y'
  AND DEFAULT = 'N'
  AND COLTYPE IN ('CHAR','VARCHAR')
 UNION
SELECT NAME,COLTYPE||'('||LENGTH||')'
   ,'NOT NULL WITH DEFAULT', COLNO
   FROM SYSIBM.SYSCOLUMNS
   WHERE TBNAME = 'some_tab'
  AND NULLS = 'N'
  AND DEFAULT = 'Y'
  AND COLTYPE IN ('CHAR','VARCHAR')
 UNION
SELECT NAME,COLTYPE||'('||LENGTH||')'
   ,'NOT NULL WITH DEFAULT',COLNO
   FROM SYSIBM.SYSCOLUMNS
   WHERE TBNAME = 'some_tab'
  AND NULLS = 'N'
  AND DEFAULT = 'Y'
  AND COLTYPE IN
     ('INTEGER','SMALLINT')
UNION
etc.
ORDER BY 4;
```

consideration are utilization of the IBM Data Base Migration Aid Utility (DBMAUI), or another product from BMC Software, known as DB2 ALTER. Both products, available at additional cost, are capable of migrating table definitions.

A more economical method of migration might be the use of the SPUFI output dataset as input for table creation. Figure 3–5 illustrates a query of the DB2 catalog tables to retrieve column definitions for the table, *some_tab*. The COLNO column is required to ensure that the columns in our new table will be in the same sequence as those of the original design.

If the record size of the output dataset is changed to 80 then it may be edited to remove SPUFI messages and used as input to subsequent SPUFI processing. Note that datasets used as input to SPUFI must have a record size of either 79 or 80.

■ VERSION 2.1 REFERENTIAL INTEGRITY

Referential Integrity has become the generally accepted locution to encompass two basic relational integrity rules: Entity Integrity and Integrity of Reference. **Entity Integrity** states that a **primary key** must be unique and may never be NULL. **Integrity of Reference** states that **foreign keys** of a **dependent table** must exactly match the primary key of a related **parent table** or the foreign key must be NULL.

Why use referential integrity? The obvious answer is, to ensure data integrity. Unfortunately, the obvious answer does not readily translate into business requirements or human resource savings. First, let's expand on data integrity; some dollars and cents issues will follow.

During the last few years, the volume and availability of computer accessible information (data) have greatly increased. Many different types of applications have gained access to data from central repositories utilizing Data Base Management Systems (DBMS). Consequently, data may be at the mercy of less computer literate people. As a result, the quality or referential integrity of data has become a critical issue. Should each application environment maintain its own referential integrity rules or should they be centralized within a DBMS, such as DB2?

Centralized referential integrity (RI) will

1. Standardize application attributes by maintaining the consistency of data regardless of access source.
2. Reduce application development time and costs by eliminating the need for each application and/or program to incorporate its own RI techniques.
3. Ensure consistency of data (right or wrong).
4. Facilitate performance and tuning by keeping computer resource requirements consistent.

Referential Integrity Terms

Referential Integrity, as implemented within DB2 Version 2.1, is designed to support relationships and constraints between tables. Figure 3–6 will simplify the pertinent terms utilized in Referential Integrity implementation.

Key abbreviations are defined as used in the preceding example. Note that all keys may consist of one or more columns.

PK   Primary Key
fk   Foreign Key
key   Standard DB2 key column(s)

In Figure 3–6, BOOKS, PUBL (Publishers), and AUTHORS are **parent tables**. A parent table may have its **primary key** (PK) referenced by **foreign key**(s) (fk) of one or more directly **dependent table**(s). A DB2 index must be created for primary keys, and it <u>must be unique</u>. Moreover, primary keys may not be NULL nor can any columns of a composite key contain NULLs.

AUTHORS, MKT DATA (Marketing Data), and AUTH DATA (Author Data) are **dependent tables**. A dependent table directly references a parent table by using its **foreign key** (fk). A dependent table may have multiple

FIGURE 3–6
REFERENTIAL INTEGRITY TERMS AND RELATIONSHIPS

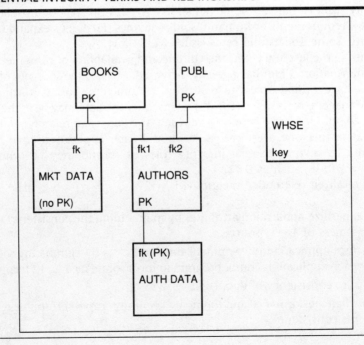

foreign keys that point to rows in different parent tables. In the previous example, AUTHORS is a dependent of both the BOOKS and PUBL tables and is also the parent table of AUTH DATA. Foreign keys are <u>not</u> <u>required</u> <u>to</u> <u>be</u> <u>unique</u> and are not required to be indexed. However, it is strongly recommended that a DB2 index be created for all foreign keys, as they will automatically be referenced for referential integrity checking. Note that one index could be composed of more than one foreign key of a dependent table.

Descendents represent the hierarchic structure of all dependent tables, such as AUTHORS and AUTH DATA. Subsequent discussions will demonstrate that descendents play a critical role in UPDATE and DELETE processing. Also, the authors will use the term descendents in later chapters to refer to hierarchic dependents for ROWS, TABLES, and TABLESPACES.

The AUTH DATA table's primary key and foreign key is the same element or field (i.e., author ID). Primary keys may be foreign keys and vice versa, but primary keys must still have a unique DB2 index defined for them.

Foreign keys must exactly match their respective parent keys. Length, scale, and data type of each column of the key, as well as the column sequence itself, must be identical. The authors suspect that key comparisons are executed using character comparisons (i.e., assembler CLC), another reason why DB2 allows only packed signs of either 'C' (positive) or 'D' (negative).

WHSE (Warehouse) is an **independent** table in that it is not involved in any relationships with any other tables. It is neither a parent nor a dependent table.

DB2's implementation of referential integrity requires additional terms to define table relationships. The actual relationship between two tables is considered a **path**. A set of tables that are either parents or dependents, or dependents of themselves is a **referential structure**. Referential structures may be composed of several different types of paths, such as Self-referencing,

FIGURE 3–7
SELF-REFERENCING TABLE

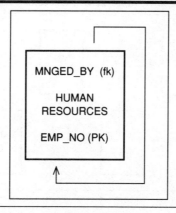

FIGURE 3–8
CYCLE STRUCTURE

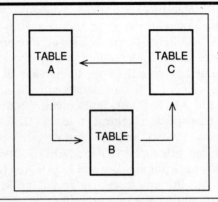

Cycle, and Multiple path. A table that is a dependent and a parent of itself is considered Self-referencing. Figure 3–7 illustrates a Self-referencing table.

A Self-referencing table would have a **Self-referencing row** if one row's foreign key has the same value as its primary key.

A Cycle Structure connects a table to itself through another table. The path of dependencies must all flow in the same direction. As such, it is recursive in nature. Figure 3–8 depicts a Cycle Structure that consists of three tables. A Cycle Structure must utilize two or more tables.

A referential structure is considered to be Multiple Path if any table has more than one direct parent or more than one direct dependent.

In Figure 3–9, Tables B and C have multiple paths to other tables. Table B has Tables A and C as direct parents, and Table C has Tables B and D as direct dependents.

FIGURE 3–9
MULTIPLE PATH STRUCTURE

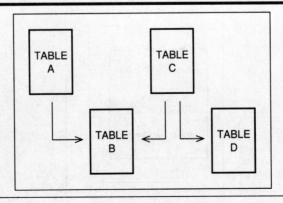

Entity and Referential Integrity

In the current relational model, rules or **constraints** are defined to enforce specific relationships between parent and dependent tables (i.e., primary and foreign keys). Note that these rules (applicable to DELETE, INSERT, UPDATE activity) are for the relational model and are not necessarily implemented within DB2 Version 2.1. As we describe each rule, we will explain how it is implemented within DB2 and the restrictions placed on certain types of referential structures.

DELETE

Every foreign key has its own delete rule that consists of one of the following three options: **RESTRICT**, **CASCADE**, or **SET NULL**. Even though the DELETE rule is defined on a foreign key of a dependent table, it serves either to deny the delete action or to control the flow of the delete action through the dependent table and possibly to other descendents.

RESTRICT   A parent table row may not be deleted if any related foreign keys contain the same value as the primary key of the parent table.

CASCADE   A delete of a parent table row will propagate deletes to dependent table rows whose foreign keys match the parent table's primary key. All associated deletes must complete or the entire operation fails. As such, a parent and a dependent with a DELETE option of CASCADE are said to be **delete-connected.**

SET NULL   When a parent table row is deleted, all foreign keys with the same value(s) as its primary key will be set to NULL.

The DB2 implementation of the DELETE rule supports all options. The default is RESTRICT. In order to prevent delete anomalies, restrictions apply for Self-referencing, Cycle, and Multiple Path Structures.

A Self-referencing structure must specify a delete option of CASCADE. In the Human Resources example in Figure 3–7, the deletion of the CEO would result in all personnel being deleted!

A Cycle Structure may not be delete–connected to itself. At least two of the tables in a cycle must specify either RESTRICT, SET NULL, or both. Therefore, a two-table Cycle Structure may never specify CASCADE for any of its paths.

A Multiple Path Structure may never utilize the SET NULL option. All foreign keys of the lowest-level descendent in a Multiple Path Structure must specify the same delete option.

INSERT

The INSERT rule is implicit in that there are no explicit options. The relational model INSERT rule dictates that no foreign key may be inserted that does not equal a primary key unless it is NULL. Therefore, the parent row must exist prior to inserting the dependent row, or the foreign key must allow NULLs. Recall that primary keys must be unique and may not be NULL.

The DB2 implementation of the INSERT rule is fully supported.

UPDATE

The relational model UPDATE rule also has RESTRICT, CASCADE, and SET NULL options.

RESTRICT A parent table primary key may not be updated if any dependent row foreign key(s) contain the same value. Before the UPDATE may be processed, a separate operation must either delete all the dependent rows where any foreign keys equal the primary key or set all the related foreign keys to NULL.

CASCADE If a primary key is updated, then all dependent foreign keys with the same value will also be updated! Therefore, if any descendents' foreign keys specify CASCADE as an UPDATE option, they will be modified to reflect the same value(s) as the corresponding primary key.

SET NULL If a primary key is updated, then all dependent foreign keys with the same value will be set to NULL. What happens if the dependent's foreign key is also its primary key?

DB2 implements only the RESTRICT option of the UPDATE rule. The potential update anomalies for CASCADE and SET NULL are overwhelming.

Referential Integrity Design Recommendations

Primary and foreign key design are of the greatest concern when designing a table with referential constraints. Beyond constraint definition, the next greatest concern is the actual loading of table data.

Minimally, every DB2 table must have a primary index. Referential integrity requires that all primary keys composing the primary index be unique. The only way to guarantee uniqueness for a table (with or without constraints) is with a unique index. An exception to this rule might be for independent tables. If the resulting index key is so large that performance will be impacted, sacrifice uniqueness.

Primary key columns should not be allowed to default to zero, space, date, or time values. The only viable default is TIMESTAMP, which can maintain its uniqueness during single row inserts. Load processing will use the same timestamp on all rows.

Since DB2 supports only the RESTRICT option of the UPDATE rule for primary keys, it is wise to enforce a standard that primary keys may never be updated. Furthermore, a philosophical interpretation of Third Normal

Form would imply that a change to a primary key would effectively alter its related data. Also, a **partitioned** DB2 table may not have its sequencing **(CLUSTER)** key column(s) updated. Therefore, a primary key modification should only be accomplished by deleting the row in question and then inserting it with the new key value(s) and the same data.

Primary keys should not contain additional columns to encourage index-only data retrieval. Not only would this increase the primary index size, but all dependent tables and their foreign key indices would be larger. Every additional column would have to exist in at least four separate DB2 objects (i.e., primary table and index, and dependent table and index).

All columns of a composite foreign key should be defined as either NULL or NOT NULL. If one or more columns of a foreign key are NULL, the entire foreign key is considered NULL. Moreover, DB2 will not check the referential integrity of column(s) of the composite key that contain a nonNULL value(s) if one or more of its composite columns is NULL.

Avoid the situation where primary and foreign keys share columns. A DML restriction for DB2 referential integrity will not allow multiple row UPDATEs. Further, UPDATE WHERE CURRENT OF is not allowed on primary key columns.

One foreign key within a Cycle Structure should be defined to allow NULLs. Otherwise, a row may not be inserted if its foreign key(s) does not have a matching parent primary key value(s). The initial primary row to be inserted must allow its foreign key(s) to be NULL. In figure 3–10, a new BOOK, AUTHOR, PUBLISHER relationship could not be added if NULLs were not defined as valid for any foreign keys.

If all foreign keys in Figure 3–10 may never be NULL, then all tables within this referential structure must be fully populated with the LOAD utility. Please see the **Utilities chapter** for load scenarios when loading referential structures.

FIGURE 3–10
CYCLE STRUCTURE INSERT ANOMALY

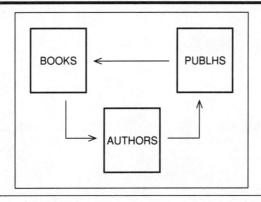

A single referential structure may reside within multiple tables in one simple TABLESPACE, multiple tables in a segmented TABLESPACE, or multiple TABLESPACEs. A referential structure that spans more than one TABLESPACE is considered a TABLESPACE structure. Note that other documents may refer to a tablespace structure as a table space set. The following factors must be considered when a referential structure is utilized:

Time of constraint creation
LOAD utility option: **ENFORCE [NO]**
CHECK utility

Referential constraints may be defined at the time a table is created or with the DDL ALTER statement. If constraints are established after a table is populated, no DML (SELECT, INSERT, etc.) accesses will be allowed until all constraints are verified by the CHECK utility. All related tables will be in CHECK PENDING status until the CHECK utility has executed.

If ENFORCE NO was specified during table load, then all tables within the structure will also be in CHECK PENDING status. The CHECK utility must be executed to reset the CHECK PENDING status.

See the Appendix to the **Utilities chapter** for information on the LOAD, CHECK, REPORT, and REPAIR utilities specifically related to referential integrity issues.

Data Definition Language (DDL)

DB2 acts upon objects which range in significance hierarchically from data bases and stogroups to tables, indices, and views. A DB2 object is classified as something defined in the DB2 catalog that can be manipulated by a SQL statement. It is precisely this manipulation of DB2 objects with respect to creation and performance considerations that will be presented in this chapter.

DB2 Version 2.1 provides a security mechanism that greatly extends object ownership. In prior releases, AUTHIDs with grouped authorities (e.g., **SYSADM, DBADM**) could create objects for other users. Unfortunately, the actual owner was not registered in the DB2 catalogs. Version 2.1 furnishes a facility that allows one user to create an object for another user. Furthermore, the event will be saved within the applicable DB2 catalog tables. Please see the **SECURITY** chapter for specific information about grouped authorities.

■ STOGROUPS

A DB2 **STOGROUP** is merely a set of DASD volumes (from 1 to 133) associated with one Integrated Catalog Facility (ICF) catalog named by the user for use by DB2. DB2 uses stogroups to allocate space for tablespaces and indices, to define VSAM datasets for the same, and to extend or delete the VSAM datasets as required. When allocating stogroups, estimate the number of bytes of stored data and multiply by a factor of two for an approximation of the amount of storage required in the stogroup (i.e., the number of volumes that should be assigned to the stogroup). The factor of two may appear a bit excessive, but this takes into consideration indices and DASD overhead associated with inter record block gaps.

The user should be aware of several requirements for stogroups.

1. DB2 will return a dynamic allocation error if all volumes within a sto-group are not mounted at the time of a CREATE request for a tablespace or index.

2. All volumes <u>within</u> a stogroup must be of the same device type.[1] This requirement clearly does not prevent the allocation of multiple stogroups to utilize different device types.

3. Multiple stogroups may include the same DASD volume.

4. Indices may utilize different stogroups from those utilized by tablespaces to distribute the load more evenly.

5. If the ICF catalog is password protected, the same password must be specified for the stogroup create request.

6. An IBM system default stogroup is defined at installation time as SYSDEFLT. Therefore, the user can quite easily use a stogroup without ever having allocated one.

7. DB2 uses the VSAM REUSE attribute to enable the DSN1COPY utility to restore datasets without having to delete and define VSAM clusters.

8. Volumes in a stogroup are used serially; this means that a volume is used in total before the next volume is accessed. DB2 makes no attempt to balance the load from a storage perspective.

For performance purposes, a user should be sure to allocate high-use DB2 objects (i.e., tables) on faster or less I/O-intensive devices than would be used for low-access objects. It may also be advisable to maintain different applications in different ICF catalogs (therefore, separate stogroups).

Information about stogroups and the volumes allocated to them may be found in the DB2 catalog tables, SYSIBM.SYSSTOGROUP and SYSIBM.SYSVOLUMES, respectively.

The STOSPACE utility must be run to update space statistics when using stogroups.

The syntax for the creation of a stogroup is shown in Figure 4–1.

FIGURE 4–1

```
CREATE STOGROUP stogroup-name
    VOLUMES
    (volume1,volume2,...,volume133)
    VCAT ICF-catalog-name
    [PASSWORD password]
    ;
```

[1] Any 3380 is considered to be the same device type.

- *stogroup-name* — must be unique among stogroups, although it may be used to name other DB2 objects.

- *volume1–133* — represents the volume serial number(s) of the DASD volume(s) to be included in the stogroup. The volumes included in the stogroup may be added or removed later through use of the ALTER STOGROUP command. However, current storage configurations will not be affected; only future storage assignments will reflect the change to the stogroup. A volume may not be removed until all DB2 objects have been dropped from the volume.

- *ICF-catalog-name* — is the catalog name or alias of the ICF catalog associated with the stogroup to be created. All volumes within a stogroup must be associated with the same ICF catalog. This catalog name will become the high-order qualifier for all VSAM datasets associated with this catalog.

- *password* — is the control or master password of the ICF catalog associated with the stogroup.

A user may desire to define his or her own VSAM datasets rather than allow DB2 to handle it through stogroup utilization. Using Access Method Services (AMS) IDCAMS facility, the user must define a dataset for each simple tablespace (or partition of a partitioned tablespace) and simple index (or partition of a partitioned index). Additionally, any additional datasets required due to dataset growth must also be allocated by the user. Usually, these datasets are defined as Entry Sequenced Datasets (ESDSs). VSAM linear datasets (LDSs) are also supported.

Direct user allocation of VSAM ESDS datasets, rather than allocation via the stogroup mechanism, enables the user to maintain closer control over the physical storage of tables and indices; including their placement and allocation type. In turn, DB2 tablespace definition defines VSAM datasets. In either case, however, you will not be able to use the AMS EXPORT, IMPORT, REPRO, or PRINT commands after the datasets have been formatted. When stogroups are used, DB2 will automatically delete datasets when the tablespace is dropped, extend datasets when necessary, and create new datasets when the old ones are full. Thus there is a tradeoff between the two approaches in dataset management.

User allocation of DB2 datasets also means that the modification of space allocations will be easier. This is significant for tables that are expected to rise or fall dramatically in size, making the DB2 allocations unsuitable.

Large tables that must reside on multiple volumes or in multiple datasets are excellent candidates for user allocation. User allocation will allow any related datasets of these tables to be recovered with the DSN1COPY utility. Recall that simple tablespaces utilizing stogroups will allocate additional datasets when their current primary and secondary allocations are exhausted.

Furthermore, it is much easier to move datasets from one device type to another when DB2 stogroups are not utilized. This aspect should be considered for datasets likely to undergo massive growth or size reduction in the future.

DB2 allocates datasets within stogroups using record space allocation; whereas user allocation processing may request track or cylinder space allocation of datasets. Note that if the number of kilobytes for both primary <u>and</u> secondary space allocations is divisible by the device type cylinder size (e.g., 600K on a 3380 device), then cylinder allocation will be requested by AMS.

User definition of VSAM datasets also means that the automatic deletion of datasets on a time basis may be inhibited through the use of the TO/FOR options in the DEFINE CLUSTER statement.

User dataset definitions may also specify linear VSAM datasets. This option will be available for stogroup allocation with the release of DB2 version 2.

Finally, installations that are using MSS devices (Mass Storage System, device type 3850) may desire staging options other than the defaults (i.e., STAGE and NODESTAGEWAIT) which DB2 employs.

Users who choose to allocate their own VSAM ESDS datasets should be aware that DB2 checks to make sure that your definitions are correct.

1. All dataset definitions must be complete before the create request for an index or tablespace is issued.

2. Both the cluster and data component names must be specified. Naming of the datasets must conform to the following structure.

    catname.DSNDB*x*.*dbname*.*tsname*.I0001.*Annn*

where:

- *catname* — is the ICF catalog name or alias used in the USING VCAT clause of the create request.

- *x* — C for cluster or D for data component.

- *dbname* — is the data base used in the create tablespace request, the data base associated with the table for which an index is defined, or the system default, if used.

- *tsname* — is the tablespace or indexspace name used in the create request. It must be unique within the data base. If your index name is not exactly eight characters long, DB2 will generate an indexspace name using parts of the index name.

- *nnn* — is the dataset numbering sequence (most clearly demonstrated by the partition numbers of a partitioned dataset). Note that additional datasets, if allocated, must follow this numbering sequence by incrementing each new allocation name by one. Simple or partitioned tablespaces may utilize multiple datasets.

The password provided in tablespace or index dataset creation does not correspond to the VSAM catalog password since DB2 will not need to know it for user allocations. Rather, this password is the highest level password.

All datasets including index datasets must be defined as NONINDEXED with a RECORDSIZE of 4089 and CONTROLINTERVALSIZE of 4096, REUSE, and SHAREOPTIONS (3,3).

DB2 will ignore several options of the DEFINE CLUSTER command even if they have been applied to a user-allocated dataset. These options include: SPANNED, EXCEPTIONEXIT, SPEED, BUFFERSPACE, and WRITECHECK.

The SYSADM ID assigned during DB2 installation will be assigned as the owner of the cluster definition, unless otherwise specified by the user.

Index or tablespaces that are dropped must have their corresponding datasets deleted by the user, unless they are to be reused by issuing the COMMIT command first. DB2 will destroy the old data when reuse/COMMIT is specified by writing over it. Similarly, if a user deletes a tablespace or index dataset, he or she is also responsible for dropping the corresponding DB2 object; DB2 will not handle it automatically.

As has been demonstrated, there are some advantages to direct user allocation of DB2 datasets in lieu of allocation through stogroups. However, DB2 is unable to perform several manipulation functions automatically against user-allocated datasets, so direct user-allocation should be chosen only sparingly, if at all, and with sound justification and thorough follow-up.

There is even less justification in DB2 Version 2 for direct user-allocation of DB2 datasets, as datasets allocated via stogroups may be extended and specific space allocation may be requested. Additionally, DSN1COPY has been improved to more fully support STOGROUP.

■ DATA BASES

A DB2 **data base** is a means of referencing sets of tablespaces and index spaces for operational and security purposes. A DB2 data base may be the unit of access to tables and indices, thereby minimizing the impact on applications that do not require use of the data base and its related objects. DB2 security mechanisms may also grant authorization at the data base level.

DB2 data base creation is simple because there are only two options that DB2 will accept in a data base CREATE request. These options will then be available as defaults for subsequent creation of tablespaces and indexspaces within that data base. The syntax for the creation of a data base is shown in Figure 4–2.

FIGURE 4–2

```
CREATE DATABASE data-base-name
     STOGROUP stogroup-name
     BUFFERPOOL bufferpool-name
     ;
```

- *data-base-name* — must be unique among all data bases within a DB2 system and must not begin with the characters DSNDB. DSNDB is the prefix for all data bases under which the system catalog tablespaces are defined.

- *stogroup-name* — names an existing storage group that may provide DASD space as necessary. If the parameter is omitted, the default will be SYSDEFLT.

- *bufferpool-name* — names the default bufferpool (BP0, BP1, BP2, or BP32K) for objects that will be defined within this data base. The default is BP0.

Both STOGROUP and BUFFERPOOL specifications may be overridden in subsequent CREATE TABLESPACE and INDEX statements. Therefore, when specified here they are defaults to be taken when they are omitted from an individual object CREATE statement.

For clarity, it is recommended that STOGROUP and BUFFERPOOL be required entries for DATABASE, TABLESPACE, and INDEX statements.

Normally, the use of bufferpool BP0 is granted to everyone (PUBLIC) while the use of STOGROUP SYSDEFLT is not granted to everyone. Our poor first time user, in an attempt to create a table/tablespace, will specify a DATABASE and BUFFERPOOL but not a STOGROUP. Since the DATABASE statement did not include a STOGROUP, he receives: 'SQLCODE-551 AUTHID xxxxxxx NOT AUTHORIZED TO USE STOGROUP SYSDEFLT'. Not knowing the default, our user becomes totally confused. Worse still, if the use of SYSDEFLT were granted to public, it would become the dumping ground for all sorts of useless information. Similar problems will be discussed later for other defaults.

Definition of objects within DB2 data bases may occur only when applications do not involve any objects referred to by the definitional request. Furthermore, DB2 will not permit any concurrent access to a data base for applications requesting BIND activities, dynamic SQL requests, or many DB2 utilities. (Note that DB2 will create a table when a SAVE DATA request is issued under QMF for a non-existent table name. Therefore, QMF users may also be subject to the same contention.) It is recommended that users allocate dedicated data bases as a means of avoiding contention that their specific data requirements are apt to cause or cannot tolerate.

DB2 will store information pertinent to a data base in the DB2 catalog table, SYSIBM.SYSDATABASE. Additionally, most utilities will update other system catalog tables. These tables use a strict clustering technique based on DATABASE name. Several concurrently running utilities or BIND operations will cause catalog contention if processing against the same data base. Therefore, it may be advisable to allow only one tablespace per data base. DB2 Release 3 allows up to 800 data bases to be concurrently in use in an MVS/XA environment. If the one-tablespace-per-data-base option is to be enforced, then the data base naming convention should allow generic names to be specified in START/STOP DB commands. See the "Naming Conventions" section in the **Logical Design** chapter for a suggested approach.

By the way, if a data base is dropped (deleted), all its dependent objects are also dropped. That would include tablespaces, tables, views, and indices, but not synonyms. All plans that referenced tables within this data base would be invalidated.

■ TABLESPACES

A DB2 **tablespace** is a named set of VSAM spaces populated by one or more DB2 tables and composed of one or more VSAM ESDS datasets associated with the creator of the tablespace, although the dataset names are not prefixed by the AUTHID of the creator. DB2 tablespaces are not likely to be explicitly referenced by the average user, except when they are being created.

Tablespaces nonetheless must be dealt with implicitly as

1. A unit of locking.
2. The unit of data involved in some utilities.

Tablespaces may be defined as simple, segmented, or partitioned: a **simple tablespace** contains one or more DB2 tables; a **segmented tablespace** also contains one or more tables, stored in (from 4 to 64) contiguous pages called **segments**; a **partitioned tablespace** may contain only one DB2 table, divided by key range values into multiple partitions during the CREATE process for the table's clustering index.

Because each partition of a partitioned tablespace is allocated to a different VSAM ESDS dataset, partitioned tablespaces may represent an advantage over simple tablespaces in that they may be assigned to multiple physical devices for performance enhancement. Also, a partitioned tablespace provides more flexibility for the execution of certain DB2 utilities because individual partitions may be the unit of recovery or reorganization. The ability to limit access to individual partitions may dramatically reduce utility execution time, despite the fact that the entire tablespace will be locked for the duration of the execution. Obviously, large tables are good candidates for partitioning if ranges of the primary key may be segregated appropriately for potential utility usage.

A potential disadvantage to the use of tablespace partitioning is that, once defined, the individual partitions themselves may not be deleted or redistributed. Even the clustering index for a table residing in a partitioned tablespace cannot be dropped unless the table to which it relates is dropped first. Given that execution of utilities over partitions as opposed to entire tables may save processing time, it may be more effective to allocate an alternate table in a different tablespace to act as an index rather than to define an index over the partitions, because the entire tablespace will be locked during utility execution and an application may not tolerate such unavailability for larger tables.

Partitioning requires that only <u>one</u> <u>table</u> may be defined for a given tablespace, a <u>clustering</u> <u>index</u> must be defined for the table, and the values of the key used for the purposes of partitioning <u>may</u> <u>not</u> <u>be</u> <u>updated</u> during processing.[2]

Be aware that the clustering index defined for the partitioned tablespace will act as a delimiter which specifies the upper limit (or lower limit, for descending sequences) for key values allowed within a given partition. In this sense, the index acts as an integrity check upon row placement.

As previously stated, multiple tables may be defined within a given tablespace. However, there are several reasons why such a definition may not be the wisest approach for simple or segmented tablespaces.

1. Locking specified at the tablespace level will hold a lock over all tables within that tablespace. Although this is not a new concept, care must still be given to ensure that all tables to be simultaneously locked are logically related such that they may tolerate the lock duration. In addition to being related, the tables should not vary in size (i.e., one large table and multiple smaller ones) because then a few lock requests could cause unnecessary duration of locking for all tables.

2. A SQL LOCK TABLE statement on a simple tablespace will also cause a full tablespace lock to occur. This is dangerous for the reasons just presented and because such statements are typically issued by application code that, unaware of the composition of the tablespace, will not be sensitive to the full impact of the request. Since such a request should typically require the locking of only one table by the application, the unavailability of all other tables within the tablespace is needlessly inefficient.

3. Full tablespace scans, whether intended or defaulted by the inability of DB2 to utilize an index, will actually scan all tables within a simple tablespace. Obviously, as the number and size of tables increases, the potential I/O processing and degradation of performance increases.

4. As with other forms of tablespace locking, execution of the RECOVER and REORG utilities will lock an entire simple or segmented tablespace even though the utility itself may have been concerned with only one of the tables within the non-partitioned tablespace. Note that outstanding conditions such as COPY PENDING, IMAGE PENDING, and CHECK PENDING apply to entire simple or segmented tablespaces and not to individual tables.

5. Also, the LOAD/REPLACE utility refreshes an entire simple tablespace and should not be considered for tables within a common tablespace if

---

[2] Note that such processing may be simulated by the use of DELETE and INSERT requests in most instances. This prohibition of UPDATE requests does somewhat temper the transparency of tablespace definition to the average user as stated at the outset of this section.

they are to be replaced at different times. Grouping the tables by logical relationship is critical to performance of this utility.

6. Dropping a table within a multi-table tablespace permits no reclamation of unused space until a reorganization occurs.

7. Under normal circumstances, a clustering index will not cause data to be redistributed in clustering sequence during a REORG if multiple tables exist within a simple tablespace.

8. A mass-delete (i.e., DML DELETE with no WHERE clause) of a table within a segmented tablespace will not allow space reuse if referential constraints are in effect.

9. Tuning segmented tablespaces may be difficult, due to the inability to specifically place tables on DASD.

Despite the previously stated disadvantages of defining multiple tables within simple or segmented tablespaces, there are some instances when such action is justified.

1. Tables logically related by frequent references such as JOINs and UNIONs may tolerate the unavailability of several tables due to the locking of a few as appropriate to the application. Simultaneous locking may be required to ensure the integrity of the relationship, particularly when common primary keys are utilized; therefore, they might just as well reside in a common tablespace.

2. Tables sharing a common tablespace should all be uniformly small, having approximately 1000 rows of about 65 bytes each. This would mean that locking any one table (the invocation of a utility), would not lock all other tables within the tablespace for an inordinate amount of time.

   Perhaps the best reason for grouping many small tables within one tablespace (as opposed to creating them in individual tablespaces) is to reduce I/O and storage requirements, as well as virtual storage and allocation/deallocation costs.

3. Tables may also share a common tablespace to advantage if they are seldom or never updated by application processing. Lack of updating (or deletion) would mean that most lock requests could be issued on a share basis. Share locking, in turn, would not inhibit concurrency since share locks are usually not the point of contention in table processing.

4. Tables that can be loaded by interleaving their data rows throughout a simple tablespace will enable the greatest access efficiencies. This is accomplished by sorting the keys of all tables prior to load execution such that a row of one table is followed by the respective rows of alternating tables. Be aware, however, that this interleaving of data is totally user-dependent, as DB2 will not support this sequence upon future insert requests or access path determination. Consequently, interleaving is best if all tables within the tablespace are subject to read-only access.

5. All tables of one referential structure may be placed in one segmented tablespace. Then all related tables may be populated with one execution

of the LOAD (ENFORCE CONSTRAINTS) utility. The related tables will not be in CHECK PENDING status. Thus, additional operations will not be required to establish constraints (ALTER) or validate constraints (CHECK UTILITY).

6. A SQL "Lock Table" statement on a segmented tablespace will cause locks to be taken only on all pages of one table. Thus concurrency is increased.

7. Dropping a table within a segmented tablespace permits immediate reuse of the newly available space.

8. A mass-delete (i.e., DML DELETE with no WHERE clause) of a table within a segmented tablespace allows space reuse of all pages if no referential constraints are in effect.

The definition of multiple tables within a tablespace will minimize the number of VSAM ESDS datasets to support and, therefore, should not be altogether disregarded as an alternative. However, each table (for any tablespace type) will still require a separate index, which must be allocated as a separate dataset. To summarize, the disadvantages of having multiple tables per tablespace normally dictate that one table per tablespace is optimal. Definitely follow this guideline if there is any doubt about the exceptions indicated above.[3]

FIGURE 4–3
NON-PARTITIONED TABLESPACE

```
CREATE TABLESPACE tablespace-name
    [IN data-base-name]
    [USING VCAT catname |
           STOGROUP stogroup-name
                    [PRIQTY integer
                    SECQTY integer
                    ERASE YES | NO]]
    [FREEPAGE integer] [PCTFREE integer]
    [BUFFERPOOL bufferpool]
    [SEGSIZE page-int]          V2.1
    [LOCKSIZE PAGE | TABLESPACE | ANY |
                    TABLE]             V2.1
    [CLOSE  YES | NO]
    [DSETPASS password]
```

---

[3] Please refer to the section on views later in this chapter for an alternative technique for achieving multiple row definitions within one tablespace/table and minimizing the number of indices.

FIGURE 4–4
PARTITIONED TABLESPACE

```
CREATE TABLESPACE tablespace-name
    [IN data-base-name]
    [USING VCAT catname |
            STOGROUP stogroup-name
                    [PRIQTY integer
                    SECQTY integer
                    ERASE YES | NO]]
    [FREEPAGE integer] [PCTFREE integer]
    NUMPARTS integer
            (PART integer1 USING ········
            ,PART integern USING ········
            )
    [BUFFERPOOL bufferpool]
    [LOCKSIZE PAGE | TABLESPACE | ANY]
    [CLOSE YES | NO]
    [DSETPASS password]
```

Figures 4–3 and 4–4 present the format of the DDL statement to define a tablespace. Figure 4–4 differs from Figure 4–3 by its inclusion of the NUMPARTS parameter.[4]

Briefly, these parameters are discussed as follows.

- *tablespace name* — may be any tablespace name not already defined as part of the data base specified in the IN clause.

- *data-base-name* — must be a data base already in the DB2 catalog (default DSNDB04) and must not include DSNDB03 or DSNDB06 (or DSNDB07 unless in stopped mode).

- *catname* — Use of this parameter indicates that the user, and not DB2, will define the datasets for the tablespace. The AMS cluster definition for the first dataset (i.e., catname.DSNDBx......A001) must be completed prior to execution of this CREATE statement.

- *stogroup-name* — indicates that DB2 will define the datasets for the tablespace. The stogroup name must be in the DB2 catalog and the user must have SYSADM authority or the USE privilege over it. The default for STOGROUP name is the stogroup specified for the data base within which the tablespace is to reside. If there is no stogroup defined for the data base the system default stogroup, SYSDEFLT will be used.

---

[4] Note that some parameters are similar to IDCAMS cluster definition.

- PRIQTY *integer*—indicates the primary quantity of space in kilobytes to be allocated for the DB2 datasets. Kilobytes is employed for device independence. The primary quantity must be available on the first volume of the stogroup. The default is 3 since DB2 uses the first two pages for internal purposes and there is only one page left for data storage. Do not let this parameter default, as the tablespace will inevitably expand into secondary space allocations that will not be adjacent to the primary allocation. Cylinder allocations will be made if **both** the primary and secondary request are divisible by the number of bytes per cylinder for the device. A 3380 cylinder accommodates 600 K bytes. Therefore, if both quantities are divisible by 600 you will achieve cylinder allocations for any 3380 device type.

- SECQTY *integer* — indicates the secondary space allocation allotted to the DB2 dataset. The default for this parameter is also 3. Avoid the situation where the tablespace will require use of secondary space allocations, as they won't be adjacent to the primary allocations and will yield less favorable performance.[5]

- ERASE YES | NO — indicates to DB2 whether to erase the data in the tablespace when it is dropped. If specified, the data will be written over with hex zeros (X'00'). This is largely useless except for obliterating remnants of sensitive production data.

  Note: the USING parameters are the same for both partitioned and non-partitioned tablespaces, subject to a hierarchical interpretation. A USING clause defined for a specific partition will override, for that partition, the USING values defined for the tablespace as a whole. Similarly, the USING clause defined for a tablespace as a whole will override the default values.

- FREEPAGE *integer* — indicates how often DB2 should leave available a free page of storage during the load of a table within the tablespace. DB2 will attempt to locate nearby storage when additional space is required. For a segmented tablespace, *integer* must be less than the SEGSIZE-*page int* specification.

- PCTFREE *integer* — indicates the percentage of each page to be left available for storage during the load of a table within the tablespace. The higher the PCTFREE parameter, the higher the possible access concurrency to the tablespace, since fewer pages will ultimately have to be locked for update processing. The PCTFREE approach is more efficient than that of FREEPAGE when additional space allocation can be

---

[5] Cylinder allocations will be forced if both primary and secondary space requests are divisible by the number of bytes available on the cylinder for that device type (e.g., 600,000 bytes on a 3380 type device).

```
PRIQTY 1800  SECQTY 600  (CYL, (3,1))
```

anticipated. PCTFREE and FREEPAGE should be set to zero if the table(s) will be read-only.

- NUMPARTS *integer* — simply indicates the number of partitions to be allocated for a partitioned tablespace.

- *bufferpool* — determines tablespace page sizes. The parameters are **BP0, BP1,** or **BP2** for a 4K page size or **BP32K** for a 32K page size. You should almost always code BP0 for all DB2 data. The other bufferpools may be accessed by DB2 for internal purposes or may be used to isolate an index or tablespace for tracing. If the table row size is greater than 4,074 (including row overhead), then BP32K must be specified.

- SEGSIZE *page-int* — (Version 2.1) indicates the number of pages per segment for a segmented tablespace. From 4 to 64 pages (in multiples of 4) may be specified. Segments will be allocated from contiguous empty pages as needed. Each segment will only contain rows of one table. All tables within one tablespace must utilize the same segment size. The *page-int* value must be greater than the FREEPAGE *integer* specification.

- LOCKSIZE — indicates which locking level DB2 should employ on the tablespace. This, in turn, determines the amount of data to be locked during data access and the resulting maximum level of concurrency.

  Prior to DB2 Version 2.1, use of the smallest unit of locking (i.e., PAGE) was preferable to provide maximum concurrency. PAGE locks usually do not allow escalation by DB2[6] and thus, provide a way of circumventing DB2 control over locking; page locks can be used, where appropriate, to maximize concurrency for the application. Page locking provides the maximum of concurrency at the cost of CPU processing by DB2 and the IMS Resource Locking Mechanism (IRLM) and thus should be used in conjunction with frequent commit requests to free resources.

  New with Version 2.1 is the LOCKSIZE TABLE specification. It may only be used in conjunction with the SEGSIZE parameter for segmented tablespaces. LOCKSIZE TABLE will not reduce the actual number of locks taken, but will reduce the related number of calls to the IRLM. One call to the IRLM will lock all pages of all the segments of a table; formerly, only one page or one dataset (tablespace) per call would have been locked.

  The authors recommend that locksize ANY be used to allow DB2 to escalate the locking unit from PAGE to TABLE or TABLESPACE when the number of page locks per tablespace exceeds the installation maximum. This action causes all former page locks to be released. Therefore, the ANY option serves to balance concurrency with performance.

  TABLESPACE locking reduces CPU costs at the expense of concurrency and is therefore most appropriate for read-only tables that are

---

[6] Refer to the **Application Design** chapter for an instance where page locking may be escalated to tablespace locking.

never subject to concurrency issues. Tablespace locking is more appropriate in batch processing where entire tablespaces will be scanned,
thus greatly reducing locking overhead. Although it reduces the IRLM
requirements, IRLM does not release the tablespace lock until the program terminates or commits. The user may thus be locking more data
for a longer duration than is otherwise necessary — despite the CPU cost
savings.

- CLOSE YES | NO — indicates to DB2 whether or not it should close
  datasets of the tablespace when there is no current access of the
  tablespace, not the actual table.

  NO — should be used when there are multiple users concurrently accessing the tablespace, since frequent open and close operations may provoke
  high supervisor overhead costs. Every open tablespace ACB requires 2.3K
  of memory below the already cluttered MVS 16 meg line. This figure will
  range from 1.2K to 2.3K with subsequent releases of MVS X/A, depending
  upon the release of DFP. In a testing environment where every developer
  has his/her own set of test tables, there could conceivably be over 200
  datasets (tables & indices) in use. That adds up to 460,000 bytes of highly
  sought after memory.

  YES — is appropriate when few accesses to the tablespace are anticipated,
  and the unnecessary allocation of virtual storage cannot be justified.

Note that DB2 will automatically allocate and name a tablespace if none
was specifically requested. However, this approach is not recommended
because DB2 will use nonstandard naming conventions and will allocate
tablespaces one track at a time.

Furthermore, note that stogroups and bufferpool parameters may be
designated at the data base definition level and will remain in effect for
tablespace creation if no overriding parameters are specified.

Particular caution in this regard should be exercised. Failure to specify
a parameter, permitting a default value to be used, could place the creator
in a position of not having the authority to access the default object. In a
typical situation where the data base name is not specified, the name would
default to DSNDB04. If the person trying to create the table/tablespace is not
authorized to use DSNDB04, then DB2 would return a SQLCODE − 551
(unauthorized use), which can be very confusing.

■ TABLES

A DB2 **table** is a named set of unordered rows, each composed of the same
sequence of columns. The column sequence itself is not critical,[7] and the
values within the columns are variable. The table name is prefixed by the

---

[7] Except perhaps from a performance perspective—not the issue at this point.

AUTHID of its creator. From the point of origin forward, tables are intimately tied to that creator. Table row order is guaranteed by DB2 only after a reorganization. The LOAD utility places rows into a table in the sequence in which they are received. If load input was in cluster sequence then the table will be in cluster sequence.

Tables are the single form of external data presentation in the DB2 environment. Even DB2 catalog information is presented to the user in the form of tables, and can be manipulated on the same basis as any other DB2 table. Additionally, table structure is often the primary point of control and contact for the average user. Security is often administered at the table level by granting authorization or denial of access to a table. It follows that logical and physical table design and administration have wide-sweeping consequences for DB2 performance and integrity.

Logical design falls victim to a tradeoff between the practical issues involved in application requirements and design issues of good normalization techniques.[8] In proper normalization methodology, increased levels of normalization are sought to reduce redundancy and table maintenance (i.e., update overhead). This design progression almost certainly will yield the highest number of DB2 tables for physical implementation. The proliferation of tables, however, is in direct conflict with performance considerations that would arise in an application known to require multiple table accesses if the normalized data model were used. Performance may suffer in situations where multiple tables must be joined (in fact, denormalized) to accomplish application objectives. Therefore, a delicate balance must be maintained between update overhead of less than ultimate normalization data models and the performance reduction of fully normalized data models.

One method of reducing the number of tables with minimal impact on normalization is to eliminate the use of tables that act as indicators into other tables for the actual retrieval of data. This situation typically results in frequent table joins in order to obtain the entire data picture. Consider a situation where state abbreviations and little else are stored in one table that must be frequently joined with at least one other table to obtain zip code, area code, and sales tax information. In this case the designer, having realized the potential for performance degradation, should merge the two tables and permit minor redundancy to prevent unnecessary table joins. Pursuit of normalization, which seeks to minimize redundancy, may be overridden by qualifying information about application requirements. To achieve the proper balance of normalization and performance considerations, the designer must realize that on a practical level, **not all redundancy is bad**.

Consider the definition of a view to store data derived from two or more other columns which compose the view when the data does not require its own physical existence. A view is particularly desirable if these

---

[8] Please refer to the **Conceptual Model** chapter for a thorough discussion of normalization technique.

derived columns are not needed consistently, and the use of a view would not degrade performance.

Each table should be designed with at least one primary key defined as unique to ensure that each row of a table can be distinguished from all others in the table. Foreign keys may be utilized to associate the table with one or more others, based on columns which are analogous between them. These foreign keys, in turn, may be employed to assign indexing or to enable join functions that otherwise would have been difficult.

Referential Integrity Considerations

In DB2 Version 2.1, referential integrity enables the definition of and adherence to **constraints** between tables, which essentially guarantee the validity of such references without the intervention of application coding as was necessary in prior releases of DB2. Referential constraints are defined during the creation of a new table or during a subsequent **ALTER** request on an existing table. They are automatically deleted when an object of the relationship in a constraint no longer exists (i.e., is dropped). Referential constraints are automatically enforced for SQL INSERT, UPDATE, and DELETE processing as well as during LOAD processing with the ENFORCE option (new with DB2 Version 2.1). DB2 will never allow a violation to occur (even temporarily). Furthermore, the outcome from an operation must occur consistently, regardless of processing sequence (i.e., DELETE processing especially), or the operation will not be allowed.

Note that referential constraints defined for existing tables cannot be enforced for previously existing violations. Consequently, DB2 places the tablespace in CHECK PENDING status until the violations are eliminated.[9] The CHECK DATA utility (also new with DB2 Version 2.1) is executed to identify constraint violations and remove the CHECK PENDING status once violations have been corrected.

Utilization of referential integrity in DB2 Version 2.1 requires that all primary keys have *entity integrity*—defined as unique and not nullable. Only one primary key (composite or single column) may be defined for any primary (parent) table. This primary key must always exist for any given row in the parent table. Further, each foreign key value must match a primary key value in another table or be NULL. For composite primary keys, each component of the foreign key must match the corresponding component of the primary key in data type, size, and column sequence. A unique index on the primary key involved in the referential constraint is required; an index on the corresponding foreign key is highly recommended for performance reasons, although not required. A table created without a primary key unique

---

[9] Note that other circumstances may place a tablespace in CHECK PENDING status. Execution of the LOAD utility without enforcement of the referential constraints (i.e., ENFORCE NO, a new LOAD option) is an example of such a situation.

FIGURE 4–5
PARENT TABLE CREATE SYNTAX

```
CREATE TABLE table-name
(
PRIMARY KEY (col-nam1,...., col-namN)
    col-nam1 data-type NOT NULL
        .
        .
    col-namN data-type NOT NULL
    additional column definitions
)
IN database-name.tablespace-name
;
CREATE UNIQUE INDEX pri-index-name
    on table-name (col-nam1,...
                        , col-namN)
    CLUSTER.....
;
```

index will be flagged as unusable in DB2 catalog tables until such an index is created. For additional referential integrity design considerations and implementation restrictions, see the "Referential Integrity" section of the **Logical Model** chapter.

The table creation parameters specific to referential integrity are detailed in Figures 4–5 and 4–6. Additional CREATE TABLE parameters and design considerations are expounded upon in Figure 4–7.

The general format for the creation of the primary (parent) table of a constraint relationship follows.

• PRIMARY KEY *(col-nam1, . . . , col-namN)* — identifies the table columns of the primary index. If more than one column is specified, they should be contiguous. No column may be declared more than once. Primary key columns may never be NULL, and a UNIQUE index is required on the specified columns. As with all index definitions, the total number of bytes may not exceed 254; the total number of columns may not exceed sixteen.

The general format for the creation of the dependent table of the constraint relationship follows. Note that a dependent table in one relationship may be the parent table of another relationship or even within the same relationship (i.e., self-referencing). Also, a dependent table may have more than one parent table.

FIGURE 4–6
DEPENDENT TABLE CREATE SYNTAX

```
CREATE TABLE table-name
(
PRIMARY KEY (col-nam1,...,col-namN)

FOREIGN KEY [constraint-name-1]
    (column-name-1,
    ,column-name-n)
REFERENCES par-table-1
[ON DELETE SET NULL I RESTRICT I CASCADE]

FOREIGN KEY [constraint-name-2]
    (column-name-a,
    ,column-name-z)
REFERENCES par-table-2
[ON DELETE SET NULL I RESTRICT I CASCADE]

    col-nam1    data-type NOT NULL
    ,col-namN    data-type NOT NULL

    ,column-name-1   data-type
    ,column-name-N   data-type

    ,column-name-a   data-type
    ,column-name-z   data-type
)
IN database-name.tablespace-name
;

CREATE UNIQUE INDEX pri-index-name
 on table-name (col-nam1,...,col-namN)

    CLUSTER......
;

CREATE INDEX fk-index-name-1
 on table-name (column-name-1
                    ,column-name-N)....
;

CREATE INDEX fk-index-name-2
 on table-name (column-name-a
                    ,column-name-z)....
;
```

- FOREIGN KEY *[constraint-name-1] (column-name-1, . . . , column-name-n)* — identifies the constraint name and the table columns of the first foreign key for this table. The *constraint-name-1* may be a maximum of eight characters; if specified, it will be the explicit name for this constraint. Constraint names will be referenced during constraint violations; they should therefore be explicit and unique. The default is the first eight characters (or less) of the foreign key's first column (i.e., *column-name-1*). *(column-name-1, ... , column-name-n)* are the column(s) that make up the first foreign key. Foreign key columns may be NULL. If any column is NULL the entire foreign key is treated as NULL and no referential integrity check to a parent table primary key will be performed. Except for the actual column name and the NULL attribute, dependent foreign keys must exactly match their respective parent primary keys, including column sequence.

- REFERENCES *par-table-1* — identifies the parent table for this constraint. The parent table must exist prior to the creation of this constraint.

- ON DELETE SET NULL | <u>RESTRICT</u> | CASCADE — establishes the DELETE RULE option for this relationship. The default is RESTRICT. DB2 implements both the UPDATE and INSERT RULES with an implicit option of RESTRICT. Therefore, no parameter is provided for either rule.

- CREATE INDEX *fk-index-name-1* — is a standard index creation statement. Indices on foreign keys are not required but strongly recommended.

Primary and foreign key columns may overlap. Key column overlap should be carefully analyzed to prevent anomalies during update or delete processing.

Non-Referential Integrity Considerations

Another aspect of design is table row size. Every row requires 8 bytes of overhead and every page has a 22 byte header. Furthermore, a **VARCHAR** (variable length) column requires two additional bytes for length, and a column that may be null has a one byte indicator. Therefore, a column that is both variable and nullable will have three additional bytes of overhead.

DB2 offers data pages and related bufferpools of either 4K or 32K bytes. DB2 does not allow table rows to span data pages; the size of the rows chosen, and therefore the data page size required, will determine whether a table must be processed in a 4K or 32K bufferpool.

Since a 32K bufferpool will require considerably more virtual storage, it is preferable to restrict all data pages to just less than 4,074 bytes (or fractional equivalents of 4K such as two 2,029-byte rows). This may mean reducing row size by dividing a table's rows into two or more tables with smaller rows in order to take advantage of the 4K bufferpools. Otherwise (unless row size is neatly divisible into 32K increments) there will be too much wasted space within the data page in which no more records can be stored.

On the other hand, rows should not be defined to contain fewer than 24 bytes (excluding row and column overhead) since DB2 can not store more than 127 rows within a data page. Rows smaller than 24 bytes will cause much wasted space on a page.

Here, as in the "Tables" section of this chapter, we must point out the compromise between design efficiency and application requirements. The actual composition of the rows (i.e., the column data structures) must be associated in accordance with the specified design. In order to obtain the most efficient data definitions, all columns that may be compared with each other should have the same length wherever possible. For numeric items, this means that both the precision (total number of digits) and scale (number of positions to the right of the decimal point) should be equal. If they are not, a full scan of the tablespaces associated with the columns under comparison may ensue—DB2 will probably not elect to use any indices defined for the tables. Where multiple tables are present within a tablespace, the ramifications of such a seemingly small point are much more severe. Moreover, in many installations, design will be the last area ever responsible for such evaluations. Inefficiencies introduced at this point will likely remain in the system indefinitely.

Consider also that a variable length column, which may reduce physical storage requirements (DASD), nonetheless utilizes an amount of virtual storage equal to its maximum size plus a two byte overhead amount. In instances where DB2 must move the row to another page during update (i.e., its length has increased beyond available storage on its current page), significant overhead may be incurred in subsequent processing of the row. Pointers to the new location of the row will reside in its former location on the original page, meaning that additional I/O will occur for every retrieval. For the preceding reasons, unless a column will exceed 20 bytes, it may be more efficient to define it as a fixed-length column. Also, do not overspecify the maximum length of the column, as this will increase the amount of virtual storage required for processing the row containing the column. Index entries will always be padded to account for the maximum length, and you may be prohibited from adding additional columns to the row containing the variable length column if the row's new maximum length will exceed the allowable size for the page.

Nulls should be employed where a default value (zero, blank, zero length) would produce unacceptable results. If used, an additional byte of DASD storage is required for an internal DB2 indicator. This byte must be interrogated in retrieval attempts in order to ascertain whether a column value is present, adding complexity to the application program. In cases where a column value is not available at the time of load but a default value is acceptable for application purposes, specify NOT NULL WITH DEFAULT. This will avoid the presence of the one-byte attribute on nullable fields and will allow the column to participate in built-in functions. Use of NULLs is discussed in more detail in the **Application Design** chapter.

A user-written edit routine, if defined for a table, serves to compress data and reduce DASD and I/O requirements for processing the table. However, an edit routine receives control with every attempt at data manipulation (i.e., retrieval, update, insert) and could substantially degrade performance if not carefully designed. Furthermore, edit routines may not be added or dropped once a table has been created, nor may columns be subsequently added to a table with an edit routine defined for it. Consequently, be sure that the DASD and I/O savings safely justify the restrictions of edit routine utilization, especially in the long run.

User-written validation routines screen data within a table, based on criteria defined in the routine. Like edit routines, validation routines may cause significant performance degradation in that they receive control with every request for data update, insertion, or deletion. Also, validation routines must be coded in assembler and may not issue any SQL requests. Although a validation routine may reduce the amount of code required by an application program, it is likely that a more effective solution would be to process the validation criteria within the program. A validation routine may be added or dropped after table creation; however, records already existing within the table will not be retroactively evaluated with respect to an added routine.

Field procedures are typically defined to encode or decode data within a column for security or collating purposes. As with the other types of procedures, CPU utilization may increase because the procedure will be invoked for all accesses of the column. A field procedure may be added with the addition of a column, but it may not be dropped. Again, be sure that application requirements justify the CPU utilization resulting from the invocation of a field procedure.

Figure 4–7 outlines the syntax of the TABLE CREATE function (exclusive of DB2 Version 2.1 referential constraint parameters as demonstrated in Figures 4–5 and 4–6). Note that the definition as presented may be submitted via SPUFI, DSNTEP2, DSNTIAD, or as embedded code within an application program. The user must be authorized for the CREATETAB privilege; have SYSADM authority; or have DBADM, DBCTRL, or DBMAINT authority for the data base referenced in the definition of the table.

Most significant is the qualification of the table name. If the table name is qualified in the definition (prefixed with an AUTHID), then the user associated with that qualification name will become the creator of the table and will possess all rights attributable to that table. Should the table not be explicitly qualified within the definition, the creator is the user executing the CREATE, and his/her AUTHID becomes the AUTHID of the definition's

FIGURE 4-7
BASIC TABLE CREATE SYNTAX

```
CREATE TABLE table-name
(column-name
 data-type
       [NOT NULL I NOT NULL WITH DEFAULT I
        no specification]
       [FIELDPROC program-name(constant)]
)

[IN [database-name.]tablespace-name
 I IN DATABASE database-name]
[EDITPROC program-name]
[VALIDPROC program-name]
```

execution (e.g., TSOID if submitted via SPUFI). Privileges of the creator may not be revoked, although the creator may grant other users privileges of access to the table. In Figure 4-8 the AUTHID, TSOID01, is being used to qualify table TBAC_CLM explicitly, while table TBAC_NOT will be explicitly qualified with the ID of the person invoking the create statement.

FIGURE 4-8

```
            Qualified and unqualified
                  table names
              TSOID01.TBAC_CLM
                  TBAC_NOT
```

- *table-name* — is a user-supplied name of the table being defined. The resulting fully qualified name must be unique relative to any other fully qualified table, view, or synonym name currently residing in the DB2 catalog.
- *column-name* — is a unique name for the column within the table. Note that being unique within the table does not preclude its use as a name for corresponding columns within other tables. This is especially useful in demonstrating relationships between tables for the purposes of joins, unions, foreign key definition, and the like.

  A maximum of 300 columns may be defined for a table.

- *data-type* — specifies the storage representation of the column within the table. As previously discussed within this section, make certain to create compatible definitions for columns that will be the participants in comparisons.[10]

  The choices are:

  - INTEGER — halfword binary up to 4 digits.
  - SMALLINT — fullword binary up to 9 digits.
  - FLOAT (*integer* | REAL | DOUBLE PRECISION) — single or double precision.
  - DECIMAL (*precision, scale*) — packed data, to 15 digits.
  - DATE / TIME default formats are determined at DB2 install time and may be retrieved in any of the formats listed below. They must be inserted using the format specified at install time.
  - DATE — dates returned in edited format.

ISO	YYYY-MM-DD
USA	MM/DD/YYYY
EUR	DD.MM.YYYY
JIS	YYYY-MM-DD
LOCAL	any site defined format

  - TIME — time returned in edited format.

ISO	HH.MM.SS
USA	HH:MM {AM / PM }
EUR	HH.MM.SS
JIS	HH:MM:SS
LOCAL	any site defined form

  - TIMESTAMP — timestamp returned in edited format where the date piece will be in one of the above DATE layouts.

    ISO YYYY-MM-DD-hh.mm.ss.nnnnnn

  - CHAR(*integer*) — up to 254 characters, fixed length.
  - VARCHAR(*integer*) — variable length, up to 254 characters.
  - LONG VARCHAR(*integer*) — up to 32,704 characters.
  - GRAPHIC(*integer*) — up to 127 double byte characters, fixed length.
  - VARGRAPHIC(*integer*) — up to 127 double byte characters, variable length.

- LONG VARGRAPHIC — variable length, up to 16,352 double byte characters.

- NOT NULL — disallows the presence of null values within the column. Data must always be provided during load or insert processing.

---

[10] Please refer to the presentation of the data types in the IBM manual, *IBM Database2 SQL Reference*.

- NOT NULL WITH DEFAULT — disallows the presence of null values within the column and states that, wherever a value is not specified for a column during load or insert processing, a default value will be substituted.

  The default value is dependent on column definition. Numeric data types will be defaulted to zero, fixed length strings will default to spaces, and variable length strings will receive a data content length of zero. (Recall that variable length columns are prefixed by a two-byte length of field value.)

  Note that failure to specify either form of the NOT NULL clause will mean that the column may accept NULL values and will default to the null value whenever a specific value for this column is omitted in insert or load processing.

- IN *database-name.tablespace-name* | IN DATABASE *database-name* — are optional specifications of the data base and tablespace targeted to receive the table being defined. The default is <u>DSNDB04</u>. If the default data base is not used, a user-specified data base must reside within the DB2 catalog prior to invocation of the table CREATE request.

  Use of the implicit form of tablespace specification means that a DB2 will define a tablespace for the table based on the name of the table, with all attributes of the non-optional tablespace CREATE statement. Since actual creation of a tablespace is being requested, the user must have DBADM, DBCTRL, or DBMAINT authority for the data base, hold the CREATETS privilege for the data base, or possess SYSADM authority.

  A tablespace explicitly named must relate to the data base specified (or DSNDB04 if the default was used). It may not name a tablespace that is partitioned and already contains a table. Reference to a tablespace implies its use and, therefore, the user must have SYSADM authority, DBADM authority for the data base, or the USE privilege for the tablespace.

- EDITPROC — names the program to be used as the edit routine for the table. This program may also be used as a data compression routine. Refer to the preceding discussion of edit procedures for a thorough discussion of their use. There is no default for this specification.

- VALIDPROC — names the program to be used as the validation routine for the table. Refer to the preceding discussion of validation procedures for a thorough discussion of their use. There is no default for this specification.

- FIELDPROC — names the program to be used as the field procedure for the column with which it is associated. Refer to the preceding discussion of field procedures for a thorough discussion of their use. There is no default for this specification.

  The constant value represents a parameter to be passed to the field procedure when it is invoked during the CREATE TABLE request. The constant is an optional parameter of the field procedure specification.

Note that a CREATE TABLE request may not be issued concurrently with the running of a DB2 utility that controls the tablespace in the same data base targeted by the request (implicitly or explicitly).

■ INDICES

An index is an ordered set of pointers[11] to rows in a DB2 data table; its name is prefixed by the AUTHID of the index creator (unlike data bases or tablespaces). DB2 indices exist for internal use by DB2 only and thus are never explicitly referenced by the user or SQL statements.

There are likely to be three primary objectives in establishing indices over data tables.

1. To ensure uniqueness of column values used as the indexing column(s). This is a referential integrity requirement for a primary key.
2. To guarantee the clustering (or physical) sequence of data within the table when particular access paths are known to be required.
3. To avoid a situation where an entire tablespace scan will be performed where no index is otherwise to be considered.

An index defined as **unique** will guarantee that no duplicate values will be allowed to exist within the column(s) specified as the indexing columns. This also applies to null values. Duplicate values of key columns encountered during the load phase will cause the load to fail and the index not to be populated.[12] Columns designated, after table population has occurred, to make up a unique key should be screened prior to index definition and reorganization to prevent load failure.

A **clustering** index will cause rows within the table to be physically positioned during insert and update processing as closely as possible to the sequence specified for the clustering index. Also, the table will physically be in clustering sequence after a REORG/RELOAD execution. A clustering index should be specified when columns are frequently used in a certain order. SQL statements such as ORDER BY, GROUP BY, and WHERE clauses, with large groupings of data required, are indicative of this type of situation. By accessing data in clustered sequence, DB2 may be able to avoid a sort prior to satisfaction of the SQL request.

Note that judgement should be used in designating clustering criteria; it may be preferable to assign the column that is the object of a WHERE clause rather than one that is the object of an ORDER BY or GROUP BY clause because it may be more efficient to retrieve the data first via the index based on the WHERE criteria, and then sort it into proper groupings, rather

---

[11] Row IDs, commonly referred to as RIDs.
[12] See LOAD, REPAIR, and CHECK utilities in the **Utilities** chapter for a method that will identify and correct indices in error. Version 2 allows deletion of duplicate rows

FIGURE 4–9
CHRONOLOGICAL INDEX CREATION

```
T1      CREATE UNIQUE INDEX BALIXUCL
        ON TDDA_BAL
            (column info )
            USING···········
                   ···········;
        CREATE INDEX BALIXANC
        ON TDDA_BAL
            (column info )
            USING···········
                   ···········


T2      DROP INDEX BALIXUCL

T3      REORG tablespace·······

T4      CREATE UNIQUE INDEX BALIXUCL
        ON TDDA_BAL
            (column info )
            USING···········
            CLUSTER·········;
```

than to select the data via an ordering criteria to fulfill the WHERE criteria. The resulting sort may be insignificant due to the small number of rows retrieved.

Furthermore, note that if no clustering index is specified, the first index created (in a chronological sense) will automatically be used by DB2 as a clustering index for REORG purposes. There is potential for DB2 to subtly degrade performance for some processing requests.

In Figure 4–9 four separate events are shown. The first event (T1) creates two indices. Neither one specifies CLUSTER, which means the first index, BALIXUCL, will by default be the clustering index. The second event (T2) drops what was the clustering index. Event 3 (T3) REORGs the tablespace that contains the table, TDDA_BAL, over which both indices were created. At the end of event 3 the table is in the sequence specified for index BALIXANC. The next day, users experience very bad response times. After careful analysis, it is decided that the BALIXUCL index must be recreated and that it must also be the clustering index. When the DBA performs event 4 (T4) response times do not improve!

The table is still in the sequence from the last reorganization. Since CLUSTER had not yet been specified for any existing index, the REORG utility used the first chronologically defined index to determine the physical reload sequence. Even though the BALIXUCL index was created with the CLUSTER specification, correct clustering of the rows will not occur until another REORG is executed. If CLUSTER had been specified for event 1, someone may have thought twice before dropping it. In short, always specify CLUSTER; do not leave it to chance.

Because indices are exclusively for DB2 internal use, it is not obvious to the user whether a particular index will be used to satisfy a particular retrieval request, even though the index has been created with a specific access path in mind. DB2 chooses the access path and therefore the index utilization during the bind process. Access Path Selection (APS) is based largely on potential CPU usage and I/O processing.

Before continuing this discussion on indices we must define the types of access DB2 can use. There are five APS methods.

1. Tablespace Scan — no index is used and all data pages in the entire tablespace are scanned.
2. Matching Index Scan — the index tree is evaluated with respect to the SQL predicate. Only leaf pages matching the predicate criteria are accessed.
3. Non-matching Index Scan — the index is accessed without the tree search. All leaf pages will be evaluated but only data matching the predicate will be accessed.
4. Matching Index without Data Reference — Similar to the Matching Scan with the exception that the index alone is sufficient to satisfy the SQL predicate. No data pages are accessed (e.g., COUNT(*) or EXISTS).
5. Non-matching Index Scan without Data Reference — Similar to the Non-matching Index Scan with the exception that the index alone is sufficient to satisfy the SQL predicate. No data pages are accessed.

With respect to performance, a matching index access strategy is preferable due to the minimization of I/O processing and the degree of data transfer necessary to satisfy the predicate. Where data requests are limited to index columns, a scan will be attempted without data reference, maximizing efficiency by reducing all cost factors. This is particularly true for large tables where I/O, data transfer, and CPU costs are most dramatically affected. When a matching index strategy is not possible, a non-matching index scan without data reference is the next best alternative. Tablespace scans are normally the least effective access strategy, unless one row or more per page will be retrieved.

If an average page contains 25 rows and a query is anticipated to return 4% or more rows of the table, then APS assumes a random distribution of

FIGURE 4–10
POTENTIAL DB2 DATA MOVEMENT

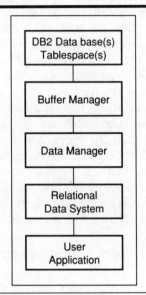

rows will be processed and scans every page in the table! This is not as terrible as it sounds; on the average, you are indeed processing every page in the table. Consider that 4 percent of a 25-row page is one row. Therefore, every page can be anticipated to be retrieved. Moreover, useless index I/O will be avoided.

In general, the type of predicate involved in the data processing request will strongly influence whether an index will be used. In the normal scheme of things, DB2 data bases are passed from the Buffer Manager component of DB2 to the Data Manager component, where they will eventually be routed to the Relational Data System component prior to release to the user application (see Figure 4–10). It is best to minimize the amount of data transferred between the Data Manager and the Relational Data System.

Predicates fall into two broad categories: those that can be processed by the Data Manager (sargable predicates[13]) and those that, due to their complexity, cannot (non-sargable predicates) and must be passed to the Relational Data System component for processing. With sargable predicates, the Data Manager screens the data so that only data pages which meet the criteria of the predicate will be transferred. Otherwise, all data pages will be transferred to the Relational Data System component.

In summary, access path selections and DB2 processing components are very relevant to cost considerations. Optimal performance will minimize I/O requests, the number of data rows processed by the Data Manager, and the

---

[13] *Sargable* is a term constructed from the merge of search and argument.

number of data rows received and processed by the Relational Data System. It is achieved through use of matching index scans or scans without data reference where sargable predicates are at issue.

To illustrate, a typical SELECT scenario would unfold as follows.

1. Data Manager accesses the data—an index or tablespace scan is employed.
2. Data Manager reduces the data available for transfer through application of any sargable predicates. The resulting data rows are then transferred to the Relational Data System.
3. Relational Data System, operating only on the rows transferred in Step 2, completes the processing of any remaining predicates (i.e., non-sargable) and performs a sort if required to present the output to the user as requested (e.g., ORDER BY).
4. The result data tables are passed to the user.

As demonstrated throughout the preceding discussion, it is not intuitively obvious whether DB2 has nominated the index of your choice in its access strategy; and regardless of that choice, the costs associated with the chosen access strategy are equally difficult to anticipate. Fortunately, DB2 has tempered its control by providing the EXPLAIN parameter as a window into its thought processes with respect to selection of indices. Using EXPLAIN, the user can be guided in the way to restructure his SQL requests in an attempt to manipulate index utilization, cost levels, efficiency of design, and concurrency issues.

The performance effects of indices vary according to table and tablespace size; cardinality (or proportion of distinct key values) of the index; the number of insert, update, and delete processing requests; and the frequency of index use. The following instances do not necessarily justify the creation of an index.

1. A small table (less than 5 data pages) that is frequently accessed but is predominantly read-only when accessed.
2. A small table (less than 10 data pages) that is not frequently accessed but is predominantly read-only when accessed.
3. A small table (less than 15 data pages) that is frequently accessed for insert, update, or delete activity.
4. A table in which more than 5 percent of the rows have key columns containing nonunique data and for which no clustered index exists. (This case would require more I/O with an index than for a tablespace scan.)

Additionally, a small table (under 150 pages) that is heavily accessed will more than likely retain most of its pages in the buffer pool. On the other hand, a large table should almost always have at least one index as an alternative to a tablespace scan, and smaller tables failing the criteria listed above should also be considered for index definition.

Consideration should be given to the temporary availability of indices where permanent support cannot be justified. Some tables are static except for a single month-end process during which they are subject to variable inserts, deletes, and updates. For such a table, an index could be created for month-end processing and dropped immediately thereafter.

If an **index** is appropriate according to the preceding criteria, it should be created prior to the actual load of the table whenever possible. Otherwise, DB2 must create index entries during the index CREATE process instead of during the tablespace LOAD process. Additionally, the index CREATE process itself will provoke a scan of the entire tablespace. Not only is this condition much less efficient for a populated table, but in earlier releases of DB2 it has also required up to twice the number of index pages as would be used in an index defined prior to load. The performance degradation caused by increased I/O will be significant. CREATE processing also requires the access of several DB2 catalog tables and should, if possible, be executed during periods of low system utilization.

Furthermore, all data input to a load process should, prior to the load, be sorted by key sequence specified by the clustering index. This will reduce tablespace page splits when additional rows are inserted.

The syntax for creating both non-partitioned and partitioned indices is shown in Figures 4–11 and 4–12, respectively.

FIGURE 4-11
NON-PARTITIONED INDEX FORMAT

```
CREATE [UNIQUE] INDEX index-name
       ON table-name

       (column_name_1 ASC I DESC...
       ,column_name_n ASC I DESC
       )
       USING VCAT catname I STOGROUP
                                    stogroup-name
                           PRIQTY int
                           SECQTY int
       [CLUSTER]
       [SUBPAGES int] [BUFFERPOOL bufferpool]
       [CLOSE YES I NO]
```

FIGURE 4–12
PARTITIONED INDEX FORMAT

```
CREATE [UNIQUE] INDEX index-name
        ON table-name
      (column_name_1 ASC I DESC...
      ,column_name_n ASC I DESC
      )
      USING VCAT catname I STOGROUP
                                    stogroup-name
                          PRIQTY int
                          SECQTY int
      [FREEPAGE int] [PCTFREE int]
      CLUSTER
          (PART int-1 VALUES(constant-1,
                                ,constant-n)
                  [USING ··········]
                  [FREEPAGE int] [PCTFREE int]
          ,PART int-n VALUES(constant-1,
                                ,constant-n)
                  [USING ··········]
                  [FREEPAGE int] [PCTFREE int]
          )
      [SUBPAGES int] [BUFFERPOOL bufferpool]
      [CLOSE YES I NO]
```

For a non-partitioned index UNIQUE and CLUSTER are optional. For a partitioned index, as shown in Figure 4–12, UNIQUE is optional, but **CLUSTER** is required. See the examples at the end of this chapter for completed tablespace, table, and table CREATE statements.

- UNIQUE — specifies that the key column(s) within this index must be unique (i.e., contain a unique value for each row). As previously mentioned, any key column with a high degree of cardinality should be considered for definition as unique to ensure that no duplicate values of the key column(s) will exist. Uniqueness of key column values will promote the use of the index by DB2, all other things being equal. More than one unique index per table may be created.

- *index-name* — is a user-defined name for the index being created, which is implicitly or explicitly qualified with an AUTHID. The fully qualified name must be unique within a DB2 system. If no AUTHID is specified then the userid of the person invoking this statement will become the qualifying AUTHID. If index-name is explicitly qualified with an AUTHID other than that of the person executing this statement, then the userid of the executor must hold the DBCTRL, DBADM, or SYSADM authority. Thus, indices may be created for other users. For example

1. Unqualified index (Creator is TSOIDA)

    ```
    CREATE UNIQUE INDEX          BALIXUCL
    ```

2. Qualified index where the AUTHID is the userid (Creator is TSOIDA)

    ```
    CREATE UNIQUE INDEX TSOIDA.BALIXUCL
    ```

3. Qualified index where the AUTHID is not the userid (any authorized creator)

    ```
    CREATE UNIQUE INDEX TSOIDX.BALIXUCL
    ```

Examples (1) and (2) would yield the same fully qualified index name. The unqualified portion of the index-name (BALIXUCL) is used by DB2 to generate an internal indexspace name. If the unqualified portion of the index name is exactly eight characters, it will also become the internal indexspace name. This indexspace name will, in turn, become part of a fully qualified VSAM dataset name *(catname.DSNDBx.dbname.ixspname.I0001.Annn)* where *ixspname* is generated by DB2. For this reason it is strongly recommended that index-name be restricted to exactly eight non-delimiter characters. This will facilitate DASD space management and limit confusion when VCAT is specified and a VSAM user dataset must be defined.

*   *table-name* — must be an existing table and may or may not be qualified. If you are not the owner of this table you may still create an index provided you have the INDEX privilege for this table, have DBADM authority over the data base it is in, or have SYSADM authority.

*   *column_name_1* ASC | DESC — identifies the column(s) for the index and whether each will be in ascending or descending sequence. Ascending is the default. The following is a valid column list for an index.

    ```
    (BAL_ACCT_NO ASC
    ,BAL_BR_NO ASC
    ,BAL_ACTY_DT DESC
    )
    ```

Since the latest dates will be the most frequently retrieved, BAL_ACTY_DT is specified with DESC. It may be very tempting to sequence the index in branch/account/date sequence instead of account/branch/date. **If the branch (BAL_BR_NO) were first, this index would probably never be used!** Instead, a leaf page scan would be used. The number of discrete values (cardinality) of the first column of an index determines whether the index will be chosen by Access Path Selection. The account number, although not unique to each row, will be sufficiently variable to justify index utilization, whereas the branch number will not.

- USING VCAT *catname* | STOGROUP *stogroup-name* — indicates whether user-defined (VCAT) or DB2 (STOGROUP) dataset(s) will be used. Dataset attributes and physical location are more easily controlled with user-defined datasets and recovery is always assured. Accidently dropped objects may not be recoverable if STOGROUPs are employed. (The DSN1COPY utility may recover a dropped tablespace from an image copy.) Dataset placement can be controlled by specifying different stogroups for other objects.

- PRIQTY *int* SECQTY *int* — requests space in kilobytes. These parameters are used only with STOGROUPs.

An index is composed of at least one root page and possible multiple levels thereafter, depending on the number of entries in the index and thus on the number of page splits that have occurred, as well as on factors such as the number of subpages requested and whether an index key is unique. Each page consists of 4K bytes. The lowest level of any index is that of the leaf pages, which point directly into the key of the table and contain a four byte row id (RID). Primary and secondary space allocations for index creation should be chosen to minimize waste while considering the number of index pages and levels.

Note that space allocations may also have to consider applications that populate tables with SQL INSERTs. An index entry for a row inserted after table load will use up to twice as much index space as an entry for a row that was placed in the table by table load. This is caused by page splitting. This excess space can be reclaimed by reorganizing the index.

- PCTFREE — reserves a percentage of each subpage of an index as free space during LOAD, REORG, AND RECOVER (index) processing; this free space will be filled in subsequent insert or update requests. Lack of available free space will cause additional index entries to be stored on another index page whose location is not predictable. Consequently, performance will be degraded as the number of index pages physically out of sequence increases.

For indices defined over tables that may anticipate moderate insert and update activity, reduce the occurrence of index page splits by increasing the default PCTFREE to 5 percent or more. On the other hand, reduce PCTFREE to 0 percent if a table for which an index has been defined will be used as read-only.

- FREEPAGE — specifies the frequency with which DB2 is to reserve a free page of index space during load processing; this free space will be used by subsequent insert and update requests. FREEPAGE is most significant when index page splits are frequent; it keeps the resulting split pages in better sequence than would have occurred randomly. In this way, FREEPAGE allocations for indices are much more effective than its allocations for tables.

- SUBPAGES — are the units of locking on an index during update processing. Index leaf pages are divided into a number of subpages (1, 2, 4, 8, or 16) based on this parameter. The default value is four subpages.

  The higher the parameter value, the larger the number of subpages per index leaf page and, therefore, the smaller the unit of locking. However, concurrency is increased only at the cost of processing and fixed storage overhead. Thus, the greater the number of subpages, the larger the size of the index overall. Reduced contention (increased concurrency) is more important if frequent update, insert, or delete activity is anticipated with multiple user participation. Maximum concurrency may be achieved by specification of SUBPAGES 16 and PCTFREE of 50 per cent. Read-only tables should have SUBPAGES 1 since locks will be taken at share level only, and there will consequently be no contention.

- CLUSTER — has been thoroughly discussed at the outset of this section. Be aware that a clustering index is only possible in situations where there is one table per tablespace, and only one clustering index per table (tablespace) is allowed. Furthermore, all partitioned tables must have a clustering index.

- BUFFERPOOL — specifies which buffer pool will be used for an index. An index is only allowed assignment to a 4K-byte buffer pool. The current recommendation is BP0.

- CLOSE YES | NO — specifies whether or not a dataset should be left open when not in use. When an index is frequently accessed, CLOSE NO should be specified to minimize I/O by limiting the number of times the dataset must be opened and closed. This option is recommended for all production environments. CLOSE YES should be specified for indices with infrequent access, to minimize the allocation of virtual storage when not needed. This option is recommended for test environments.

Please see the concluding "DDL Performance Summary" section in this chapter for additional information on indices.

■ VIEWS

A DB2 **view** is a logical representation of data that exists in one or more underlying DB2 tables.[14] This data may be composed of all or a subset of the columns and/or rows defined for one or many tables. Figure 4–13 depicts a possible implementation of multilevel views.

For most purposes, the definition and access of a view is transparent to the user (i.e., identical to the definition and access of a table). Physically, however, a table is distinct from a view in that a table has a physical storage

---

[14] Note that the term *underlying* does not exclude the possibility of data being extracted from another view representation, although the physical basis will always be a table at some point.

FIGURE 4-13
TABLE AND VIEW RELATIONSHIP

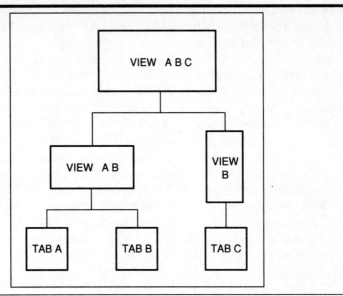

representation, while the view relating to that table does not. DB2 stores the view definition in a DB2 catalog table (SYSIBM.SYSVIEWS) where it will reside awaiting an access request for the view. When a view is requested, the definition of the view will be retrieved by DB2 and executed against the physical table(s) in the definition. This execution will in most cases produce a temporary results data table similar to the physical table that would have existed in the absence of an available view. In this manner, DB2 succeeds in eliminating redundant data storage until actual access of the data is required.

There is no specific authorization required to create a view; rather, it is implied with other privileges or authorizations. Any user may create a view over any tables for which they hold the SELECT privilege. Views may be created if DBADM authority is held over the respective data bases(s) or, of course, if SYSADM authority is held. A user with SYSADM authority may also create a view for another user. Furthermore, table creation implicitly grants the privilege of view definition over that table.

Given that all views have a physical basis as a table at some point, questions may arise as to the significance of the view mechanism. The following four features may suggest some uses for it.

1. *Reduction and/or combination of table columns specific to a user group.* A view definition allows actual SQL commands to join multiple tables to be avoided for non-technical users; the view by definition does the joining. Since DB2 will execute the definitional requirements upon request for the view, most differences are undetectable to the average user.

Users who do not desire access to all columns and/or rows within a table set may effectively eliminate those columns, for their processing, by use of a view. The major restriction of this type of functionality occurs during insertion attempts into the base table via a view (to be discussed later within this section).

2. *Security requirements.* Given that it is not desirable to make all table data redundant in terms of physical storage, security requirements may dictate that it is necessary to restrict access to other data via the view mechanism. In this way, a user group may be allowed access to only those columns and/or rows appropriate for its level of authorization.

3. *Insulation of applications from physical table changes.* A view will not have to be modified for changes to columns of underlying tables that are not included in the view definition. This could represent significant functionality enhancement for applications that would otherwise fall victim to high rates of design fluctuation, even in testing stages.

4. *Storage considerations.* Redundant data may be less desirable than the CPU cost of translating the view definition into a results table to simulate the physical storage of a base table.

The primary disadvantage of views occurs with the use of dynamic SQL. Catalog contention could occur during a dynamic bind since two popular catalog tables (i.e., SYSIBM.SYSTABLES and SYSIBM.SYSCOLUMNS)[15] must be accessed a minimum of two times.

A subselect in a view may not contain a UNION or an ORDER BY.

The most important administrative consideration when using views is the adherence to naming standards. Pay special attention to the *view_column_list*

FIGURE 4–14
VIEW SYNTAX

```
CREATE VIEW view_name
    [(view_column_list)]
AS
    SELECT select_column_list | *
        FROM table_1[,...,table_n]
        [WHERE predicate(s)]
            [GROUP BY group_list]
            [HAVING predicate(s)]
[WITH CHECK OPTION]
;
```

[15] SYSIBM.SYSCOLUMNS did not have an index prior to DB2 Version 2.1.

and the *select_column_list* parameters (see Figure 4–14). If the view column names are not carefully chosen, application development (QMF, COBOL, SPUFI, PL1, etc.) will turn into a nightmare. Refer to the naming standards at the beginning of this chapter for additional guidelines. The parameters are

- *view_name* — a user-defined name (long identifier) for the index being created. Like table names, the fully qualified name may not be the same as another fully qualified TABLE, SYNONYM, or another VIEW. See the CREATE TABLE statement in this chapter for more information on qualified names.

- *view_column_list* — a list of names for columns in this view. This list corresponds positionally on a one-to-one basis to the columns in the subselect. It is not required unless the result of the subselect contains duplicate names or has derived columns from an arithmetic expression, function, or a constant.

- *select_column_list* | * — is a standard column list for a SELECT statement. The order of the names will correspond positionally on a one-to-one basis with the columns named in the *view_column_list*. In the following example (Figure 4–15), CUST_ACCT_NO will be known as CBAL_ACCT_NO when processing through view VDDA_CBAL. If an asterisk were specified and the view column list omitted, then the view would use the column names as they were originally defined in the CREATE definition of the table.

    Avoid numeric constants. If a zero value must be returned, subtract a column from itself:

    TDDA_BAL - TDDA_BAL.

If a column function (e.g., SUM) is used with a view column name that is a numeric constant, a negative SQLCODE will be returned, as when a base table and a view participate in a UNION.

FIGURE 4–15

```
CREATE VIEW VDDA_CBAL
    (CBAL_ACCT_NO, CBAL_NAME,
    CBAL_ADDR, CBAL_BAL_AMT)
        AS
SELECT CUST_ACCT_NO, CUST_NAME,
    CUST_ADDR, BAL_OS_BAL_AMT
    FROM TDDA_CUST, TDDA_BAL
    WHERE CUST_ACCT_NO = BAL_ACCT_NO
    AND CUST_ACCT_NO LIKE '01%';
```

- WITH CHECK OPTION — when specified for an updatable view, will prevent modification or insertion of a row whose columns' values do not conform to all of the conditions in the WHERE predicate.

A comprehensive example of a view definition follows. Note that the names in the view column list are prefixed with the view acronym, CBAL. The remainder of the name is derived from the column names within the table. Figure 4–15 illustrates a condition where a view, VDDA_CBAL, has been defined to join two tables, TDDA_CUST and TDDA_BAL, on the basis of a common column named, CUST_ACCT_NO and BAL_ACCT_NO, respectively. Only those accounts (or rows) that begin with the characters 01 are to be accessible to the user of this view. Further, only information pertaining to the account, name, address, and outstanding balance will be available for the rows returned. The columns returned have been renamed with a prefix of CBAL, although DB2 catalog information will still supply the physical characteristics of the columns.

As previously stated, access to this view by the average user is identical to access to the actual physical tables themselves. However, there are restrictions to view access that, if pertinent, may require the user to be more familiar with the view definition and tables underlying it.

1. A view that is defined as the join of multiple tables may not participate in any update, delete, or insert processing requests through that view.
2. A view that uses column functions such as SUM, AVG, MIN, MAX in its definition may not participate in any insert, delete, or update processing requests through the view.
3. A view that is defined as the grouping of data or elimination of duplicate data using GROUP BY, HAVING, or DISTINCT clauses also may not participate in any update, insert, or delete processing requests through the view.
4. A view that contains a column where information has been derived through constants or arithmetic and scalar functions is restricted from participation in an update request for that column. An example would be the column CBAL_BAL_AMT in our previous view definition if it had been derived as DECIMAL(BAL_OS_BAL_AMT/100,15,2) to present the cents position.
5. A view that does not include all columns of the underlying table that are defined as NOT NULL (with no default) may not perform insertions into the base table through the view. This is because the view is powerless to substitute values for columns that it is not defined to include. Consequently, DB2 will attempt to nullify a column that prohibits nulls and does not provide a default value.

In summary, if the physical sequence of a table is modified, short of excluding rows, or if a column does not reflect its original attributes or value, then that view is strictly available for "READ ONLY" access.

The preceding restrictions against processing through the view mechanism may appear more reasonable when you consider that either most of the conditions described would have produced data in the views that was not consistent with column definitions in the original base tables, or that the view changed the composition of rows and/or columns which were in the original tables (e.g., AVG, GROUP BY, and DISTINCT).

For update or deletion of a row via a view, it is not necessary for a view to contain the same number of columns or rows as its base table. However, the view should relate to the base table through its primary key (i.e., the view should contain the primary key of the table) in order to prevent the update from corrupting the base table's relationships.

The user of a view is able to perform functions against the base table that would violate the access to the tables authorized via the view definition. DB2 does not verify that the actual values of the columns being inserted or updated through a view are consistent with the definition of the view itself.

In the definition for the view (VDDA_CBAL) illustrated in our example, the user was clearly prohibited from access to any accounts which did not begin with the digits 01. However, the user would have been able to insert an account number beginning with 22 into table TDDA_CUST if it had not been joined to table TDDA_BAL and did not conflict with any of the other restrictions indicated previously.

The only way to provide integrity for the base table against such update and insert violations is through the use of the WITH CHECK OPTION feature of the view definition. Note that this check will be performed for every update and insert request through the view, and could represent significant performance costs for views heavily used in this manner.

The adaptation in Figure 4–16 of the original definition for view VDDA_CBAL illustrates the inclusion of the WITH CHECK OPTION clause.

This view will allow updates on table, TDDA_CUST, as long as the first two characters of column CUST_ACCT_NO are 01.

FIGURE 4–16

```
CREATE VIEW VDDA_CBAL
    (CBAL_ACCT_NO, CBAL_NAME,
    CBAL_ADDR)
        AS
SELECT CUST_ACCT_NO, CUST_NAME,
    CUST_ADDR
    FROM TDDA_CUST
    WHERE CUST_ACCT_NO LIKE '01%'
        WITH CHECK OPTION;
```

■ USING VIEWS IN PLACE OF SMALL TABLES

Every system will have need for a few small tables. The usual requirement is reference data such as STATE CODES, ACCOUNT TYPE CODES, INTEREST RATE CODES, and the like. The authors have worked on one system where one table consisted of four rows! Since most site standards require every table to have a unique index, those four rows would have utilized two datasets. Wouldn't it be more efficient to keep all small tables together and not incur the additional overhead of multiple indices? Regardless of the type of tablespace (simple or partitioned) or table (simple or segmented), every index must have a separate indexspace/dataset.

Figures 4–17 through 4–24 show how views can, in effect, support multiple row definitions in one table. The reference data table (TDDA_REF) consists of 32 columns and is the base for six views. The total number of rows will not exceed 200. The total number of data pages is less than fifteen. The system date view (VDDA_SYDT) requires only one row. None of the views need all the columns defined in the base table, but every column will be used by at least one of the six different views.

FIGURE 4–17
COMMON REF DATATABLE EXAMPLE

```
  --
   CREATE TABLE      TDDA_REF
   ( REF_CD                   CHAR(02) NOT NULL
   , REF_ROW_CD               CHAR(01) NOT NULL
   , REF_TXT                  CHAR(30) NOT NULL
   , REF_COLL_DB_CR_CD        CHAR(01) NOT NULL WITH DEFAULT
   , REF_CASH_DB_CR_CD        CHAR(01) NOT NULL WITH DEFAULT
   , REF_GL_OR_BANK_CD        CHAR(01) NOT NULL WITH DEFAULT
   , REF_MAN_ENT_CD           CHAR(01) NOT NULL WITH DEFAULT
   , REF_FUNC_FUNC1_NM        CHAR(08) NOT NULL WITH DEFAULT
   , REF_FUNC_STAT1_CD        CHAR(01) NOT NULL WITH DEFAULT
   , REF_FUNC_FUNC2_NM        CHAR(08) NOT NULL WITH DEFAULT
   , REF_FUNC_STAT2_CD        CHAR(01) NOT NULL WITH DEFAULT
   , REF_FUNC_FUNC3_NM        CHAR(08) NOT NULL WITH DEFAULT
   , REF_FUNC_STAT3_CD        CHAR(01) NOT NULL WITH DEFAULT
   , REF_FUNC_FUNC4_NM        CHAR(08) NOT NULL WITH DEFAULT
   , REF_FUNC_STAT4_CD        CHAR(01) NOT NULL WITH DEFAULT
   , REF_FUNC_FUNC5_NM        CHAR(08) NOT NULL WITH DEFAULT
   , REF_FUNC_STAT5_CD        CHAR(01) NOT NULL WITH DEFAULT
   , REF_FUNC_FUNC6_NM        CHAR(08) NOT NULL WITH DEFAULT
```

FIGURE 4–17 (*continued*)

```
    ,REF_FUNC_STAT6_CD      CHAR(01) NOT NULL WITH DEFAULT
    ,REF_FUNC_FUNC7_NM      CHAR(08) NOT NULL WITH DEFAULT
    ,REF_FUNC_STAT7_CD      CHAR(01) NOT NULL WITH DEFAULT
    ,REF_FUNC_FUNC8_NM      CHAR(08) NOT NULL WITH DEFAULT
    ,REF_FUNC_STAT8_CD      CHAR(01) NOT NULL WITH DEFAULT
    ,REF_LAST_UPDT_TS       TIMESTAMP NOT NULL WITH DEFAULT
    ,REF_LAST_UPDT_USR      CHAR(8)  NOT NULL WITH DEFAULT
    ,REF_LAST_UPDT_TRM      CHAR(4)  NOT NULL WITH DEFAULT
    ,REF_PRV_SYS_DT         DATE
    ,REF_CUR_SYS_DT         DATE
    ,REF_NXT_SYS_DT         DATE
    ,REF_PRV_MO_SYS_DT      DATE
    ,REF_CUR_MO_SYS_DT      DATE
    ,REF_NXT_MO_SYS_DT      DATE
    )
    IN AUDDA01.T$REF001;
--
    GRANT SELECT ON TDDA_REF TO PUBLIC;
--
    COMMENT ON TABLE TDDA_REF IS
      'COMMON REF DATA TABLES';
--
    LABEL   ON TABLE TDDA_REF IS
      'COMMON REF DATA TABLES';
```

FIGURE 4–18
INDEX EXAMPLE

```
    CREATE UNIQUE INDEX    REFIXUCL
        ON      TDDA_REF
    ( REF_CD         ASC
     ,REF_ROW_CD     ASC
    )
      USING  STOGROUP T142SGA
          PRIQTY 600 SECQTY 600
      CLUSTER
          SUBPAGES 1 BUFFERPOOL BPO
          CLOSE YES;
```

FIGURE 4–19
ACCOUNT TYPE NAME VIEW EXAMPLE

```
    CREATE VIEW      VDDA_ANAM (
      ANAM_CD  ,ANAM_ROW_CD  ,ANAM_TXT
      ,ANAM_RPT_SEQ_CD
      ,ANAM_SHRT_NAM
      ,ANAM_LAST_UPDT_TS
      ,ANAM_LAST_UPDT_USR
      ,ANAM_LAST_UPDT_TRM
    )     AS
    SELECT   REF_CD,  REF_ROW_CD,  REF_TXT
    ,SUBSTR(REF_FUNC_FUNC1_NM,1,2)
    ,SUBSTR(REF_FUNC_FUNC2_NM,1,3)
    ,REF_LAST_UPDT_TS
    ,REF_LAST_UPDT_USR
    ,REF_LAST_UPDT_TRM
            FROM TDDA_REF
    WHERE REF_ROW_CD = 'A'
      AND REF_CD           LIKE 'X%'
  WITH CHECK OPTION;
  --
  GRANT SELECT ON VDDA_ANAM TO PUBLIC;
  --
  COMMENT ON TABLE VDDA_ANAM  IS
      'ACCOUNT TYPE NAME   VIEW';
  --
  LABEL   ON TABLE VDDA_ANAM  IS
      'ACCOUNT TYPE NAMES';
```

FIGURE 4–20
ACCOUNT TYPE CODES VIEW EXAMPLE

```
    CREATE VIEW      VDDA_ATYP    (
      ATYP_CD ,ATYP_ROW_CD ,ATYP_TXT
      ,ATYP_FUNC_FUNC1_NM ,ATYP_FUNC_STAT1_CD
      ,ATYP_FUNC_FUNC2_    ,ATYP_FUNC_STAT2_CD
      ,ATYP_FUNC_FUNC3_NM ,ATYP_FUNC_STAT3_CD
      ,ATYP_FUNC_FUNC4_    ,ATYP_FUNC_STAT4_CD
      ,ATYP_FUNC_FUNC5_NM ,ATYP_FUNC_STAT5_CD
      ,ATYP_FUNC_FUNC6_NM ,ATYP_FUNC_STAT6_CD
      ,ATYP_FUNC_FUNC7_NM ,ATYP_FUNC_STAT7_CD
      ,ATYP_FUNC_FUNC8_NM ,ATYP_FUNC_STAT8_CD
      ,ATYP_LAST_UPDT_TS   ,ATYP_LAST_UPDT_USR
      ,ATYP_LAST_UPDT_TRM
    )    AS
      SELECT   REF_CD,  REF_ROW_CD,  REF_TXT
      ,REF_FUNC_FUNC1_NM ,REF_FUNC_STAT1_CD
      ,REF_FUNC_FUNC2_NM ,REF_FUNC_STAT2_CD
      ,REF_FUNC_FUNC3_NM ,REF_FUNC_STAT3_CD
      ,REF_FUNC_FUNC4_NM ,REF_FUNC_STAT4_CD
      ,REF_FUNC_FUNC5_NM ,REF_FUNC_STAT5_CD
      ,REF_FUNC_FUNC6_NM ,REF_FUNC_STAT6_CD
      ,REF_FUNC_FUNC7_NM ,REF_FUNC_STAT7_CD
      ,REF_FUNC_FUNC8_NM ,REF_FUNC_STAT8_CD
      ,REF_LAST_UPDT_TS   ,REF_LAST_UPDT_USR
      ,REF_LAST_UPDT_TRM
            FROM TDDA_REF
      WHERE REF_ROW_CD = 'A'
        AND REF_CD        NOT LIKE 'X%'
              WITH CHECK OPTION;
  --
    GRANT SELECT ON VDDA_ATYP TO PUBLIC;
  --
    COMMENT ON TABLE VDDA_ATYP IS
      'ACCOUNT TYPE CODES  VIEW';
  --
    LABEL ON TABLE VDDA_ATYP IS
      'ACCT TYPE CODES';
```

FIGURE 4–21
RATE IDX NAME VIEW EXAMPLE

```
CREATE VIEW      VDDA_IDXN (
  IDXN_CD ,IDXN_ROW_CD ,IDXN_NAM
  ,IDXN_LAST_UPDT_TS     ,IDXN_LAST_UPDT_USR
  ,IDXN_LAST_UPDT_TRM
)  AS
  SELECT   REF_CD, REF_ROW_CD,  REF_TXT
  ,REF_LAST_UPDT_TS ,REF_LAST_UPDT_USR
  ,REF_LAST_UPDT_TRM
        FROM TDDA_REF
  WHERE REF_ROW_CD = 'I'
WITH CHECK OPTION;
--
GRANT SELECT ON VDDA_IDXN TO PUBLIC;
--
COMMENT ON TABLE VDDA_IDXN  IS
    'RATE IDX NAME VIEW';
--
LABEL   ON TABLE VDDA_IDXN  IS
    'RATE IDX NAM VW';
```

FIGURE 4–22
STATE CODE VIEW EXAMPLE

```
CREATE VIEW      VDDA_ST (
  ST_CD ,ST_ROW_CD ,ST_NAM
  ,ST_LAST_UPDT_TS  ,ST_LAST_UPDT_USR
  ,ST_LAST_UPDT_TRM
)  AS
  SELECT   REF_CD,  REF_ROW_CD,  REF_TXT
  ,REF_LAST_UPDT_TS ,REF_LAST_UPDT_USR
  ,REF_LAST_UPDT_TRM
        FROM TDDA_REF
  WHERE REF_ROW_CD = 'S'
WITH CHECK OPTION;
--
GRANT SELECT ON VDDA_ST TO PUBLIC;
--
COMMENT ON TABLE VDDA_ST  IS
    'STATE CODE VIEW ';
--
LABEL   ON TABLE VDDA_ST  IS
    'ST CD VW ';
```

FIGURE 4–23
CURRENT SYSTEM DATA VIEW EXAMPLE

```
CREATE VIEW      VDDA_SYDT    (
   SYDT_CD ,SYDT_ROW_CD ,SYDT_TXT
  ,SYDT_PRV_SYS_DT ,SYDT_CUR_SYS_DT
  ,SYDT_NXT_SYS_DT ,SYDT_PRV_MO_SYS_DT
  ,SYDT_CUR_MO_SYS_DT ,SYDT_NXT_MO_SYS_
)    AS
  SELECT    REF_CD,   REF_ROW_CD,   REF_TXT
  ,REF_PRV_SYS_DT ,REF_CUR_SYS_DT
  ,REF_NXT_SYS_DT ,REF_PRV_MO_SYS_DT
  ,REF_CUR_MO_SYS_DT ,REF_NXT_MO_SYS_D
        FROM TDDA_REF

WHERE REF_ROW_CD = '['
    AND REF_CD       = '[['
    AND REF_PRV_SYS_DT          IS NOT NULL
    AND REF_CUR_SYS_DT          IS NOT NULL
    AND REF_NXT_SYS_DT          IS NOT NULL
    AND REF_PRV_MO_SYS_DT       IS NOT NULL
    AND REF_CUR_MO_SYS_DT       IS NOT NULL
    AND REF_NXT_MO_SYS_DT       IS NOT NULL

  WITH CHECK OPTION;
--
  GRANT SELECT ON VDDA_SYDT TO PUBLIC;
--
  COMMENT ON TABLE VDDA_SYDT  IS
    'CURRENT SYSTEM DATE VIEW';
--
  LABEL   ON TABLE VDDA_SYDT  IS
    'CURT SYS DT VW';
```

The most important benefit of this design is that there is only one table and, more importantly, only one index. The index will not exceed one level, which will heavily influence its ability to remain resident within a bufferpool.

Figure 4–17 creates the only base table. The first two columns (REF_CD and REF_ROW_CD) will be common to all views. They represent the unique sequence for this table and its dependent views. The REF_ROW_CD will be

FIGURE 4–24
TRANS CODE DESC/VERIFICATION VIEW EXAMPLE

```
   CREATE VIEW      VDDA_TC (
      TC_CD    ,TC_ROW_CD    ,TC_TXT
     ,TC_COLL_DB_CR_CD  ,TC_CASH_DB_CR_CD
     ,TC_GL_OR_BANK_CD  ,TC_MAN_ENT_CD
     ,TC_LAST_UPDT_TS   ,TC_LAST_UPDT_USR
     ,TC_LAST_UPDT_TRM
   )   AS
     SELECT    REF_CD,  REF_ROW_CD,   REF_TXT
        ,REF_COLL_DB_CR_CD  ,REF_CASH_DB_CR_CD
        ,REF_GL_OR_BANK_CD  ,REF_MAN_ENT_CD
     ,REF_LAST_UPDT_TS        ,REF_LAST_UPDT_USR
     ,REF_LAST_UPDT_TRM
           FROM TDDA_REF
     WHERE REF_ROW_CD = 'T'
   WITH CHECK OPTION;
--
   GRANT SELECT ON VDDA_TC    TO PUBLIC;
--
   COMMENT ON TABLE VDDA_TC      IS
      'TRANS CODE DESC/VERIFICATION VIEW';
--
   LABEL    ON TABLE VDDA_TC      IS
      'TRAN CD DESC/VFY VW';
```

used in conjunction with the WITH CHECK OPTION to ensure view integrity. REF_CD will be first in the index to ensure greater first-column cardinality.

The VDDA_SYDT view (Figure 4–23) will allow only one row to exist within the base table. Its WHERE clause tests the index columns for one specific value. Therefore, a select from this view will not require a WHERE predicate.

■ MULTIPLE ROW DEFINITION SUMMARY

Use of views eliminates the necessity for multiple indices and their related overhead. Granted, extra DASD space is required due to the number of columns in the base table, but this is reduced by some of the columns defined as nullable. Additional space may be saved if other columns are either nullable or VARCHAR.

Since DB2 will not use an index if a table is joined to itself, a tablespace scan will be used by the optimizer where two or more of the views must be joined. If joins are required, do not use this method in cases where the base table is larger than 150 pages.

■ SYNONYMS

A DB2 **synonym** is an alternative means of referencing a table or view owned by another user, without use of the fully qualified name otherwise required.[16] The alternative reference is actually a name designated by the creator of the synonym to act as a substitute for the fully qualified name.

The most common use of this facility is in a testing environment. As source code is migrated from one testing level to another, synonyms eliminate the need to change source code to modify embedded or declared table names.

However, the synonym has significance only for the AUTHID of its creator. The synonym is stored in the DB2 catalog in association with the AUTHID of the creator and will act as an alternative to a fully qualified table or view name only when referenced by its creator. A user attempting to use a synonym for which he or she is not the creator must qualify the synonym with the AUTHID of the creator. This requirement defeats the purpose of synonym definition in most cases. The only exception to this condition exists when a user having SYSADM capability defines synonyms for other users (e.g., systemwide tables such as a company calendar table).

There is no specific authorization required to create a synonym; it is implied by privileges or authorizations for the tables or views to which they correspond. The synonym may be created but table access will be denied if the appropriate privilege is not held.

Synonym creation may be embedded or issued interactively through QMF or SPUFI. The syntax for the CREATE SYNONYM statement is shown in Figure 4–25.

FIGURE 4–25
SYNONYM CREATE SYNTAX

```
CREATE SYNONYM synonym_name
      FOR authid.tablename |
          authid.viewname
```

---

16 A synonym may also be defined by a user for his/her own tables or views.

- *synonym_name* — a SQL identifier that must be different from other synonyms defined by the creator and the unqualified name of any table or view owned by the creator. See the "Table" section of this chapter for additional naming considerations.

- *AUTHID.tablename* | *AUTHID.viewname* — the fully qualified name of the table or view to be referenced by the synonym. It must exist in the DB2 catalog as specified.

A synonym can be dropped only by its creator. A synonym that is dropped is deleted from the DB2 catalog and invalidates all application plans referencing it. Note, however, that the dropping of a DB2 object (i.e., table or view) upon which a synonym is dependent does not also cause the synonym to be dropped in a cascading effect. This condition will greatly facilitate synonym maintenance in test environments, where tables are constantly being redefined. The explicit use of the DROP statement is required to delete a synonym from the DB2 catalog.

The syntax for the DROP statement is shown in Figure 4–26. Parameters apply as defined for the CREATE statement.

FIGURE 4–26
SYNONYM DROP SYNTAX

```
DROP SYNONYM synonym_name
```

■ ALTER

The importance of the ALTER statement has greatly increased with DB2 Version 2.1. In addition to adding columns to a table, modifying free space, changing bufferpools, and so on, referential constraints may be added and/or removed. The population of some referential structures would be impossible without the ALTER statement.

The ALTER statements for referential constraints must be executed in the sequence shown in Figure 4–27. A primary key must be established for a parent table (*par-table-1*) before a foreign key of a dependent table (*table-name*) may reference it.

- PRIMARY KEY *(col-nam1,..., col-namN)* — identifies the table columns of the primary index. No column may be declared more than once. The total number of bytes may not exceed 254; the total number of columns may not exceed sixteen. Primary key columns may never be NULL, and a <u>UNIQUE</u> index <u>must</u> <u>exist</u> on the columns specified.

FIGURE 4–27
ALTER STATEMENT SYNTAX

```
1.   ALTER TABLE par-table-1
     PRIMARY KEY (col-nam1,....,col-namN)
     ;

2.   ALTER TABLE table-name
     FOREIGN KEY [constraint-name-1]
        (column-name-1, ,column-name-n)
     REFERENCES par-table-1
     [ON DELETE SET NULL I RESTRICT I CASCADE]
     ;
```

- FOREIGN KEY *[constraint-name-1] (column-name-1,....,column-name-n)* — identifies the constraint name and the table columns of the foreign key for a table. The actual *constraint-name-1* may be a maximum of eight characters; if specified, it will be the explicit name for this constraint. Constraint names will be referenced during constraint violations; they should therefore be explicit and unique. The default is the first eight characters (or less) of the foreign key's first column (i.e., *column-name-1*). *(column-name-1,.....,column-name-n)* are the column(s) that make up the foreign key. Foreign key columns may be NULL. If any column is NULL, the entire foreign key is treated as NULL and no referential integrity check to the parent table primary key will be performed. Except for the NULL attribute, dependent foreign keys must exactly match their respective parent primary keys, including column sequence. The column names may, of course, be different.
- REFERENCES *par-table-1* — identifies the parent table for this constraint. The parent table must exist prior to the creation of this constraint. It must have a primary unique index.
- ON DELETE SET NULL I RESTRICT I CASCADE — establishes the DELETE RULE option for this relationship. The default is RESTRICT. DB2 implements both the UPDATE and INSERT RULES with an implicit option of RESTRICT. Therefore, no parameter is provided for either rule.

■ DATA DEFINITION LANGUAGE (DDL) PERFORMANCE SUMMARY

1. Use the DB2 catalogs as a control dictionary.
2. Table names: Ensure that output member name from DCLGEN is the same name as its respective DB2 table name. This will obviate

confusion and facilitate automated creation (e.g., via TSO CLIST) of tables and DCLGENs.

3. Synonym names: *AUTHID.objnam* must be unique within a DB2 system. Never allow more than one synonym per AUTHID for the same base table or view, and ensure that it is the same name (less AUTHID) as the base object.

4. View names: Ensure that the output member name from DCLGEN is the same name as its respective DB2 view name.

5. Data base names: Use the last three sequence characters to allow functionally related data bases to be sequentially referenced in a one-database-per-tablespace environment.

6. Stogroup names: Use a different stogroup for each test environment within an application.

STOGROUPS

1. When allocating stogroups, estimate the number of bytes of stored data and multiply by two.

2. DB2 will return a dynamic allocation error if all volumes within a stogroup are not mounted at the time of a CREATE request for a tablespace or index.

3. Indices and tablespaces may use different stogroups to distribute the load more evenly.

4. Volumes in a stogroup are used serially; DB2 makes no attempt to balance the load from a storage perspective.

5. Allocate high-use or less I/O-intensive DB2 objects on faster devices, low-use DB2 objects on slower devices.

6. Run the STOSPACE utility to update space statistics when using stogroups.

7. Use the "ALTER STOGROUP" command to add or remove stogroup volumes.

8. Allocate user VSAM ESDS datasets to maintain closer control over the physical storage of tables and indices.

9. Use stogroups for automatic dataset deletion, extension, and creation.

10. Data may be difficult to recover for STOGROUP datasets.

DATA BASES

1. Use DB2 data bases as the units of stop or start of access to tables and indices.

2. DB2 security mechanisms may also be employed to grant authorization at the data base level.

3. Avoid DB2 catalog contention; provide each developer with his or her own data base.
4. It may be advisable to allow only one tablespace per data base, particularly where large tables are involved.

TABLESPACES

1. Tablespaces are significant as
    a. A unit of locking
    b. The unit involved in some utilities.
2. Partitions may be assigned to different physical devices for performance enhancement.
3. A partitioned tablespace provides more flexibility for the execution of certain DB2 utilities.
4. Individual partitions may not be deleted or redistributed, once defined.
5. A clustering index for a partitioned tablespace cannot be dropped unless the table to which it relates is dropped first.
6. The index over a partitioned tablespace acts as an integrity check upon row placement.
7. Multiple tables defined within a given tablespace may not be the wisest approach (prior to DB2 Version 2.1).
    a. Locking specified at the tablespace level will hold a lock over all tables within that tablespace.
    b. A SQL LOCK TABLE statement actually causes a full tablespace lock to occur, unless tablespaces are segmented. Then only the segmented area (TABLE) is locked.
    c. Tablespace scans will scan all tables within a tablespace, unless tablespaces are segmented.
    d. Execution of the RECOVER and REORG utilities will cause the lock of the entire tablespace; execution of the LOAD/REPLACE utility refreshes the entire tablespace (segmented or not).
    e. Reclamation of unused space in simple tablespaces having multiple tables will not occur until a reorganization occurs. (This is no longer true with DB2 Version 2.1 segmented tablespaces.)
    f. Under normal circumstances, a clustering index will not cause data to be redistributed in clustering sequence during a REORG.
8. Defining multiple tables within a tablespace may be justified if
    a. Tables are logically related by frequent references such as JOIN's and UNION's.
    b. Tables approximate the same small size.
    c. Tables are seldom or never updated.

    d. Tables can be loaded by interleaving their data rows throughout the tablespace for read-only access.

    e. Multiple tables within a tablespace will minimize the number of VSAM ESDS datasets to support.

9. Definitional parameters:

- PRIQTY *integer* — do not let this parameter default. Allocate in device track or cylinder increments. (i.e., 40K or 600K increments).
- SECQTY *integer* — do not let this parameter default. For a 3380, increments of either 40 or 600 are suggested.
- PCTFREE *integer* — Higher PCTFREE parameters permit higher concurrency within the tablespace — more efficient than FREEPAGE.
- PCTFREE and FREEPAGE should be set to zero if the table(s) will be read-only.
- *bufferpool* always reflect BP0 for all DB2 data.
- LOCKSIZE—Use locksize ANY to allow DB2 to escalate the locking unit. TABLESPACE locking is most appropriate for read-only tables and some batch processing.
- CLOSE NO for multiple users with concurrent access of the tablespace.
- YES for few accesses to the tablespace.
  Do not default tablespace.

TABLES

1. Balance <u>update</u> <u>overhead</u> and <u>performance</u> <u>reduction</u> of normalization. **Not all redundancy is bad.**
2. Use a view if derived columns are not needed consistently. (Year-to-date amounts or other summary data are examples of candidate view applications.)
3. Design each table with at least a unique primary key for identification of rows. (DB2 Version 2.1 referential integrity requires that all primary keys be unique.)
4. Foreign keys may also be utilized to associate the table with one or more others.
5. Foreign keys should be indexed and allowed to be NULL.
6. The keys may be employed to assign indexing or enable JOIN functions.
7. DB2 does not allow table rows to span data pages; a row greater than 4,074 bytes will not fit into a 4K page.
8. Rows should not be defined to contain less than 24 bytes.
9. Columns which may be compared should have the same length.
10. A variable length column no longer than 20 bytes should be defined as a fixed length column.

11. Do not overspecify the maximum length of a variable length column.
12. Avoid variable character column definitions when constant fluctuation in column length is anticipated.
13. Avoid long variable character (LONG VARCHAR) columns. You will not be able to use the DDL ALTER statement to add additional columns.
14. Numeric data column definitions: SQLCODE-802 (arithmetic overflow) may occur.
15. Position variable length columns (NULL or VARCHAR) at the end of a row.
16. Position frequently referenced columns at the beginning of the row.
17. Specify NOT NULL WITH DEFAULT during load of columns with values to be determined at a future time.
18. An edit routine compresses data but could substantially degrade performance.
19. Validation routines screen data but also could degrade performance; use the application program to screen data.
20. Note that a table CREATE request may not be issued in one tablespace concurrently with the running of a DB2 utility that controls a different tablespace in the same data base.

INDICES

1. DB2 will not use an index if a table is joined to itself (including the use of multiple views of the table).
2. Indices are primarily useful in enhancing performance and ensuring uniqueness among column values.
3. Indices should be monitored to verify that expectations of index access and results of such access are realized.
4. The EXPLAIN function provides information regarding the Access Path Selection of DB2. Query the DB2 catalog table SYSIBM.SYSPLANDEP to see if all indices are used as anticipated.
5. An index should be dropped when it is no longer in use.
6. RUNSTATS must be executed to update the statistics available for analysis by the EXPLAIN function.
7. Reorganization of indices should be considered based on the number of index levels, the sequence of leaf pages, and data disorganization.
8. An index should be dropped when there are fewer than six data pages to the table for which it is defined.
9. FREEPAGE: 10 is recommended for situations where frequent index page splits can be anticipated. PCTFREE (i.e., free space on the same page) is still preferable overall.

10. Note that values specified for PCTFREE and FREEPAGE may be modified after table load, but the associated impact will not be felt until REORG/RELOAD has occurred.

11. Appropriate use of free space may accomplish faster data reference, but at the cost of DASD space utilization and increased number of index pages and levels, as well as possible increased length of tablespace scans.

12. Composite keys should be used for indexing to provide uniqueness.

13. A host variable described in a manner inconsistent with the attributes of the column to which it is meant to correspond will prevent access of an index for that column.

14. Indices defined for columns longer than 40 bytes should be avoided.

15. Cardinality of a column will impact index use.

16. Columns that are subject to frequent UPDATE should participate in a minimum number of indices.

17. Columns that are designated to compose a unique key column should be screened to prevent load failure.

18. A clustering index should be specified when columns are frequently used in a certain order.

19. The first index created (in a chronological sense) will automatically be used by DB2 as a clustering index for REORG purposes if no index was specifically defined with the CLUSTER option.

20. Use EXPLAIN to tune access strategies.

21. A matching index access strategy is preferable.

22. When a matching index strategy is not possible, a non-matching index scan without data reference is the next best alternative.

23. Tablespace scans are normally the least effective alternative access strategy unless sequential prefetch is used and one (or more) rows per two pages will be retrieved.

24. In general, the type of predicate involved in the data processing request will strongly influence whether an index is used.

25. A large table should almost always have at least one index to provide an alternative to a tablespace scan. Additionally, smaller tables failing the previous criteria should also be considered candidates for index definition.

26. Consideration should be given to the creation of temporary indices where permanent support can not be justified (e.g., for a monthly job that must process in an unclustered sequence).

27. An index should always be created prior to the actual load of the table.

28. Data input to a load process should be previously sorted by key sequence to be reflected by the clustering index.

VIEWS

1. Create a view for
   a. Reduction and/or combination of table columns specific to a user group.
   b. Restriction of access to some, but not all, data as appropriate for a user group level of authorization.
   c. Insulation of applications from physical table changes.
2. Redundant data may be less desirable than the CPU cost of translating the view definition into a results table upon demand.
3. Views should be reconsidered with the use of dynamic SQL.
4. A subselect in a view may not contain a UNION or an ORDER BY.
5. View restrictions: if the physical sequence of a table is modified, short of excluding rows, or a column does not reflect its original attributes or value, then that view is READ ONLY.
   a. Avoid numeric constants (for zero, subtract a column from itself).
   b. A view that is defined as the join of multiple tables may not participate in any update, delete, or insert processing requests through that view.
   c. A view that uses column functions may not participate in any insert, delete, or update processing requests through the view.
   d. A view that is defined as the grouping of data or elimination of duplicate data using GROUP BY, HAVING, or DISTINCT clauses also may not participate in any update, insert, or delete processing requests through the view.
   e. A view that contains a column where information has been derived through constants or arithmetic and scalar functions is restricted from participation in an update request for that column.
   f. A view that does not include all rows of the underlying table that are defined as NOT NULL (with no default) may not perform insertions into the base table through the view.
6. A view should relate to the base table through its primary key.
7. Provide protection (at the possible cost of performance) for the base table against update and insert violations through the use of the WITH CHECK OPTION feature of the view definition.
8. Use views in place of several small tables.

DESIGN GUIDELINES

When dealing with DB2 application design, you must take into consideration both the DB2 environment and the TP monitor with which all applications must interface. One IMS/VS call or CICS/VS command will require fewer resources than a badly coded SQL query.

Even batch programs may execute as a background TSO task. In any batch environment, especially for programs that will run concurrently with online programs, great care must be taken to avoid potential contention problems. Online program design will be strongly influenced by the respective TP monitor (i.e., IMS/VS, CICS/VS, or TSO/E). Commit or checkpoint processing must be controlled and coordinated through the TP monitor. In an IMS/VS environment, for instance, resources could be held for several thousand transaction iterations.

■ PROGRAM DESIGN

There are two overriding DB2 program design objectives: limit the number of rows accessed by a SQL query, and minimize lock duration. SQL provides no explicit SQL calls to limit the total number of rows being retrieved or to control lock duration. Instead, the actual number of rows being processed is implied by the WHERE predicate of a DML (SQL) statement; the number of locks being taken will be proportional to the number of manipulated rows. DML coding standards intended to optimize table access and indirectly minimize I/O and locking will be presented later in this chapter.

■ I/O CONSIDERATIONS

With regard to row retrieval, DB2 tends to get a bad reputation from its purported excessive appetite for resources, specifically I/O. To evaluate this reputation, we must consider just how this DBMS is being utilized. When

FIGURE 5–1

```
SELECT CLM_ACCT_NO ,CLM_LAST_NAM
,CLM_ADDR1_LN
   FROM TDDA_CLM
   WHERE CLM_LAST_NAM >= :CLM-LAST-NAM
   ORDER BY CLM_ACCT_NO
```

are these I/Os being completed—as the rows are being presented or at some other point in the DB2 process?

When using DB2, people tend to lose sight of the specific criteria governing an I/O request. For example, users often have an attitude of "Give me all names and phone numbers," rather than just the one really needed. Depending on table size and availability of indices, a request of this type may generate several thousand I/Os. The SELECT statement shown in Figure 5–1 is a typical example.

If the host variable (CLM-LAST-NAM) contains the name ADDAMS, DB2 will create a results table consisting of a row for every name that is greater than or equal to ADDAMS. In an average distribution, this would probably be over 95% of the table. Moreover, all the related table I/O and sorting will have to be completed before the first row is even presented to the application query request! The response time may be unacceptable.

Obviously, an additional clause is needed to control the total number of rows being retrieved. The query illustrated in Figure 5–2 would satisfy the requirement and be more efficient.

The additional clause

```
AND CLM_LAST_NAM <  'A99999999999999'
```

was added to limit the rows in the results table to rows that contain the

FIGURE 5–2

```
SELECT CLM_ACCT_NO ,CLM_LAST_NAM
,CLM_ADDR1_LN
   FROM TDDA_CLM
   WHERE CLM_LAST_NAM >= :CLM-LAST-NAM
     AND CLM_LAST_NAM < 'A99999999999999'
ORDER BY CLM_ACCT_NO
```

names of ADDAMS through AZZINNARI. Thus, fewer resources will be consumed.

An even more efficient approach would utilize a LIKE clause.

```
WHERE CLM_LAST_NAM LIKE 'AD%';
```

to limit the results to last names that begin with the characters AD.

Is the excessive I/O and response time encountered in the request of the original query (Figure 5–1), attributable to DB2 or to poor program design? One response may be, "That's obvious, program design, but what about JOINs and UNIONs?" With a little more effort invested in retrieval criteria, similar resource deductions can be achieved.

■ LOCKING CONSIDERATIONS

The other area of concern is lock duration and quantity. Locking is required to prevent access to uncommitted data. However, its actual impact may far exceed the stated design criteria. The exorbitant number of rows being returned in Figure 5–1 probably caused the IS-lock (INTENT SHARE) on the tablespace to escalate to an S-lock (SHARE). This tablespace S-lock would prohibit other updates within the entire resource (tablespace) until its release at either COMMIT or DEALLOCATE time. Such a restriction was probably not necessary; page locks would have been sufficient.

DB2 uses block level sharing via the IMS/VS Resource Lock Manager (IRLM) to control locking. The IRLM supports block/CONTROLINTERVAL and dataset/CLUSTER locking. To DB2, this translates to either a PAGE or TABLESPACE locking protocol.

Given the impact of program design on lock duration and number, when are page and tablespace locks held and when are they released? In response, the term *results table* must be defined. In general, a **results table** is required whenever the rows being returned are not in the same sequence as that of the underlying base table(s). Specifically, GROUP BY, ORDER BY, JOIN, or UNION will require the creation of a results table. Please note that some documentation will refer to a results table as an *answer table* and that the terms may be used interchangeably in other publications. The omission of a column name(s) or the sequence of column names in a SELECT column list does not change row sequence and will not necessitate a results table.

■ BIND PARAMETERS

Before discussing locking it is necessary to review BIND parameters that influence locking. Recall the BIND DSN subcommand syntax, shown in Figure 5–3.

FIGURE 5–3
BIND SYNTAX

```
BIND ·······
   ISOLATION( RR | CS)
   ACQUIRE( USE | ALLOCATE)
   RELEASE( COMMIT | DEALLOCATE)
```

Isolation level (ISOLATION) will affect page lock duration. The isolation level of CS (cursor stability) is intended to hold and release page locks as pages are processed; RR (repeatable read) holds page locks until a commit point is reached.

The ACQUIRE and RELEASE parameters also influence tablespace lock duration. ACQUIRE(ALLOCATE) will allocate and force a tablespace level lock of all resources when the first SQL call is processed. ACQUIRE(USE) will allocate and lock (tablespace) resources as they are used. COMMIT releases tablespace locks at a commit point. DEALLOCATE releases tablespace locks when a PLAN is released. In an IMS/VS or CICS/VS environment, this could last for several transaction iterations, perhaps all day. Page locks are always released at a commit point.

■ LOCKING LEVELS

Locking level may be set at either page, table, or tablespace. It is established with the LOCKSIZE parameter of the CREATE TABLESPACE DDL statement in conjunction with the LOCKS PER TABLESPACE (NUMLKTS) installation parameter. For LOCKSIZE you may specify either PAGE, ANY, TABLE, or TABLESPACE. LOCKSIZE PAGE requests that only page locks be used. LOCKSIZE TABLE is used in conjunction with segmented tablespaces to lock all segments of a table. LOCKSIZE TABLESPACE will ensure that tablespace locks are always in effect. LOCKSIZE ANY will use page locks until the total number of locks (including all index locks) for a tablespace exceeds the NUMLKTS value. At this point, all page locks are released and a tablespace or table lock will be taken. This ascent to a higher locking level is known as *lock escalation*.

At this writing, table locks will not escalate to tablespace locks. However, a table lock will require that its respective tablespace hold, at least, a minimum *mode* lock. This point will be clarified in the subsequent "Table Locks" section of this chapter.

■ PAGE LOCKS

DB2 employs three types or modes of page locks: SHARE (S), UPDATE (U), and EXCLUSIVE (X). A SHARE page lock allows programs to read the same page concurrently, but none may change it. An EXCLUSIVE (X) page lock occurs when a row within a page satisfies the criteria for the WHERE clause of a DELETE or UPDATE statement. INSERTs will also cause an X-lock to be taken. Since no other program may acquire any locks on a page that is held with an X-lock, access by other programs cannot occur.

The purpose of UPDATE (U) locking is to serialize update intent and thus greatly reduce the likelihood of a deadlock situation. A program acquires a U-lock on a page when it *intends* to modify data. As processing passes over pages, U-locks are taken and either promoted to an X-lock if an UPDATE/DELETE is attempted or released when the next page is returned.

The significant difference between a U-lock and an S-lock is the concurrency of share locking. Multiple S-locks may be obtained on a page concurrently with one U-lock, although the U-lock may not be promoted to an X-lock until all S-locks on the current page are released. Concurrent U-locks are not allowed. Ultimately, the S-locks will be released and the program with a U-lock will proceed. The U-lock was new in DB2 Version 1.2.

A program may not explicitly acquire a page lock; rather, page locks are

FIGURE 5–4
HELD PAGE LOCK STRATEGY

```
  1. Page S-locks at beginning of SQL statement:
                 single row select
  2. Page S-lock as DB2 passes from page to page
         using Cursor Stability/Repeatable Read:
                 no results table
  3. Page U-locks as DB2 passes from page to
         page using Cursor Stability and
         'FOR UPDATE OF', UPDATE, or DELETE:
                 no results table
  4. All pages S-locked at OPEN CURSOR using
         Cursor Stability/Repeatable Read:
                 results table was required
  5. Exclusive X-locks are taken as page(s)
         are modified by UPDATE, DELETE, OR INSERT
         with or without CURSORs.
```

FIGURE 5–5
PAGELOCK RELEASE STRATEGY

```
1.Page S-locks released at end of SQL statement:
              single row select
2.Page S-lock released as DB2 passes from
     page to page using Cursor Stability:
              no results table
3.Page U-lock released as DB2 passes from
     page to page and data is not changed using
     Cursor Stability:
              no results table
4.Page S-locks released at CLOSE CURSOR using
     Cursor Stability:
              results table (VER.1.2)
5.Page S-locks released after all table rows
     are read:
     prior to results table sort or other
              processing (VER.1.3)
6.Page S-locks released at COMMIT with
     Repeatable Read:
              with or without results table
7.All exclusive X-locks released at COMMIT
```

---

implied by the type of SQL process being performed. The three types of page locks are acquired as shown in Figure 5–4.

Correspondingly, page lock release is dependent on the process that acquired it, isolation level (CS or RR), and whether or not a results table is required (see Figure 5–5).

■ TABLESPACE LOCKS

DB2 employs five modes of tablespace (TS) locks: INTENT SHARE (IS), SHARE (S), INTENT EXCLUSIVE (IX), SHARE INTENT EXCLUSIVE (SIX), and EXCLUSIVE (X). Tablespace locks, in conjunction with BIND and DDL CREATE parameters, control the lock mode of resources that a program will utilize upon initialization.

If all CREATE LOCKSIZE parameters specify PAGE or ANY and the Isolation Level specified at BIND is CS, then all related resources will have an initial TS lock of either IS or IX. On the other hand, if a LOCKSIZE specifies

TABLESPACE, or an Isolation Level of RR is selected, then read processing will use a tablespace S-lock and modify (UPDATE, DELETE, INSERT) processing will use a tablespace X-lock.

Initial TS lock modes are also impacted by the BIND ACQUIRE parameter. ACQUIRE(ALLOCATE) will pick the most restrictive mode for each tablespace within a program. If a program has five SELECTs and one UPDATE for the same tablespace, then IX will be chosen for that tablespace. If ACQUIRE(USE) is specified, then IS will be the initial mode, and it will be promoted to IX only if the UPDATE statement has been executed. Note that ACQUIRE(ALLOCATE) will obtain the most restrictive locks for all tablespaces when the program issues its first SQL request. Thus, lock duration will be longer and more restrictive.

Tablespace lock release is dependent on the BIND RELEASE parameter. The two choices for release are COMMIT and DEALLOCATE. COMMIT is the easiest to understand; the program either issues a commit or returns to the invoking task (e.g., COBOL GOBACK). A DB2 COMMIT will be forced when either an IMS/VS checkpoint or CICS/VS syncpoint is requested.

DEALLOCATE is dependent on when the controlling TP monitor releases its task-related resources. Under IMS/VS, tablespace lock duration will be impacted by the APPLCTN and TRANSACT installation macros. Within CICS/VS, transaction arrival rates and thread reuse parameters, as defined in the Resource Control Table (RCT), will control tablespace lock deallocation.

Tablespace locks are used in combination with page locks. For example, when a few rows are being read from a table, a tablespace IS-lock is taken and held at least until a commit point is reached. This tablespace IS-lock is acquired before any page S-locks are taken. As such, a tablespace IS-lock is a form of notification that a tablespace is active or open. If a page is to be read, a page S-lock must still be acquired. An IS-lock will be promoted to a tablespace IX-lock if a U-lock or X-lock is obtained on any page within that tablespace.

A tablespace share S-lock allows concurrent read access of a DB2 table/tablespace. No program may update any data while any other program holds a tablespace S-lock. One tablespace S-lock eliminates the requirement to obtain individual page S-locks for pages within the tablespace. A tablespace S-lock will be promoted to a tablespace X-lock if a U-lock or X-lock is obtained on any page within that tablespace.

A TS lock of INTENT EXCLUSIVE (IX) does not imply exclusive use of the entire tablespace, but rather that a program intends to update one or more rows. An IX-lock will allow concurrent access to all pages and concurrent updates of different pages in the same tablespace. Other programs with tablespace IS-locks or IX-locks on the current tablespace may access any pages within the tablespace that do not hold a U-lock or X-lock.

A tablespace SHARE INTENT EXCLUSIVE (SIX) lock will allow concur-

FIGURE 5–6
TABLESPACE LOCK COMPATIBILITIES

PGM 1	PGM 2		MODE		
MODE	IS	IX	S	SIX	X
IS	Y	Y	Y	Y	N
IX	Y	Y	N	N	N
S	Y	N	Y	N	N
SIX	Y	N	N	N	N
X	N	N	N	N	N

rent access to all pages of a tablespace, but only one program may modify data within that tablespace. This is in contrast to an IX-lock, which will allow different pages to be modified by different programs, and the S-lock, which permits read-only access for all programs.

An EXCLUSIVE (X) lock allows only one program any access to a tablespace. No other program may access an X-locked table. Caution: A program that modifies data and has an Isolation Level of RR will have its tablespace lock mode promoted to EXCLUSIVE (X) during the BIND process. This will occur despite a CREATE LOCKSIZE specification of PAGE or ANY.

Figure 5–6 summarizes DB2's responses to all possible sequences of TS lock acquisition requests made by two programs. PGM 1 is the program making the first of two requests; Y indicates that DB2 will grant PGM 2's request, and N indicates that DB2 will deny PGM 2's request.

To minimize the number of locks and their duration, SQL DML statements must be coded so as to limit the number of rows/pages being accessed, and to commit or deallocate your processing as soon as possible. To reduce the impact of lock promotion (X-locks), data modification statements should be located as close as possible to program termination (implied commit) or to a commit.

DB2 locking is not the easiest subject to grasp. The following illustrations will clarify the interrelationships between page and tablespace lock as well as the impact of lock promotion. In these examples, lowercase letters designate page locks, and uppercase letters indicate tablespace locks. The TSO examples refer to either foreground or background invocations of TSO.

Figure 5–7 depicts a single row SELECT. The BIND ACQUIRE (ALLOCATE) parameter will allocate all resources for this program/PLAN at

FIGURE 5–7
SINGLE ROW SELECT (TSO)

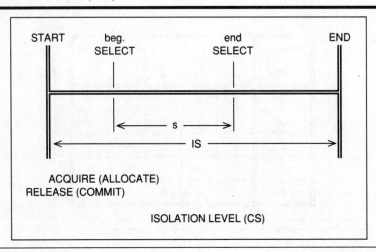

the first SQL process. The page S-lock is held for the duration of the DML SELECT statement. The tablespace IS-lock will be held until the program terminates (commit). If the program had issued a COMMIT, the tablespace lock would have been released at that time.

In Figure 5–8 a column function (AVG, COUNT, etc.) is being utilized. All rows within a page (if any) that match the WHERE clause criteria will

FIGURE 5–8
SELECT WITH COLUMN FUNCTION (TSO)

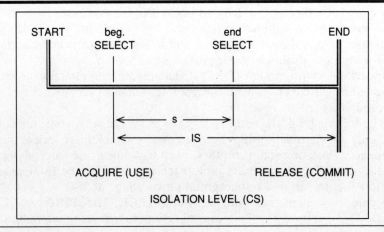

FIGURE 5–9
SELECT WITH FOR UPDATE OF DELETE OR UPDATE W/O A CURSOR (TSO)

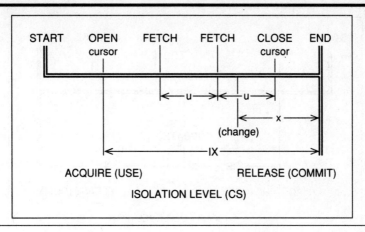

be S-locked as they are retrieved and released when the final results row
(not results table) is presented. The BIND ACQUIRE(USE) parameter limits
the duration of the tablespace IS-lock. If COUNT(*) were the only column
function specified and the related WHERE clause referenced indexed columns
only, the tablespace would not be read and no page locks would be required.

Figure 5–9 shows the impact of a FOR UPDATE OF or a DELETE or
UPDATE. Only page U-locks are held. The U-locks are held and released as

FIGURE 5–10
SELECT WITH 'ORDER BY' USING A CURSOR (VER 1.2)

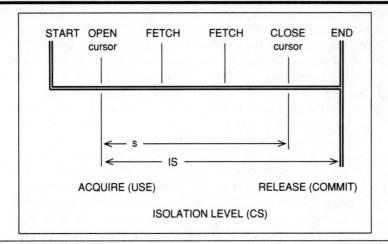

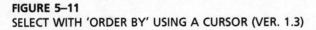

FIGURE 5–11
SELECT WITH 'ORDER BY' USING A CURSOR (VER. 1.3)

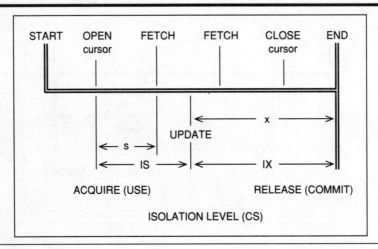

processing proceeds from page to page. If a page is modified, the U-lock is promoted to a page X-lock and is not released until commit time.

The operations depicted in both Figures 5–10 and 5–11 will produce a results table from which rows will be FETCHed. In Version 1.3 all page share locks will be released before first FETCH, so the rows may be modified by another program prior to their retrieval by the first program. The purpose of this is to increase concurrency. Any subsequent UPDATE(s) based on these retrievals must ensure that row data was not modified. Due to ACQUIRE(USE), the tablespace IS-lock will be promoted to an IX-lock when the first UPDATE is issued. If ACQUIRE(ALLOCATE) had been specified in Figure 5–11, then the tablespace IX-lock would be held from the first SQL call for any DB2 resource. The page X lock will be held on the updated page until a commit is reached (i.e., end of the program or SQL COMMIT).

See the "Program Design Recommendations" section in this chapter for a discussion of a method that utilizes timestamps to guarantee data integrity.

In Figure 5–12 the tablespace lock mode is determined by the access strategy. If a tablespace scan is used, a TS S-lock will be held, which will not allow changes by any program. The page S-locks will be held when the cursor is opened because a results table is to be created.

In Figure 5–13 the tablespace lock mode is again determined by the access strategy. If a tablespace scan is utilized, then an EXCLUSIVE lock will be held. The SHARE INTENT EXCLUSIVE (SIX) lock prohibits other programs from changing any data, but still allows read access on non–X-locked pages. When page rows are actually updated, the page S-lock is promoted to a page X-lock. Note that if the tablespace lock is promoted to EXCLUSIVE, then no page locks are required.

FIGURE 5–12
SELECT USING A CURSOR AND A RESULTS TABLE WITH ISOLATION LEVEL (RR)

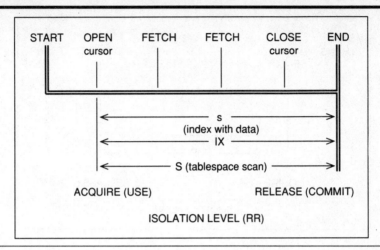

FIGURE 5–13
CURSOR SELECT, SINGLE UPDATES AND A RESULTS TABLE WITH ISOLATION LEVEL (RR)

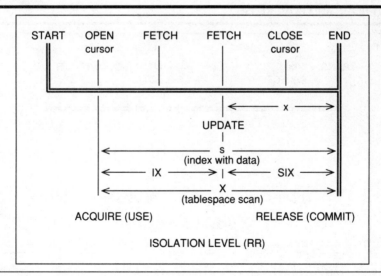

FIGURE 5–14
CICS THREAD AND PLAN REUSE

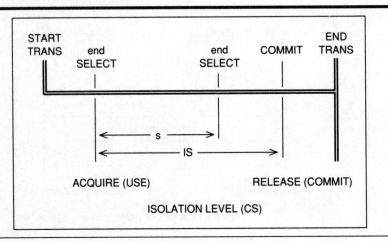

In Figure 5–14 the BIND RELEASE(COMMIT) parameter will release the IS tablespace lock at a COMMIT OR PROGRAM TERMINATION.

FIGURE 5–15
CICS THREAD AND PLAN REUSE

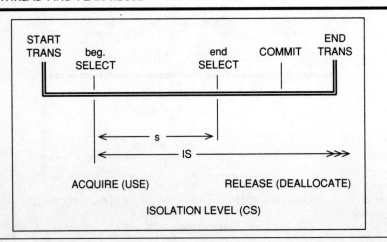

In Figure 5–15 the BIND RELEASE(DEALLOCATE) parameter will release the IS tablespace lock at PLAN/thread termination. Imagine the consequences of a tablespace lock that is promoted to an SIX-lock or X-lock!

FIGURE 5–16
TABLESPACE/TABLE LOCK DEPENDENCIES

DDL LOCKSIZE	REQUIRED PLAN LOCK	TABLESPACE	TABLE
PAGE/ ANY	IS IX S X	IS IS IS IS	IS IX S X
TABLE	IS S IX X	IS IS IS IS	S S X X
TABLESPACE	IS S IX X	S S X X	none

■ TABLE LOCKS

Table locks are new to Version 2.1 and are only used in conjunction with segmented tablespaces. Table lock modes are determined and promoted in the same manner as tablespace lock modes. However, all lock modes for a segmented tablespace require that its respective tablespace hold an INTENT SHARE lock. Figure 5–16 illustrates the mode dependencies between tables and tablespaces.

If the DDL LOCKSIZE parameter specified TABLESPACE, then no locks are taken on any of the tables within the segmented tablespace. The entire tablespace will be in either SHARE or EXCLUSIVE mode.

■ PROGRAM DESIGN RECOMMENDATIONS

During the course of several DB2 project life cycles we have paid our dues. The following are some of our most important program design considerations.

1. Always use unqualified table names within programs. Let the bindors AUTHID qualify the TABLE, VIEW, or SYNONYM names.

Reason: As programs migrate from test environments to production, no source code changes will be required.

2. All SELECT statements must use a column list. No "SELECT *" statements should be used within programs. Do not SELECT more columns than needed.
   Reason: Performance and ease of change. Results tables will be smaller, which will decrease sort time and reduce cross memory overhead.

3. All WHERE clauses should include predicates for indexed columns.
   Reason: Will allow DB2 to use indices and decrease I/O.

4. When using column functions (e.g., MAX, AVG), consider using NULL indicators.
   Reason: If the WHERE clause is so restrictive that no rows are returned, DB2 will return NULL(s). If the program does not provide a NULL indicator, then a negative SQLCODE will be returned.

5. Avoid the use of leading '%' or '_' characters in a LIKE predicate.
   Reason: DB2 will have to scan the entire index, which will result in more I/O.

6. Avoid the use of subqueries within an IN predicate.
   Reason: DB2 will access the subquery table with a full tablespace or indexspace scan.

7. Avoid the use of NOT LIKE, NOT IN, NOT BETWEEN, or NOT EXISTS predicates.
   Reason: Performance; DB2 will not use the index structure—an indexspace or tablespace scan will be chosen.

8. Close cursors as soon as processing is complete for each open cursor or when an end of TABLE condition (SQLCODE = 100) is detected.
   Reason: Resource utilization; results tables are kept until their related cursors are closed.

9. When a results table is required, do not retrieve more rows than necessary. Within the WHERE predicate, establish beginning and ending values.
   Reason: Locking and resource utilization will be minimized. In Version 1.3, all page S-locks are held until the final results table is complete.

10. Use ORDER BY when retrieving rows in a specific sequence (cluster or otherwise).
    Reason: Tables are in clustering sequence only after a REORG. Subsequent row INSERTs may be stored in any page. To guarantee the query sequence you must use an ORDER BY clause.

11. When using a single SELECT statement to check for the existence of a value, use

```
SELECT COUNT(DISTINCT COL_1)
FROM table_1
WHERE COL_1 = :   search-arg
```

Reason: Performance; DB2 will stop the statement when it encounters the first row whose COL_1 equals the value in *search-arg* of the WHERE predicate.

12. No critical batch program should take more than 15 minutes to restart in the event of an abnormal termination.

    Reason: Criticality of systems; see the **DB2 Automated Restart** chapter for suggested restart methods.

13. Always ensure that a COMMIT completes prior to sending information to a terminal.

    Reason: Locking; all locks will remain held until subsequent processing releases them or until a deadlock occurs.

14. When retrieving rows for possible UPDATE and cursors are not used, use a LAST UPDATE TIMESTAMP column:

    ```
    LAST_UPDT_TS TIMESTAMP
    ```

    Reason: Data integrity; the TIMESTAMP's value will guarantee the row's data integrity. The following UPDATE standard must be strictly adhered to:

    ```
    UPDATE  table_xxx
    SET   COL_A = :HOST-A
                •
                •
                •

    ,LAST_UPDT_TS = CURRENT TIMESTAMP
    WHERE  KEY_COL = :KEY-VALUE
    AND LAST_UPDT_TS = :WS-TS;
    ```

    The host variable (WS-TS) must contain the TIMESTAMP value from when the row was first retrieved and all other programs must properly update the "LAST_UPDT_TS" column.

DB2 AUTOMATED RESTART

■ RESTART TERMS

To discuss DB2 automated restart properly, it is necessary to define a few terms that are common to DB2. A **unit of recovery** is considered a sequence of operations between two commit points. **Commit points** occur when a unit of recovery completes and all of its data manipulation has been applied. As such, DB2 COMMITs are very similar to IMS checkpoints or CICS syncpoints. The difference between them is that commit points may also include DDL or DCL functions which are not available in either IMS or CICS. A **point of consistency** may be considered a point in time when all processing (including COMMIT) is complete and all related data is available for any other user or program. A point of consistency could be a commit point or even the successful completion of a RECOVERY utility. As such, its scope could cover one unit of recovery or several tablespaces.

When a program does more than retrieve data and its table changes require more than 30 minutes to back out, it becomes necessary to consider automated restart. The objective of **automated restart** is to restore all tables for a given unit of recovery to their last point of consistency. Ideally, this "backout" should occur with little or no operator intervention.

■ TYPES OF RESTART

The easiest method of automated restart employs the NO COMMIT-STEP RESTART policy. Put simply, the program issues no COMMIT that, in the event of an ABEND, will require DB2 to back out all table changes for the current unit of recovery. This means that if the program is executing for 20 minutes, it will probably take DB2 an additional 15 minutes to back out all the related updates. Furthermore, all related pages will hold exclusive locks until DB2 completes its backout. Recall that exclusive locks are incompatible with any other type of lock. Thus, for 35 minutes, no other programs will be able to update or **read** any of these pages. Moreover, all pages and/or tablespaces that held share locks will be unavailable for updates for the program duration. On the plus side, this method will require no operator intervention except for the necessary JCL STEP RESTART statements.

Another method of automated restart is similar to IMS/VS extended restart facility. This method will allow a program to reposition its main processing sequence, save an unlimited amount of working storage, and allow the program to do restart processing, if necessary. This technique requires no operator intervention and minimizes both lock duration and backout time. However, the program must be designed to be more sensitive than it otherwise might be to the key range values of its major processing sequence. For lack of a better name, let's call it DB2 EXTENDED RESTART.

■ THE CHECKPOINT TABLE

In Figure 6–1, a checkpoint table is outlined. The line numbers (incremented by 5) at the left of the figure will be referenced in the following discussion. The checkpoint table provides a repository for program areas (e.g., working storage fields) and positioning information at commit points. The presence of a row within this checkpoint table signals that a program is in progress, and that commit points (checkpoints) are being taken. Uniqueness within this table is ensured by the CKPT_PGM_ID and, if necessary, the CKPT_PGM_TS columns (lines 2 and 3). Up to 3,556 bytes per row may be saved at each COMMIT. If more data must be saved, multiple rows may be uniquely inserted using the CKPT_PGM_TS column. Note that each row is one DB2 page. This will greatly reduce potential locking problems.

■ DB2 CHECKPOINT RESTART APPLICATION EXAMPLE

The first save area is redefined (lines 28 through 30) to allow positioning after a commit or restart. The START-KEY and END-KEY values are used to control the number of rows returned for OPEN, FETCH, and CLOSE cursor processing. Effectively, this controls the number of locks and lock duration between commit points. If the END-KEY was not used to control the number of rows being returned, the table could conceivably be read $4^1/2$ times! At

FIGURE 6–1
CHECKPOINT TABLE

```
        01  DCTABL-CKPT
            05  CKPT-PGM-ID          PIC X(8).
            05  CKPT-PGM-TS          PIC X(26).
     5      05  CKPT-SAVE-AREA1      PIC X(254).
            05  CKPT-SAVE-AREA2      PIC X(254).
            05  CKPT-SAVE-AREA3      PIC X(254).
            05  CKPT-SAVE-AREA4      PIC X(254).
            05  CKPT-SAVE-AREA5      PIC X(254).
    10      05  CKPT-SAVE-AREA6      PIC X(254).
            05  CKPT-SAVE-AREA7      PIC X(254).
            05  CKPT-SAVE-AREA8      PIC X(254).
            05  CKPT-SAVE-AREA9      PIC X(254).
            05  CKPT-SAVE-AREA10     PIC X(254).
    15      05  CKPT-SAVE-AREA11     PIC X(254).
            05  CKPT-SAVE-AREA12     PIC X(254).
            05  CKPT-SAVE-AREA13     PIC X(254).
            05  CKPT-SAVE-AREA14     PIC X(254).
        01  FILLER REDEFINES DCLTABL-CKPT.
    20      05  FILLER               PIC X(08).
            05  FILLER               PIC X(26).
         *
         *      EACH SAVE AREA MUST HAVE A LENGTH OF 254
         *
    25   *      THE SAVE AREAS MAY BE USED TO SAVE WHATEVER
         *      WORKING STORAGE THE PROGRAM REQUIRES
         *
         *
            05  KEY-SAVE-AREA.
    30          10  START-KEY        PIC X(127).
                10  END-KEY          PIC X(127).
                10  FILLER REDEFINES END-KEY.
                 15 END-KEY-CO       PIC X(1).
                 15 END-KEY-ACCT-NO  PIC X(7).
    35      05  DATA-SAVE-AREA2      PIC X(254).
            05  FILLER REDEFINES DATA-SAVE-AREA2.
                10  SOME-TOTAL-FLD1 PIC S9(13)V99     COMP-3.
                10  SOME-TOTAL-FLD2 PIC S9(13)V99     COMP-3.
                10  SOME-TOTAL-FLD3 PIC S9(13)V99     COMP-3.
    40          10  SOME-TOTAL-FLD4 PIC S9(13)V99     COMP-3.
                10  SOME-TOTAL-FLD5 PIC S9(13)V99     COMP-3.
                10  SOME-TOTAL-FLD6 PIC S9(13)V99     COMP-3.
```

FIGURE 6–2
COBOL COPY CODE : PRIMARY PROCESSING SEQ.

```
*       DCLGEN AREA
*                        also controls start key sequence
  01   DCLTABL-CLM.
       05   CLM-CO                PIC X(1).
       05   CLM-ACCT-NO           PIC X(7).
       05   CLM-                  PIC
       05   CLM-     other data   PIC
       05   CLM-                  PIC
       05   CLM-                  PIC
```

each open cursor, a results table would be built that would consist of rows from the starting position to the end of the table. If each open was intended to process $1/8$ of the table, the first open would process the whole table, the second open would process $7/8$ of the table, the third open would process $3/4$ of the table, and so on until the table was manipulated in a recursive fashion $4^{1}/2$ times. Moreover, sort overhead attributable to "ORDER BY" clauses will be greatly reduced because of the smaller results table for each open cursor.

Figure 6–2 presents the COBOL copy code for a client master table that will control the primary processing sequence in our example. Columns in this table will be referred to by a DML "ORDER BY" clause to control start and end sequence ranges for the main row retrieval order of the program. Even though the START-KEY values are being saved in the checkpoint table, they will be moved into this copy code area prior to any open cursor statements for this table. This action will be clarified further on.

The actual test for a restart is shown in Figure 6–3. If a checkpoint row is found and returned, a restart is in progress. The program must restore its working storage areas from the current checkpoint row. Any other restart activities, such as opening and repositioning O/S files, setting the END-KEY values, or printing messages must be performed.

If a checkpoint row was not returned (i.e., a restart was not in process), control falls through to paragraph 0010-SET-UP-FIRST-SELECT (Figure 6–4), where the first range of values must be established. The first start and end row sequence values are determined as shown. The choice of subsequence ranges will be totally dependent on the underlying data; the requirements will probably be distinct for each program. One approach is the

FIGURE 6–3
TEST FOR RESTART PROCESSING

```
    PROCEDURE DIVISION.

*       TEST FOR RESTART
        EXEC SQL
        SELECT  CKPT_PGM_ID  ,CKPT_PGM_TS
         ,CKPT_SAVE_AREA1 ,CKPT_SAVE_AREA2 ,CKPT_SAVE_AREA3
            ,CKPT_SAVE_AREA4  ,CKPT_SAVE_AREA5  ,CKPT_SAVE_AREA6
            ,CKPT_SAVE_AREA7  ,CKPT_SAVE_AREA8  ,CKPT_SAVE_AREA9
            ,CKPT_SAVE_AREA10 ,CKPT_SAVE_AREA11 ,CKPT_SAVE_AREA12
            ,CKPT_SAVE_AREA13 ,CKPT_SAVE_AREA14
        INTO    :CKPT_PGM_ID  ,CKPT_PGM_TS
            ,:CKPT-SAVE-AREA1  ,:CKPT-SAVE-AREA2  ,:CKPT-SAVE-AREA3
            ,:CKPT-SAVE-AREA4  ,:CKPT-SAVE-AREA5  ,:CKPT-SAVE-AREA6
            ,:CKPT-SAVE-AREA7  ,:CKPT-SAVE-AREA8  ,:CKPT-SAVE-AREA9
            ,:CKPT-SAVE-AREA10 ,:CKPT-SAVE-AREA11 ,:CKPT-SAVE-AREA12
            ,:CKPT-SAVE-AREA13 ,:CKPT-SAVE-AREA14
        FROM    TABL_CKPT
          WHERE CKPT_PGM_ID = 'this pgm'
        END-EXEC.
        if found
            MOVE START-KEY TO DCLTABL_CLM
            END KEY was primed by select
            GO TO 0010A-MAIN_SELECT.
*  not a restart so set up initial key range
```

creation of a COBOL table where the number of occurrences would control both the number and duration of COMMITs. A more efficient approach might utilize a DML "GROUP BY" clause to dynamically project the sub-sequences for each COMMIT. This selection criterion would be part of program initialization. The INSERT and COMMIT commands are necessary to preserve restart logic and to restore any program information that was derived prior to initial DB2 processing. At a minimum, the initial range of values is saved.

The starting values are moved into the COBOL include structure for the client master table. In turn, the client master group data name (DCLTABL-CLM) is moved into the START-KEY data element (length of 127). This is permissible because controlling columns are within the first 127 bytes of the client master row.

The query detailed in Figure 6–5 controls the processing sequence of this program. The two ACCT and CO host variable fields must be ini-

FIGURE 6—4
DETERMINATION OF START/END ROW SEQ VALUES

```
0010-SET-UP-FIRST-SELECT.
    MOVE some start acct TO CLM-ACCT-NO
    MOVE some start co   TO CLM-CO
    increment acct no to establish END
    MOVE some end co     TO END-KEY-CO
    MOVE some end acct   TO END-KEY-ACCT-NO
*  prime for  restart
    EXEC SQL
    INSERT INTO         TABL_CKPT
        (   CKPT_PGM_ID  ,CKPT_PGM_TS
        ,CKPT_SAVE_AREA1  ,CKPT_SAVE_AREA2  ,CKPT_SAVE_AREA3
        ,CKPT_SAVE_AREA4  ,CKPT_SAVE_AREA5  ,CKPT_SAVE_AREA6
        ,CKPT_SAVE_AREA7  ,CKPT_SAVE_AREA8  ,CKPT_SAVE_AREA9
        ,CKPT_SAVE_AREA10 ,CKPT_SAVE_AREA11 ,CKPT_SAVE_AREA12
        ,CKPT_SAVE_AREA13 ,CKPT_SAVE_AREA14 )
        VALUES  (  'this pgm'     ,CURRENT TIMESTAMP
        ,:CKPT-SAVE-AREA1 ,:CKPT-SAVE-AREA2 ,:CKPT-SAVE-AREA3
        ,:CKPT-SAVE-AREA4 ,:CKPT-SAVE-AREA5 ,:CKPT-SAVE-AREA6
        ,:CKPT-SAVE-AREA7 ,:CKPT-SAVE-AREA8 ,:CKPT-SAVE-AREA9
        ,:CKPT-SAVE-AREA10 ,:CKPT-SAVE-AREA11 ,:CKPT-SAVE-AREA12
        ,:CKPT-SAVE-AREA13 ,:CKPT-SAVE-AREA14   )
    END-EXEC.
    EXEC SQL
    COMMIT
    END-EXEC.
```

tialized to limit the number of rows that will be returned. It is precisely
this row limitation that governs the COMMIT duration. The host variables
must be primed prior to the OPENs for cursor "xxxxxxxx." For every
CLOSE/COMMIT following a NOT FOUND condition, it will be necessary to
set the values of the four host variables in order to process the next range
of values.

The 1000-MAINLINE logic is executed until all processing for this program is complete. At that point, it is necessary to delete the related checkpoint row(s) and terminate processing. The absence of a checkpoint row for
this program signals normal completion. If the program ABENDs prior to the
GOBACK (DB2 generated COMMIT) and subsequent deletion of the checkpoint row, the last point of consistency will be preserved. The program may
be restarted.

FIGURE 6–5
PROCESSING SEQUENCE CONTROL

```
0010A-MAIN-SELECT
    EXEC SQL DECLARE xxxxxxxx CURSOR FOR
    SELECT CLM_CO ,CLM_ACCT_NO , - -, additional columns
    FROM TABL_CLM

*   following are the COMMIT control clauses

    WHERE CLM_ACCT_NO > :CLM-ACCT-NO
      AND CLM_CO        = :CLM-CO
      AND CLM_ACCT_NO < :END-ACCT-NO
      AND CLM_CO        = :END-CO

    other criteria

    ORDER BY CLM_ACCT_NO ASC   ,CLM_CO ASC
    END-EXEC.

    PERFORM 1000-MAINLINE UNTIL max end seq

    EXEC SQL
    DELETE FROM TABL_CKPT
    WHERE CKPT_PGM_ID  = 'this pgm'
    END-EXEC
    GOBACK.
```

The last requirement (see Figure 6–6) to implement DB2 EXTENDED RESTART is that all restart-related data in the checkpoint table be saved. This action must take place just prior to issuing any COMMIT requests. To reiterate, if an ABEND occurs before the COMMIT completes, the program will be able to restart at the last point of consistency. Whenever a COMMIT successfully terminates, a new point of consistency is established.

As discussed with respect to Figure 6–4, some data/program dependent logic will be required to control the ranges of values of the END-KEY and START-KEY. In any event, the start and ending values must be saved. Note the statement MOVE DCLTABL-CLM TO START-KEY. Since we know that the columns used in the WHERE clause are within the first 127 bytes, the group data name is used to facilitate saving of the starting values. There are many other methods that may be employed to minimize the actual coding effort.

FIGURE 6–6
SAVE OF CHECKPOINT TABLE RESTART DATA

```
1000-MAINLINE

      O P E N      CURSOR

      F E T C H    until not found

      C L O S E    CURSOR(S)

   increment acct no to establish END
   MOVE some end co       TO END-KEY-CO
   MOVE some end acct     TO END-KEY-ACCT-NO
   MOVE DCLTABL-CLM       TO START-KEY
   EXEC SQL
   UPDATE TABL_CKPT  SET
    CKPT-PGM-TS           = CURRENT TIMESTAMP
   ,CKPT-SAVE-AREA1       = :CKPT-SAVE-AREA1
   ,CKPT-SAVE-AREA2       = :CKPT-SAVE-AREA2
   ,CKPT-SAVE-AREA3       = :CKPT-SAVE-AREA3
   ,CKPT-SAVE-AREA4       = :CKPT-SAVE-AREA4
   ,CKPT-SAVE-AREA5       = :CKPT-SAVE-AREA5
   ,CKPT-SAVE-AREA6       = :CKPT-SAVE-AREA6
   ,CKPT-SAVE-AREA7       = :CKPT-SAVE-AREA7
   ,CKPT-SAVE-AREA8       = :CKPT-SAVE-AREA8
   ,CKPT-SAVE-AREA9       = :CKPT-SAVE-AREA9
   ,CKPT-SAVE-AREA10      = :CKPT-SAVE-AREA10
   ,CKPT-SAVE-AREA11      = :CKPT-SAVE-AREA11
   ,CKPT-SAVE-AREA12      = :CKPT-SAVE-AREA12
   ,CKPT-SAVE-AREA13      = :CKPT-SAVE-AREA13
   ,CKPT-SAVE-AREA14      = :CKPT-SAVE-AREA14
   WHERE CKPT_PGM_ID      = 'this pgm'
   END-EXEC.
   EXEC SQL
   COMMIT
   END-EXEC
   continue until max end seq
```

■ CONCLUSION

In this chapter, two methods were presented for DB2 AUTOMATED RESTART.

The first, NO COMMIT-STEP RESTART, requires the least amount of coding and design effort and will probably suffice for programs with an elapsed execution time of less than 15 minutes. If elapsed execution time exceeds 15 minutes, the number and duration of both share and exclusive locks will be unacceptable. No other programs will be able to run until this program either completes or rolls back its updates.

If it is necessary to run a recover utility (i.e., a worst case-scenario), two other utilities must also be executed. Each tablespace must have its indices recovered. DB2 requires that a new image copy be made for each recovered tablespace. These utility sets (RECOVER TS, RECOVER INDEX, COPY) may require more than an hour of execution time—more time if the tables are large.

The second technique, DB2 EXTENDED RESTART, requires more design and coding effort, but restarts will take no longer than ten minutes. Also, DB2 EXTENDED RESTART allows program compilation prior to restart—something that other CHECKPOINT RESTART facilities do not allow. Compilation and code changes are permitted, since the program refreshes its working storage from DB2 tables.

Whatever procedure is utilized, <u>temporary</u> <u>and</u> <u>SYSOUT</u> <u>files</u> <u>cannot</u> <u>be</u> <u>used</u>. MVS deletes all temporary files at the point of normal or abnormal job termination.

SYSOUT, although processed by Job Entry Systems (JES), may be corrupted by blocking factors. JES will close and print all but the last block of SYSOUT files.

DB2 DSN COMMAND

■ THE DSN COMMAND PROCESSOR

The DSN command processor runs under TSO (invoked by the DSN TSO command) which enables the processing of subcommands as well. All subcommands may be run either in TSO foreground or background, with the exception of SPUFI, which must be run in foreground under ISPF. Both foreground and background include the use of CLISTS. Note, however, that background execution prohibits the use of prompts typically issued by the DSN command for additional information or corrections.

No authorization is required to invoke the DSN command processor. However, most of the subcommands do require appropriate authorizations for execution.

The DSN command has the format shown in Figure 7–1. All three DSN command keywords (SYSTEM, RETRY, and TEST) are optional.

FIGURE 7–1
TSO DSN COMMAND

```
DSN SYSTEM(DSN | subsystem name)
    RETRY(0 | integer)
    TEST(integer)
```

- *subsystem name* — indicates the DB2 subsystem (default is DSN, modified as required for the installation).
- RETRY(*integer*) — indicates the number of attempts (in thirty second intervals) to connect to DB2 for DSN processing if DB2 is not active at the time of the original DSN request (default 0, maximum 120).

- TEST(*integer*) — starts DSN trace. Used for debugging the DSN Command Processor; used in conjunction with the ABEND DSN subcommand.

During a DSN session, foreground input will be requested by the "DSN" prompt whereas background input will be obtained from the JCL SYSTSIN DD statement. After completion of the previous processing, the DSN command reissues the prompt for new input in a cyclical manner until it encounters the end of a DSN session. A DSN session is perceived as terminated by

1. Two consecutive attention requests (e.g., PA1, PA1),
2. Use of the END subcommand which returns control to TSO,
3. The encounter of a new DSN command which starts a new DSN session.

The subcommands to be presented in this chapter are summarized as follows.

ABEND	assist in diagnosis of DSN or DB2 problems
BIND	builds an application plan
DCLGEN	produces table or view declarations
END	terminates DSN command processing
FREE	deletes application plans
REBIND	updates application plans
RUN	invokes an application program for execution

■ ABEND

This DSN subcommand is activated when the TEST parameter of the DSN command specifies a value that is greater than zero. When TEST is activated, (i.e., value greater than zero), diagnostic information is written to SYSOUT as DSN executes.

■ BIND

The DSN **BIND** subcommand functions to build an application plan. Each DB2 application program requires that a plan be created for it to obtain the resources necessary to execute its DB2 requests. The BIND subcommand, via the optimizer, chooses the access path to the data requested by SQL statements.

Execution of the BIND subcommand requires the authority appropriate for the type of BIND request being processed. ADD requires SYSADM authority or the BINDADD privilege. REPLACE similarly requires SYSADM authority, or that the requestor be the creator of the plan (implied authority), or hold the BIND privilege for that plan.

The AUTHID which is the requestor of the BIND subcommand becomes the creator of the plan, with all privileges including the GRANT option.

The following DB2 catalog tables are affected by the BIND process: SYSIBM.SYSPLAN, SYSIBM.SYSPLANDEP, SYSIBM.SYSSTMT, and SYSIBM.SYSDBRM. See Figure 7–2 for the BIND subcommand format.

FIGURE 7–2
BIND DSN SUBCOMMAND FORMAT

```
BIND [PLAN (plan-name)]
    MEMBER (DBRM-member-name,.....)
    [LIBRARY (DBRM-library-name, ...)]
    [ACTION (REPLACE | ADD)]
        [RETAIN]
    [VALIDATE (RUN | BIND)]
    [ISOLATION (RR | CS)]
    [FLAG (I | W | E | C)]
    [ACQUIRE (USE | ALLOCATE)]
    [RELEASE (COMMIT | DEALLOCATE)]
    [EXPLAIN (NO | YES )]
    [OWNER(SQLID)          VER 2.1
```

- *plan-name* — indicates the application plan to be processed. If a plan name is omitted by coding only left and right parens

      BIND().....

  then no plan will be built and the BIND subcommand functions as a test BIND.
- *DBRM-member-name* — indicates the DBRMs to be included in the application plan to be processed.
- *DBRM-library-name* — indicates the catalogued datasets from which the DBRMs are to be included as specified in the MEMBER keyword. If more than one dataset is entered, then their sequence will be the search order.
- ACTION — indicates whether the application plan being processed is to be added or replaced in the DB2 catalog tables.
- RETAIN — retain all previous authorities associated with the PLAN being processed. If ACTION(REPLACE) was specified in conjunction with RETAIN, all previous BIND and EXECUTE authorizations will be

maintained. The executor of the BIND request will be considered the new CREATOR for authorization purposes. If RETAIN was not entered, all previous EXECUTE authorities will be lost, but prior bind authorities will still be held.

- VALIDATE — indicates the point at which validity checking for the existence of tables and authorization of access to them is performed. RUN, the default, defers checking until the plan is invoked using the executor as the AUTHID for such checking. (Dynamic bind processing occurs for statements which are invalid at bind time.) BIND indicates that validity checking is to be performed at the time of bind procesing, using the AUTHID of the bindor for checking purposes.

- ISOLATION — indicates the level at which the plan is to be isolated from access requests of other executing plans. The default, RR (repeatable read), prevents the table values <u>read</u> <u>or</u> <u>modified</u> by this application plan from being modified by other plans until the plan is terminated or encounters a commit point. CS (cursor stability) limits the restriction on other applications to the page currently being used by the plan, or until a commit point, if modifications to the data are made. See the "Locking Considerations" section of the Design Guidelines chapter for more detailed information.

- FLAG — indicates the severity of the messages to be returned as output from BIND processing. The options are: only completion messages; only error and completion messages; only warning, error, and completion messages; or all messages (C, E, W, and I, respectively.) The default is all messages (I).

- ACQUIRE — indicates when resources are to be acquired by the application plan. USE, the default, acquires locks on the resources only as the resources are requested for use by the application program. ALLOCATE acquires locks on the resources when the plan itself is activated, regardless of when (if at all) the application program requests the resources for use. (The ALLOCATE parameter does not apply to dynamic SQL statements.)

- RELEASE — indicates when resources are to be released by the application plan. COMMIT, the default, releases locks and may close related tablespaces at each commit point issued by the application program. DEALLOCATE releases locks on the resources only when the plan itself is terminated. RELEASE(COMMIT) is always used for dynamic SQL statements.

- EXPLAIN — indicates whether the optimizer access strategy pertaining to SQL statement execution for the plan is to be inserted into the BIND executor's PLAN_TABLE. The PLAN_TABLE is user-allocated and must exist prior to bind execution.

- OWNER (VER 2.1) — indicates that SQLID—not the AUTHID of the person executing the BIND subcommand—is to be known as the owner of the plan. The current AUTHID must be changed prior to executing the bind using the following SET statement

```
SET CURRENT SQLID = '(SQLID)'
```

where *SQLID* is a valid secondary AUTHID known to the User Security Exit. Thus *SQLID* becomes the plan CREATOR value and the executing AUTHID becomes the BOUNDBY value in SYSIBM.SYSPLAN.

■ DCLGEN

The **DCLGEN** (DeCLare GENeration) DSN subcommand generates a COBOL or PL/I data declaration and a SQL DECLARE TABLE statement for the table or view.

Execution of the DCLGEN subcommand requires the SELECT privilege for the table or view specified for generation of the declaration (see Figure 7–3).

FIGURE 7–3
DCLGEN DSN SUBCOMMAND FORMAT

```
DCLGEN TABLE (table-name | view-name)
       LIBRARY (library-name [(member-name)]
                            [/password])
       [ACTION (ADD | REPLACE)]
       [LANGUAGE (COBOL | PL/I)]
       [NAMES (prefix)]
       [STRUCTURE (structure-name)]
       [APOST | QUOTE)]
       [LABEL (NO | YES)]
```

- *table-name* — indicates the table or view for which a declaration is to be generated.
- *library-name(member name)/password* — indicates the dataset (sequential or partitioned) for which the declaration is destined. The dataset must be available prior to the subcommand request. Failure to enclose the library name in quotation marks will cause the declaration generator to use standard TSO dataset naming conventions. The library name will be prefixed with the user's *TSOID* and appended with a language parameter in the form

```
TSOID.library-name.lang(memname)/password.
```

- ACTION — indicates whether the declaration being generated is an addition or replacement to an existing member (ADD and REPLACE, respectively). If a replacement is indicated for a partitioned dataset for which no member truly exists, then the member will effectively be added.

- LANGUAGES — indicates the host language that the DCLGEN will use for generation. May be COBOL or PL/I with COBOL begin the default

- NAMES — enables the use of a user-supplied prefix appended with ascending numeric values to substitute for table column names in the fields output by DCLGEN processing. This option is applicable for situations where the default column names of the table would conflict with data names already present in the program including the declaration. For example, a prefix of LMN would result in field names of LMN1 through LMN999, as required.

- STRUCTURE — enables the use of a user-supplied name for the generated PL/I data structure or COBOL group. SQL uses the same name as the table or view itself. The default for COBOL or PL/I structures is the table or view name prefixed by DCL. This option is applicable for situations where the default structure name would conflict with data names already present in the program using this DCLGEN.

- APOST |QUOTE — indicates the string delimiter character of the host language (apostrophe and quotation mark, respectively).

- LABEL — indicates whether to include the column names of the table or view as comments in the DCLGEN output.

■ END

The **END** DSN subcommand terminates a DSN session and passes control back to TSO.

Execution of the END subcommand (Figure 7–4) does not require any special authorization for execution.

Note that a batch "/*" or "//*" character set or foreground attention (e.g., PA1) request (entered twice) will function as a substitute for the lack of an END subcommand in a TSO input stream.

FIGURE 7–4
END DSN SUBCOMMAND FORMAT

```
END
```

■ FREE

The **FREE** DSN subcommand removes an application plan from the DB2 environment by deleting its respective table entries from the DB2 catalog tables. All authorizations and dependencies relating to the plan are also dropped, making the plan name available for susequent BIND processing as though it had not previously been used.

Execution of the FREE subcommand requires that the requestor be the creator of the plan (i.e., having issued the last bind request), hold the bind privilege for the plan, or have SYSADM authority.

A previous bindor may FREE a plan whether or not RETAIN was specified on any subsequent bind request (see Figure 7–5).

FIGURE 7–5
END DSN SUBCOMMAND FORMAT

```
FREE PLAN (plan-name,...) | (*)
         [FLAG (I | W | E | C)]
```

- *plan-name* — indicates the specific plan name(s) requested for deletion or optionally, all plans for which the user has bind authority. An asterisk (*) indicates that all plans will be freed for which the executor's AUTHID holds the bind privilege (explicitly or implicitly).
- FLAG — indicates the severity of the messages to be returned as output from FREE processing. The options are only completion messages; only error and completion messages; only warning, error, and completion messages; or all messages (C, E, W, and I, respectively.) The default is all (I).

■ REBIND

The DSN **REBIND** subcommand functions to rebind an application plan when changes have been made which impact the plan without affecting SQL statements (i.e., access strategy and validation changes). Even when a plan has not been invalidated, performance enhancements may occur from a REBIND execution. For example, an alternative index may be indicated for execution, even though the former index of the access path chosen at bind time still exists.

REBIND is customarily performed after the REORG and RUNSTATS utilities are run.

FIGURE 7–6
REBIND DSN SUBCOMMAND FORMAT

```
REBIND PLAN (plan-name,...) | (*)]
         [FLAG (I | W | E | C)]

    Following parameters will default to the
    last bind specifications

            [VALIDATE (RUN | BIND)]
            [ISOLATION (RR | CS)]
            [ACQUIRE (USE | ALLOCATE)]
            [RELEASE (COMMIT | DEALLOCATE)]
            [EXPLAIN (NO | YES)]
            [OWNER(SQLID)]        VER 2.1
```

Execution of the REBIND subcommand requires the bind privilege for each named plan (see Figure 7–6).

The DB2 catalog tables affected by the bind process are SYSIBM.SYS-PLAN, SYSIBM.SYSPLANDEP, and SYSIBM.SYSPLANAUTH.

- *plan-name* — indicates the application plan(s) to be processed. An asterisk (*) indicates that all plans will be rebound for which the executor's AUTHID holds the bind privilege (explicitly or implicitly).

- FLAG — indicates the severity of the messages to be returned as output from REBIND processing. The options are only completion messages; only error and completion messages; only warning, error, and completion messages; or all messages (C, E, W, and I, respectively.) The default is all (I).

- VALIDATE — indicates when validity checking for the existence of tables and authorization of access to them is performed. RUN defers checking until the plan is invoked, using the executor as the AUTHID for such checking. (Dynamic bind processing occurs for statements which are invalid at bind time.) Bind indicates that validity checking is to be performed at the time of bind procesing, using the AUTHID of the bindor for checking purposes. The default is the value last specified during bind processing.

- ISOLATION — indicates the level at which this plan is to be isolated from access requests of other executing plans. RR (repeatable read), prevents the table values <u>read</u> or <u>modified</u> by this plan from being modified by other plans, until such time as the plan is terminated or encounters a

commit point. CS (cursor stability) limits the restriction on other applications to the page currently being used by the plan, or until a commit
point, if modifications to the data are made. The default is the value last
specified during bind processing.

- ACQUIRE — indicates when resources are to be acquired by the application plan. USE acquires locks on the resources only as the resources
are requested for use by the application program. ALLOCATE acquires
locks on the resources when the plan itself is activated, regardless of
when (if at all) the application program requests the resources for use.
(The ALLOCATE parameter does not apply to dynamic SQL statements.)
The default is the value last specified during bind processing.

- RELEASE — indicates when resources are to be released by the application plan. COMMIT releases locks and may close related tablespaces
at each commit point issued by the application program. DEALLOCATE
releases locks on the resources only when the plan itself is terminated.
Note that use of ACQUIRE(ALLOCATE) mandates that RELEASE(DEAL-
LOCATE) be used. The default is the value last specified during bind
procesing.

- EXPLAIN — indicates whether information pertaining to access strategy
and retrieval of SQL statements in the DBRM(s) for the plan will be
added to *userid*.PLAN_TABLE. The default is the value specified during
the last bind process.

■ RUN

The DSN **RUN** subcommand invokes an application program for execution.
Execution of the RUN subcommand requires that the requestor hold the
EXECUTE privilege (see Figure 7–7).

FIGURE 7–7
RUN DSN SUBCOMMAND FORMAT

```
RUN PROGRAM (program-name) | [CP]
    [PLAN (plan-name)]
    [LIBRARY (library-name)]
    [PARMS ('string')]
```

- *program-name* — indicates the program name requested to run.
- *plan-name* — indicates the plan name for the application program. The
default is *program-name* when PROGRAM is used.

CP forces a TSO prompt to be issued. Allows programs to be executed under the TSO TEST or COBTEST facilities. Used for testing and debugging purposes. PROGRAM and CP are mutually exclusive. If CP is specified, PLAN is also required.

- *library-name* — indicates the dataset in which the program to be executed resides. The default is *TSOID*.RUNLIB.LOAD.

- *string* — passes a parameter list to the program to be executed. For PL/I, the string should take the format 'PL/I runtime parameters (if any)/application program parameters.' For COBOL, the string should take the reverse format, 'application program parameters/COBOL runtime parameters (if any).' In both instances, the slash must be coded when the first portion of the parameter string is required. Assembler language uses a simple string format since no runtime parameters are required.

■ DSN SUBCOMMAND EXECUTION

As previously mentioned in this chapter, you may use the DB2I panels to invoke most of the DSN subcommands. When developing and or maintaining a system of any magnitude, it is advantageous to automate as many DBA functions as possible. It is even more advantageous for these functions to execute in either foreground or background environments.

Such strategy may make it possible for one person to maintain three environments (i.e., Unit Test, System Test, and Production) without forcing the application team to wait for table changes or creation. DB2I panels could not be used to accomplish this. They were too slow. CLISTs and batch jobs must exist to create tables, load data, execute binds, execute DCLGENs, etc. The CLISTs should be written to allow execution in either foreground or background. Thus, one batch job would be able to invoke many CLISTs.

The CLIST in Figure 7–8 creates a table, and if invoked with a DBA TSOIDS, creates a DCLGEN.

FIGURE 7–8
CREATE TABLE AND DCLGEN CLIST

```
      PROC 1 TAB     DROP(ASK) APPL(ABL)
      /* FUNCTION:
      /* WILL CREATE ONE TABLESPACE/TABLE AS SPECIFIED BY
  5   /* THE POSITIONAL PARAMETER ''TAB''.    ADDITIONALLY,
      /* THE TABLESPACE WILL BE ''DROPPED'' IF THE INVOKER
      /* RESPONDS WITH A ''Y'' TO A GENERATED PROMPT.
      /*
```

FIGURE 7–8   *(continued)*

```
    /* PARAMETERS:
10  /*    TAB  - INDICATES WHICH TS/TB TO CREATE
    /*    DROP - Y INDICATES THAT TABLE SHOULD NOT BE DROPPED
    /*           N INDICATES THAT TABLE SHOULD BE DROPPED
    /*    APPL - INDICATES WHICH APPLICATION    ABL OR LOC
    /*
15  SET LEN NE &LENGTH(&TAB)
    IF &LEN > 4    THEN +
       DO
           WRITE &TAB    LEN > 4 CH TERMINATING
           EXIT
20     END
    IF &APPL NE ABL AND &APPL NE LOC THEN +
       DO
           WRITE &APPL NOT ABL OR LOC, TERMINATING
           EXIT
25     END
    IF &LEN > 3    THEN +
       SET TEST# = &SUBSTR(4:4,&TAB)
    IF &LEN = 4 AND &TEXT# = X    THEN +
       SET MEM = &SUBSTR(1:3,&TAB)
30  ELSE +
       SET MEM = &TAB
    SET &X012 = X012JXC
    IF &SYSUID = X012SYS THEN +
       SET &X012 = &SYSUID
35  SET  DSNCK = &SYSDN('&X012..DB2.DDL(T&APPL&MEM)')
    IF &DSNCK  NE OK THEN +
      DO
      WRITE
      WRITE ERROR PROCESSING T&APPL&MEM, TERMINATING
40    WRITE &DSNCK
      WRITE
      EXIT
      END
```

FIGURE 7–8 (continued)

```
        IF &DROP = ASK THEN +
45      DO
           WRITE     IF &SYSUID..TABL_&TAB DOES NOT EXIST
           WRITE            TYPE    Y  ELSE
           WRITENR DEPRESS ENTER....
           READ &DROP
50      END
        IF &DROP = Y THEN +
           SET &DROP = &STR(*)
        ELSE +
           SET &DROP = &STR( )
55   SET &DATABAS = NONE
     SET &ABL     = NONE
     IF &SYSUID = X012JXC THEN +
           DO
              SET &DATABAS = AU&APPL.01
60            SET &ABL      = ABL
           END
     IF &SYSIUD = X012SYS THEN +
           DO
              SET &DATABAS = AU&APPL.51
65            SET ABL       = SYS
           END
     IF &SYSUID = X012JML THEN +
              SET &DATABAS = AU&APPL.02
     IF &SYSUID = X012MGK THEN +
70            SET &DATABAS = AU&APPL.03
     IF &SYSUID = X012BMH THEN +
              SET &DATABAS = AU&APPL.04
     IF &SYSUID = X012SDC THEN +
              SET &DATABAS = AU&APPL.05
75   IF &SYSUID = X012JGD THEN +
              SET &DATABAS = AU&APPL.06
     IF &SYSUID = X012FAT THEN +
              SET &DATABAS = AU&APPL.07
     IF &SYSUID = X012CXC THEN +
80            SET &DATABAS = AU&APPL.08
```

FIGURE 7–8 *(continued)*

```
        IF &SYSUID = X012TST THEN +
                SET &DATABAS = AU&APPL.09
        IF &SYSUID = X012RXS THEN +
                SET &DATABAS = AU&APPL.10
  85    IF &SYSUID = X012PEM THEN +
                SET &DATABAS = AU&APPL.11
        IF &DATABAS    NE NONE       THEN +
             GOTO PR
        WRITE YOUR ID IS NOT AUTHORIZED TO USE THIS CLIST
  90    EXIT
        PR:   WRITE BEGINNING TABLE CREATION
          SEND '&SYSUID CREATED T&APPLE&MEM' U(X012JXC) L
          CONTROL NOFLUSH
          ERROR +
  95        DO
                SET TSTCC = &LASTCC
                GOTO CKEOF
             END
          ALLOC FI(INDD) DA('&X012..DB2.DDL(T&APPL&MEM)') SHR
 100      ALLOC FI(OTDD) DA('&SYSUID..DB2.WORK') NEW +
             SPACE(1 1) CYL  BLOCK(23440) LRECL(80) RECFM(F B)
          OPENFILE INDD INPUT
          OPENFILE OTDD OUTPUT
        GET1:  GETFILE INDD
 105      SET INREC = &STR(&INDD)
          SET &OTDD = $STR(NONE)
          SET TYPTST = &SUBSTR(3:3,&INREC)
          IF &TYPTST NE        A   AND &TYPTST NE        H    THEN +
             SET OTDD = &STR(&INREC)
 110      IF &TEST# = X  AND &TYPTST =        H       THEN +
                SET OTD = &STR(&STR(    )&SUBSTR(4:72,&INREC))
          IF &TEST# NE X   AND &TYPTST =        A       THEN +
                SET OTDD = &STR(&STR(    )&SUBSTR(4:72&INREC))
          IF &OTDD NE $STR(NONE)                     THEN +
 115        PUTFILE OTDD
          GOTO GET1
```

FIGURE 7–8 *(continued)*

```
       SETVAR: +
         IF &TEST# = X                        THEN +
           DO
120
                    set up site specific edits
           END
         ELSE +
125      DO
                    set up site specific edits
           END
130  SETCLOSE: +
         SET CL = YES
         IF &SYSUID = X012JXC OR &SYSUID = X012SYS THEN +
           SET CL = &STR(NO )
       EDIT '&SYSUID..DB2.WORK' DATA NONUM
135  C * 999 'AU&APPL.01'  '&DATABAS' ALL
       TOP
       F 'DROP'
       C *     ' '  '&DROP'
       D 1
140  C *     ' '  '&DROP'
       TOP
       C * 999 '--'  '**' ALL
       TOP
145               other site specific edits
       END S
       TEP2:  WRITE BEGINNING DSNTEP2
       ALLOC FI(SYSIN) DA('&SYSUID..DB2.WORK') SHR
150    IF &SYSENV = FORE THEN +
           ALLOC FI(SYSPRINT) DA(*)
         DSN SYSTEM(DB2)
           RUN PROGRAM(DSNTEP2) PLAN(DSNTEP13) -
             LIB('TDB2.DSN130.RUNLIB.LOAD')
155    END
       FREE FI(SYSIN)
       DEL '&SYSUID..DB2.WORK'
           /*     NOW DO DCLGEN IF DBA
           /*
```

FIGURE 7–8 *(continued)*

```
160   IF &ABL NE NONE      THEN +
      DO
          WRITE START DCLGEN
          DSN SYSTEM(DB2)
          IF &LASTCC = 0 THEN +
165           DO
                DATA
                  DCLGEN TABLE (T&APPL._&TAB) +
                    LIBRARY('X012.&ABL..COPYLIB(T&APPL&TAB)') +
                      ACTION(REPLACE)
170               END
                ENDDATA
              END
          ELSE +
              DO
175           WRITE DSN CONNECT RETURNED A COND CODE OF:   &LASTCC
              END
      END
      EXIT
                  /*
180               /*    FOLLOWING CKECKS FOR EOF FROM GETFILE
      CKEOF: IF &TSTCC  = 400 OR &TSTCC = 0 THEN +
              DO
                CONTROL FLUSH
                ERROR  OFF
185             CLOSFILE INDD
                CLOSFILE OTDD
                FREE   FI(INDD)
                FREE   FI(OTDD)
                GOTO   SETVAR
190           END
          ELSE +
              WRITE ERROR CODE: &TSTCC TERMINATING
      EXIT

195
```

Lines 15 through 43 verify that the value for the positional keyword TAB is in the correct format and that the DDL for its table exists. The DDL must exist as a member within dataset '&X012..DB2.DDL' (lines 35 and 99). Lines 100 through 116 read the PDS member and only write lines that correspond to the application table type to be created. In this case, current and history tables have the same row structure but utilize different indices. Lines 120 through 150 use a TSO edit to modify the DDL, based on the test environment level of the TSOID executing the CLIST. Note that in this example the client did not want symbolics in his DDL. Lines 150 through 158 invoke the DSN RUN subcommand to execute DSNTEP2 to process the actual DDL. Lines 160 through 180 execute a DSN DCLGEN when the CLIST is invoked by a DBA TSOID. Line 151 uses the &SYSENV TSO system variable to verify that the execution environment is foreground and to allocate the SYSPRINT DDNAME accordingly.

A CLIST was similarly written to create VIEWs. If invoked with one of the DBA TSOIDs, the CLIST also creates a DCLGEN, as in Figure 7–9.

FIGURE 7–9
CREATE VIEW AND DCLGEN CLIST

```
            PROC 1 VIEW   DROP(ASK)  APPL(ABL)
            /* FUNCTION:
            /*   WILL CREATE A VIEW AS SPECIFIED BY THE
            /*   POSITIONAL PARAMETER "VIEW".   ADDITIONALLY,
     5      /*   THE VIEW WILL BE "DROPPED" IF THE INVOKER
            /*   RESPONDS WITH A "Y" TO A GENERATED PROMPTED
            /* PARAMETERS:
            /*   VIEW - INDICATES WHICH VIEW TO CREATE
            /*   DROP - Y = VIEW DOES NOT EXIST N = WILL DROP IT
    10      /*   APPL - INDICATES WHICH APPLICATION ABL  OR  LOC
            SET LEN = &LENGTH(&VIEW)
            IF &LEN > 4     THEN +
                DO
                    WRITE &VIEW > 4 CH, TERMINATING
    15              EXIT
                END
            IF &APPL NE ABL AND &APPL NE LOC   THEN +
                DO
                    WRITE APPL = &APPL MUST BE LOC OR ABL, TERMINATING
    20              EXIT
                END
            SET &ABL  = NONE
            SET &X012 = X012JXC
```

FIGURE 7–9 (*continued*)

```
         IF &SYSUID = X012SYS THEN +
25            SET &X012 = X012SYS
         SET DSNCK = &SYSDSN('&012..DB2.DDL(V&APPL&VIEW)')
         IF &DSNCK  NE  OK THEN +
          DO
            WRITE
30          WRITE ERROR PROCESSING V&APPL&VIEW, TERMINATING
            WRITE &DSNCK
            WRITE
            EXIT
          END
35        IF &DROP = ASK THEN +
            DO
             WRITE   IF &SYSUID..VABL_&VIEW DOES NOT
             WRITE            TYPE    Y ELSE
40             WRITENR DEPRESS ENTER. . . .
               READ &DROP
             END
           IF &DROP = Y THEN +
              SET &DROP = &STR(*)
45           ELSE +
              SET &DROP = &STR( )
     PR:   WRITE BEGINNING VIEW CREATION
        FREE  FI(X)
        ALLOC FI(X) DA('SYSUID..DB2.VWORK') NEW +
50          SPACE(1 1) CYL BLOCK(23440) LRECL(80) RECFM(F B)
     REPRO IDS('&X012..DB2.DDL(V&APPL&VIEW)') OFILE(X)
     FREE  FI(X)
     EDIT 'SYSUID..DB2.VWORK' OLD DATA NONUM
     TOP
55   F 'DROP'
     C *    ' ' '&DROP'
     D 1
     C *    ' ' '&DROP'
     TOP
60   C * 999 '--' '**' ALL
     END S
```

FIGURE 7–9   *(continued)*

```
         ALLOC FI(SYSIN) DA('&SYSUID..DB2.VWORK') SHR
         IF &SYSENV = FORE THEN +
             ALLOC FI(SYSPRINT) DA(*)
65       DSN SYSTEM(DB2)
             RUN PROGRAM(DSNTEP2) PLAN(DSNTEP13) -
             LIB('TDB2.DSN130.RUNLIB.LOAD')
         END
         FREE FI(SYSIN)
70       DEL '&SYSUID..DB2.VWORK'
         IF &SYSUID NE X012SYS AND &SYSUID NE X012JXC    THEN +
             EXIT
           /*        NOW DO DCLGEN IF SYSUID = X012JXC OR X012SYS
           /*
75       IF &X012 = X012JXC THEN +
             SET &ABL = ABL
         IF &X012 = X012SYS THEN +
             SET &ABL = SYS
         IF &ABL NE NONE    THEN +
80       DO
           DSN SYSTEM(DB2)
           IF &LASTCC = 0 THEN +
             DO
             DATA
85           DCLGEN TABLE (V&APPL._&VIEW) +
             LIBRARY('T012.&ABL..COPYLIB(V&APPL&VIEW)') +
               ACTION(REPLACE)
             END
           ENDDATA
90         END
         ELSE +
           DO
           WRITE DSN CONNECT RETURNED A COND CODE OF: &LASTCC
           END
95       END
```

The create view CLIST is comparable to the create table CLIST but less complicated. The DDL did not require extensive modifications. The SPUFI comments ('- -') are changed to asterisks (*), which represent comments for DSNTEP2. This CLIST may also be executed in either foreground or background.

The next two examples are simpler. Figure 7–10 illustrates a CLIST to execute the DSN RUN subcommand. When running programs, it is necessary to verify that DB2 is active. The "&LASTCC = 0" test will invoke the RUN subcommand if DB2 is active or display a meaningful message if it is not.

When testing in a CICS/VS DB2 environment, it becomes very difficult for each developer to own and maintain a separate set of tables. On the other hand, if one person is responsible for CICS/VS test tables and the related bind executions, he or she may be overwhelmed with bind requests. The solution,

FIGURE 7–10
DSN RUN SUBCOMMAND CLIST

```
PROC 2   PGM PLAN PARM()
/* FUNCTION:
/*    EXEC A DB2 PROGRAM UNDER  A TSO TMP
/*
/* PARAMETERS:
/*    PGM    - PGM TO BE EXEC (REQ)
/*    PLAN   - PLAN NAME (REQ)
/*    PARM   - OPT. PARM FOR PGM
/*
DSN SYSTEM(DB2)
IF &LASTCC = 0 THEN +
  DO
    DATA
      RUN PROGRAM(&PGM) PLAN(&PLAN) -
        LIB('T241.ABL.LOADLIB')
      - PARMS('&PARM/')
      END
    ENDDATA
  END
  ELSE +
    WRITE DSN CONNECT COND CODE =: &LASTCC
```

FIGURE 7–11
BATCH DSN BIND SUBCOMMAND

```
//X012JXCE JOB (acct info),'BOB HEYDT',
//  MSGCLASS=H,NOTIFY=tsoid,
//  USER=TESTCICS,
//  CLASS=E
/*JOBPARM SYSAFF=DB2M
//*******
//P1 EXEC DSNRUN
//SYSTSIN  DD *
   DSN SYSTEM(DB2)
     BIND PLAN(yourplan) +
       MEMBER( DBRM010 +
               ,DBRM015 +
               ,DBRM020 +
               ,DBRM025 +
             ) +
       LIBRARY('your.dbrmlib') +
       ACTION(REPLACE) RETAIN +
       VALIDATE(BIND)  ISOLATION(CS)
   END
//
```

as suggested by Figure 7–11, requires that all team members be authorized to submit jobs and specify CICSTEST as the USER/USERID.

In this environment all team members could compile their programs under their own TSOIDs, and bind their programs using the CICSTEST DB2 tables.

DB2 COMMANDS

DB2 Commands may be issued from an MVS Console, TSO, CICS, and IMS/VS. Since it is possible to have more than one DB2 active under MVS, a protocol must exist to communicate with different DB2 subsystems. Fortunately, only the MVS console and IMS/VS may be connected concurrently to more than one DB2. A TSO session and one CICS address space may only connect to one DB2.

All DB2 commands must be preceded by a **Recognition Character (RC)**. This RC is established during DB2 installation and is typically a hyphen. An RC is mandatory for commands entered as a TSO DSN subcommand or from a CICS terminal. However, commands entered from an MVS console must use a **Subsystem Recognition Character (SRC)** as the recognition character. A separate SRC must exist for each DB2 subsystem. Commands entered from an IMS/VS terminal must follow the IMS/VS convention of being preceded by a **Command Recognition Character (CRC)** which is usually a slash ' / '. Imbedded within the IMS/VS command is an SRC or a parameter that identifies which subsystem is to receive the command. Both the SRC and the CRC can be defined by an installation and should be verified prior to attempting to execute a DB2 command.

In Figure 8–1 two different DB2s are being started. One DB2 utilizes the ' + ' character as its SRC, the other uses the '−' character.

The START DB2 command must be entered from an MVS console. DB2 cannot be started from a subsystem. All other DB2 commands may be entered from an MVS console, an IMS/VS terminal, a CICS terminal, a DB2I panel, or the DSN command processor.

The IMS/VS Command in Figure 8–2, /SSR, will allow DB2 commands to be sent to a DB2 address space. The Command Recognition Character is required by IMS, and the Subsystem Recognition Character identifies which DB2 is to receive the command.

The example in Figure 8–3 of a DB2 command entered from a CICS terminal is prefixed with the DSNC transaction code for the CICS Call Attach

FIGURE 8–1
MVS CONSOLE DB2 COMMANDS

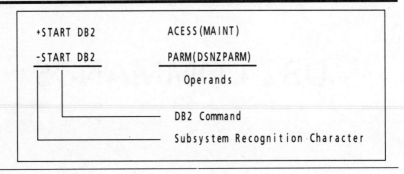

FIGURE 8–2
IMS/VS DB2 COMMANDS

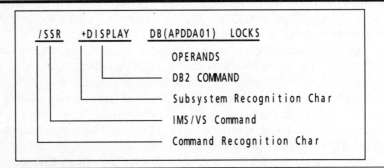

FIGURE 8–3
CICS COMMANDS

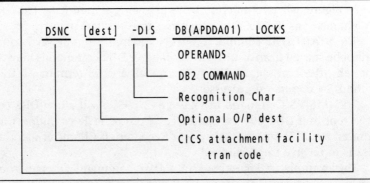

Facility (CAF). Since one CICS may connect to only one DB2 at a time, the recognition character is always a hyphen '-'.

We will present several of the more commonly referenced DB2 commands in this chapter. The examples will always be prefixed with a hyphen because this is the most common recognition character. A more detailed listing is available in the IBM *DB2 Command and Utility Reference* manual.

As a preface to the commands presentation, note that it is possible to specify values for the NAME REQUEST parameters within DB2 commands that indicate the scope of the request:

1.   One object or utility
2.   A range of objects
3.   A generic or partial request
4.   All authorized objects or utilities.

To illustrate, the DISPLAY DATABASE command (abbreviated DIS DB) will be used in the following examples.

1.   -DIS DB(APDDA01)
2.   -DIS DB(APDDA01:APDDA09)
3.   -DIS DB(APDDA*)
4.   -DIS DB(*).

If there were only nine data bases (APDDA01 through APDDA09), the second and third examples would yield the same result. If there were more than nine data bases prefixed with APDDA, example three would display all of them. The fourth example would display the status of all data bases for which the AUTHID of the command had DISPLAYDB or greater authority and would also include the data bases used by the DB2 catalog tables.

● -DISPLAY DATABASE (Abbreviated -DIS DB) — provides the status of DB2 data bases and related tablespaces and indexspaces. When used to request the status of **all** data bases, it must be entered by a userid assigned the DISPLAY privilege, or by SYSADM or SYSOPR authority. For information about a particular data base or list of data bases, the userid must be assigned the DISPLAYDB privilege for each requested data base; the DBADM, DBCTRL, or DBMAINT authority for each requested data base; or SYSOPR authority.

Information may also be returned for only those data bases which are currently active or have restricted access pending against them. Additionally, specific tablespaces and indices within one data base may be requested, as well as the connection ids (ie. userids) and correlation ids allocated to the data base components requested. Once the correlation id is known, the -DISPLAY THREAD command may be used to identify which CICS transaction is currently using the objects in question.

The "Naming Conventions" section of the **Logical Model** chapter stressed the use of an eight-character index name so that DB2 would use it to form an indexspace name. This will also make it easier to view index status on the displayed report.

Note that you may always display information about DB2 catalog tables, with the single exception of user information about data bases or tables within a tablespace that is stopped. All DB2 catalog objects are in data bases that are prefixed with DSNDB. The following DB2 command would display the current status of all the DB2 data bases, tablespaces and directories:

```
-DIS DB(DSNDB*)
```

The format of the DISPLAY DATABASE command is given in Figure 8–4. The optional keywords LOCKS, USE, ACTIVE, and RESTRICT are used to limit the output to objects that are in that respective status. The number of lines to be displayed is controlled with the LIMIT keyword. The default for integer (*int*) is 50. LIMIT(*) will limit the display to one message buffer or 12,288 characters.

FIGURE 8–4
DISPLAY DATABASE COMMAND

```
-DISPLAY DATABASE(name reg)
    [SPACENAM(name req , ····· )]
    [LOCKS I USE]
    [AFTER]  [LIMIT(  int I * )]
    [ACTIVE]  [RESTRICT]
```

● -DISPLAY THREAD (abbreviated -DIS THD) — displays information about all active or questionable connections for a specified name, the connection name of the user, or all connections as requested by the MVS console operator. SYSADM or SYSOPR authority or assignment of the DISPLAY privilege is necessary to successfully execute this command.

Note that information returned for connections is not static; that is to say that the status may have changed before the information is returned to the requestor. Since -DISPLAY THREAD requests are processed serially, information is not guaranteed to be consistent. If different TSO users enter the same display, the results will probably differ due to chronological processing by DB2.

As with the -DISPLAY DATABASE command, an (*) will return information for all DB2 connections (if requested by an authorized user). The default connection name is the name(s) associated with the trans-

FIGURE 8–5
DISPLAY THREAD COMMAND

```
DISPLAY THREAD(connection-id | *)
    [TYPE(ACTIVE | INDOUBT | *)]
```

action manager (i.e., userid of the requester). The format of the DISPLAY THREAD command is given in Figure 8–5.

● -DISPLAY UTILITY (abbreviated -DIS UTIL) — returns a status for utility jobs of active, stopped, or terminating. Each job will return its own set of messages. No special authorization is required to execute this DB2 command. Information may be requested for a single job by indicating its utility identifier (UID), a partial UID, or (*) to indicate all jobs executing to the knowledge of DB2. A range of UIDs may not be specified.

Note that the information returned is consistent with the status of the job(s) at the time DB2 received the status request. Therefore, status may vary by the time the message is output to the requester. Since DB2 will perform some I/O under its own TCBs, this display command may be the only way to tell if your utility is progressing. TSO commands may show a utility as being SWAPPED OUT when it is actually active under a DB2 TCB.

Information available beyond the actual status of the job includes the number of statements executed, the name of the utility being executed, and the phase of the utility being executed. Use the command in Figure 8–6 to determine which phase a utility was in when it abnormally terminated.

● -TERM UTILITY (abbreviated -TERM UTIL) — is capable of terminating an active utility at its next commit point, or terminating a stopped utility. In either case, most resources allocated to the job step in which termination occurred will not be released as a result of this action. As with the -DISPLAY UTILITY command, a utility is identified with a partial or complete utility ID (UID) or with (*) to indicate all utilities known to DB2.

FIGURE 8–6
DISPLAY UTILITY

```
DISPLAY UTILITY (UID | name-req | * )
```

Utility status is maintained in the SYSIBM. SYSUTIL catalog directory. Note that a terminated utility must be resubmitted to become active again. More significantly, its components may be left in an inconsistent state that must be rectified prior to resubmitting the job. For example, the COPY and RECOVER utilities must be resubmitted. LOAD processing that terminated during the reload phase must be resubmitted from the beginning. If LOG YES was specified, the terminal that requested the termination will be tied up for as long as required to back out any records previously loaded during this phase. If LOG NO was specified, the termination is immediate. LOAD processing terminated during sort or build phases must have the indices recovered for use. However, the data will remain loaded and the LOAD utility should not be rerun. REORG processing that terminates during the unload phase must be rerun from the beginning. However, termination during the reload phase means that the tablespace has already been erased and must be recovered before resubmittal can occur. If the SYSREC DD statement allocated a permanent dataset, the restart is possible from the beginning of the RELOAD phase. As with the LOAD utility, termination of the REORG utility during sort or build phases simply requires that the indices be recovered prior to access. In this case, the REORG job should not be rerun. The format of the TERM UTILITY is illustrated in Figure 8–7.

The UTIL(*) option terminates utilities that were submitted by the AUTHID of the person invoking the command.

FIGURE 8–7
TERM COMMAND

```
-TERM UTILITY (UID | name-req | *)
```

- -START DATABASE (abbreviated -STA DB) — as shown in Figure 8–8, makes available a data base that was previously the subject of a STOP DATABASE command or makes available a tablespace or index subject to a deferred restart by DB2. Availability of the data base may be restricted to utility use only, read-only access, or read-write access via the ACCESS parameter. This parameter may also be used to reset instances of previously restricted access, although care should be taken to ensure that the data base is appropriate for such an action (i.e., that there is no unresolved error or utility restriction pending against it).

Again, appending (*) to the end of the -START DATABASE request will start all data bases for which the issuer has minimally DBMAINT authority and that are not already started. Additionally, multiple data bases may be listed in the same command invocation.

FIGURE 8–8
START DATABASE COMMAND

```
-START DATABASE(dbname1, ··· | *)
    ACCESS(RW | RO | UT)
-START DATABASE(dbname) SPACENAM(spname | *)
    ACCESS(RW | RO | UT | FORCE)
```

In contrast, individual tablespaces or indexspaces may be started via use of the SPACENAM parameter. In fact, if the tablespace or indexspace was previously specifically stopped via a -STOP DATABASE command with the SPACENAM parameter, then it <u>must</u> be restarted via a SPACENAM parameter request. Even a -START DATABASE (*) request is not capable of such a restart.

Note that it is not necessary that all DASD connected with tablespaces, indices, or partitions of a data base be online when the -START DATABASE request is initiated. However, it is necessary that this same DASD be online when a tablespace of the data base is acquired by a PLAN.

The keyword option ACCESS(FORCE) can be used with only one specific data base and with either indexspace or tablespace name set, but not both. An (*) option may not be used with FORCE.

When running recoveries or reorganizations, place all tables in UT status as follows.

```
-STA DB(dbname)
    SPACENAM(*) ACCESS(UT)
```

This will ensure that none of the tables within the data base may be touched until all processing is completed. When creating image copies, put all tables in RO status as follows.

```
-STA DB(dbname)
    SPACENAM(*) ACCESS(RO)
```

This will ensure that none of the related tables will have been updated until the copy process is completed. In effect, a QUIESCE process is achieved that is similar to the new QUIESCE utility that is available in DB2 Version 2.

● -STOP DATABASE (Abbreviated -STO DB) — acts in contrast to the -START DATABASE command in that it makes unavailable data bases named in the request and *closes* their associated datasets. Optionally, specific tablespaces and/or indices may be named via the SPACENAM

FIGURE 8–9
STOP COMMAND

```
-STOP DATABASE(dbname, | *)
     SPACENAM(sp-name, ···· | *)
```

parameter. As mentioned in the -START DATABASE command section, however, these same objects must be specifically restarted via a
SPACENAM parameter invocation of the -START DATABASE command when desired for availability. The (*) parameter appended to the
basic command will stop all data bases for which the issuer has at
least the STOPDB privilege. Figure 8–9 depicts the format of the STOP
DATABASE command.

Authorization required for execution of this command must include
either SYSADM authority; DBADM, DBMAINT, or DBCTRL authority
for each data base specified; or the STOPDB privilege for each data base
specified.

Before running any of the service aid utilities, specifically DSN1COPY,
it is strongly recommended that all associated spaces be stopped. This is
the only way to guarantee that all data has been written to DASD from
the buffers.

In order to place a tablespace in a different I/O status (i.e., RO, RW,
UT), it is preferable to STOP the object first and then START it in the
required I/O status.

The keyword option SPACENAM(*) may not be used in conjunction
with DB(*). Stopping a tablespace is the only way you can guarantee
that no pages remain in the DB2 bufferpool.

CHAPTER 9

PRACTICAL PROCEDURES

■ PLAN, RUNTIME, AND MIGRATION CONSIDERATIONS

Before a program may execute, a control block known as a **PLAN** must exist. PLANs, created by the BIND[1] process will allocate resources, validate access authority and determine access strategy. The administration of PLANs is not only a security issue, but also an operational and performance concern.

DB2 program execution requires more controls and preparation than most job scheduling packages can supply. Within an MVS environment every Job, System Started Task, and TSO session must have a USERID. When connecting to DB2, this USERID is used as a default AUTHID. Since the job scheduling package will submit all production jobs, it must be authorized to execute all production PLANs. Is this a major security loophole for a DB2 installation? Worse still, is it recognized and addressed with a 'don't tell anyone' mentality?

DB2 batch programs usually execute under the TSO Terminal Monitor Program (TMP) and are invoked by the TSO DSN command. Writing JCL procedures and passing substitutions for variables will require more thought than typically given nonDB2 batch applications.

There are several products available at additional cost to assist with the migration of DDL, DCL (privileges), and actual data. The DDL source should exist within a QSAM dataset or a PDS. If privileges must be migrated from one DB2 subsystem to another, queries can be used to extract the necessary information. Moreover, the query output may be constructed to generate the required DCL statements. Of the three types of migration, data migration usually causes the greatest concern. Without the proper tools, the different column data types and internal DB2 object identifiers (OBIDs) could

---

[1] See the **DB2 DSN Command** chapter for methods to invoke the DSN BIND subcommand.

make data migration a monstrous task. Using the tools supplied with DB2, however, will make the actual transfer of data routine.

Plan Considerations

The AUTHID that binds a plan becomes the CREATOR of that plan. For a BIND request to complete successfully, that AUTHID must hold the required privileges for all objects that a plan will access. If other AUTHIDs are to execute a plan, they must be granted EXECUTE authority by the bindor (CREATOR) of the plan. Tracking the AUTHIDs who own the related tables, bind plans, and hold execute authority for the plans may become a major administration consideration.

There are two current methodologies to ease plan management. Method 1 is the use of SYNONYMs; method 2 requires that the bindor of a plan be the owner of all tables used by that plan.

SYNONYMs (method 1) are more frequently used in small applications with few tables, or where DASD space is at a premium. Recall that no special authority is required to create a SYNONYM, and that if any underlying objects are dropped, the SYNONYM is not dropped. However, the same authoritizations are required to access data with a SYNONYM as would be required without one.

If the same AUTHID (method 2) is both the bindor of a plan and the owner of all the related tables, that AUTHID implicitly holds all privileges for the related tables. No table privileges need be granted to the bindor of the plan. To facilitate operational requirements and reduce overhead associated with authorization checking, the owner of the tables should be the bindor of the program's plan.

The CICS/VS attach facility via the Resource Control Table (RCT) macro provides up to six choices for AUTHIDs. One of these choices is a literal that could be the AUTHID of the bindor of a plan that a transaction-ID (TRANID) invokes when the related program is executed. The Resource Control Table (RCT) macro example in Figure 9–1 will pass *user001* as

FIGURE 9–1
RCT MACRO WITH AUTHID = *user001*

```
DSNCRCT TYPE=INIT,.....
DSNCRCT TYPE=POOL,.....
DSNCRCT TYPE=ENTRY,AUTH=('user001'),                    X
        PLAN=someplan,TXID=(trx1,trx2,....),....
DSNCRCT TYPE=FINAL,.....
```

the AUTHID for its TRANIDs (*trx1*, *trx2*, . . .). Thus, DB2 security checking overhead is virtually eliminated.

If other TRANIDs are utilized, it would be necessary to grant each one execute authority on plan, *someplan*.

With DB2 Version 2.1, grouped AUTHIDs will facilitate plan execute authority maintenance and implementation. New security features of this release will allow a user to perform functions of a different AUTHID, thus separating the owner from the creator of a DB2 object. See the "BIND" subcommand section of the **DB2 DSN Command** chapter for complete information on PLAN BIND and ownership. Also, see the **Security** chapter for details on grouped authorities.

Runtime Considerations

Calls to DB2 are handled by Call Attach Facilities (CAF). IBM supplies CAFs for IMS/VS, CICS/VS, and TSO/E. The execution of batch programs that run under background TSO, using the IBM-supplied TSO Call Attach Facility, requires the JCL illustrated in Figure 9–2.

FIGURE 9–2
DB2 BATCH EXECUTION

```
//jobname JOB
//STEPx EXEC PGM=IKJEFT01,DYNAMNBR=
//STEPLIB DD ·····
//SYSTSPRT DD SYSOUT=A
//SYSTSIN DD *
  DSN SYSTEM(ssid)
    RUN PROG(yourprog) PLAN(someplan)-
      LIB('special.load') PARMS(·····)
//additional DD statements
```

This JCL presents two concerns.

1. The difficulty in supplying a variable (symbolic) for the keyword—
    PARMS(. . . . . .)—field.
2. The complexity in setting up JCL catalogued procedures.

The DSN RUN subcommand must be read in from the SYSTSIN DD statement. It could be placed instream as shown in the example, or it could

FIGURE 9–3
JCL SYMBOLIC SUBSTITUTION

```
//jobname JOB
//PSTEPx EXEC procname,SPARM=somevalue
```

reside on a sequential file (e.g., QSAM or PDS). In any event, operator intervention will be required to enter a special value. The trick is to make this manual operation as simple as possible. The currently acceptable method, using JCL symbolics, is to place the symbolic as the last variable to be entered, as depicted in Figure 9–3.

The person entering the substitution value does not have to be concerned with JCL syntax. Unfortunately, symbolics cannot be passed directly to input streams or sequential datasets. There are two solutions to this problem.

1. Design a program that will build the RUN subcommand and write it to a sequential dataset. Thus symbolics could be passed via this program's PARM area.
2. Design your own batch Call Attach Facility.

Solution 1 is the easiest to implement. Nonetheless, we have yet to see any of our clients implement it.

At first glance, solution 2 appears to be a major effort. A user-developed CAF must be able to handle DB2 functions such as CONNECT, OPEN, CLOSE, DISCONNECT, and assorted error handling. Fortunately, IBM has supplied an example for a user-written CAF in the *Advanced Application Guide,* which takes a lot of the mystery out of the design and coding. The benefits of a user-developed CAF include

- Elimination of TSO overhead
- Ability to run above the 16 Meg line
- Ability to run when DB2 is not active
- Utilization of event control blocks (ECB) for SQL processing
- Ability to switch plan names while executing.

Three of our clients have chosen to write their own CAFs, believing that the advantages outweigh the disadvantages.

Runtime Security Considerations

Online DB2 security has been the delight of every EDP auditor that we have met. However, batch security may present some unacceptable risks.

FIGURE 9–4
PROGRAM PREPARATION PROCESS

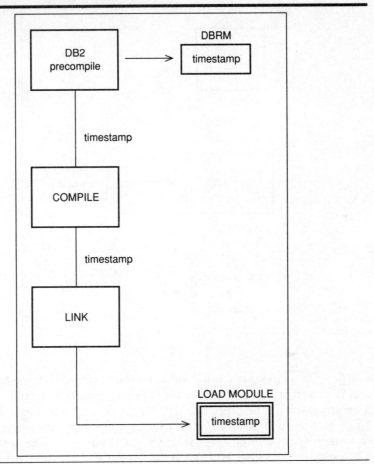

First, let's examine the program preparation and bind processes. Figure 9–4 exhibits the DB2 precompile, compile, and link process.

When programs are precompiled, the same timestamp is inserted into both the source code and the Data Base Request Module (DBRM). This identical timestamp is then passed through the entire process and ends up in the working storage of the resulting load module.

The BIND process (Figure 9–5) uses the DBRM(s) created during the precompile to create a plan. The timestamp from each DBRM is inserted into the DB2 catalog table, SYSIBM.SYSDBRM, for execution verification. A program may not begin execution if the timestamps in each program module do not match their respective plan (DBRM) timestamps.

Current program design methodologies keep source manageable by limiting program size. Therefore, a very complicated process might consist of a

FIGURE 9–5
BIND PROCESS

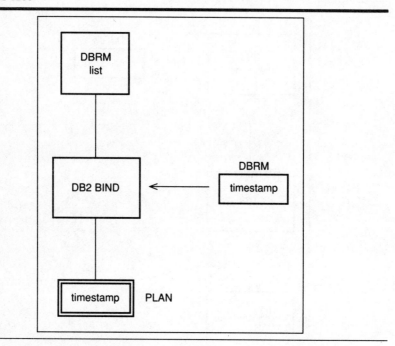

root program with several called subprograms. At this point, the first question that comes to mind is, "If a module does not contain SQL statements, must it be processed by the precompiler?" The correct technical answer is, "No." The logical answer is, "Yes!" If a root or driver program contains no SQL statements, then any program with the same name may be substituted for it. Timestamp checking will not be able stop it. The same is true for any program that is not processed by the precompiler.

We strongly recommend that <u>all</u> <u>DB2</u> <u>related</u> <u>programs</u> <u>be</u> <u>processed</u> <u>by</u> <u>the</u> <u>precompiler</u> to enforce timestamp verification as a security measure.

■ JOB SCHEDULING PACKAGES

Job scheduling packages normally have complete access via their associated USERIDs, to all production data at a given installation. If a job is scheduled, it can do anything! To prevent such a potential security disaster, the site access control facility must <u>limit</u> <u>data</u> <u>access</u> <u>by</u> <u>job</u> <u>name</u>.

For DB2-related jobs, one additional step is required. Limit JOB card USERID usage to specific jobs, as in Figure 9–6.

FIGURE 9–6
JOB CARD USER PARAMETER

```
//jobname JOB (   ),CLASS=A,
//  USER=DB2USER
//PSTEP1 EXEC YOURPROC
```

The USER parameter allows a USERID other than the submitter of the JOB to be passed to DB2. If every system requires a unique USERID and that USERID may be used with only specific job names, then access to DB2 is greatly restricted.

■ MIGRATION

The easiest way to move DDL is to copy its source. Object names (e.g., STOGROUPs, data bases, tablespaces) may change, user-defined datasets (VCATs) may be utilized, or other minor manual modifications may be required, but nothing will be catastrophic. If the DDL source is missing, run a query against the system catalogs to extract and/or build object (table) definitions. Such a query is detailed in Figure 3–5 (Table Definition Query) of the **Logical Model** chapter.

SQL (DML) may also be used to migrate privileges. The query in Figure 9–7 will generate GRANT SELECT Data Control Language (DCL) statements on VIEWS beginning with VDDA.

FIGURE 9–7
SELECT FOR AUTHORITY MIGRATION

```
1.  SELECT DISTINCT 'GRANT SELECT ON'
2.    ,SUBSTR(GRANTOR,1,5)||'.'||TTNAME
3.    ,'TO' ,GRANTEE ,';'
4.  FROM SYSIBM.SYSTABAUTH
5.   WHERE SELECTAUTH = 'Y'
6.    AND TTNAME LIKE 'VDDA%'
7.    AND GRANTOR <> GRANTEE
8.  ;
```

Before running the query with SPUFI, it is necessary to change the output dataset record size to 80 (LRECL = 80) and the recording field mode to fixed block (RECFM = FB). Then the TSO editor may be used to delete unusable print lines. No other editing is required.

Lines 1 through 3 will format the following output rows:

GRANT SELECT ON xxxxx.table TO authid ;

Line 4 must retrieve VIEW SELECT authorizations from the catalog table, SYSIBM.SYSTABAUTH. Since the naming conventions for this installation state that all VIEWs must begin with the character "V", a LIKE predicate was used. If naming standards are not enforced, then view-only selection may be guaranteed with the additional clause

```
AND STNAME <> TTNAME
```

STNAME is the name of the TABLE or VIEW in the subselect of the CREATE VIEW for TTNAME. Recall that TABLEs, VIEWs, and SYNONYMs must be unique within an AUTHID.

Line 7 specifies that the GRANTOR and GRANTEE may not be equal. When an object is created, implied privileges are established, as reflected by rows where the GRANTOR and GRANTEE are equal (i.e., the creator GRANTs him- or herself all privileges). Therefore implied privileges do not require migration. Similar queries could be utilized to build GRANT statements for other privileges.

FIGURE 9–8
DSNTIAUL EXECUTION REQUIREMENTS

```
//TMP EXEC PGM=IKJEFT01,DYNAMNBR=20
//SYSTSPRT DD SYSOUT=*
//SYSPRINT DD SYSOUT=*
//SYSTSIN DD *
  DSN SYSTEM(DBP)
    RUN PROGRAM(DSNTIAUL) PLAN(DSNTIB13) +
    LIB('DSN130.RUNLIB.LOAD')
  END
//SYSPUNCH DD DSN=
//SYSREC00 DD DSN=
//SYSIN DD *
your_table [WHERE col_a = 'some value']
```

Mention data migration and the first response is Data Base Migration Aid Utility (DBMAUI). Other responses are Data eXTract (DXT) and the service aid utility, DSN1COPY. Another alternative exists. A dynamic SQL assembler program, DSNTIAUL, is available among the DB2 sample programs. The function of this program is to unload tables into sequential datasets and create LOAD utility control statements for the unloaded tables. This unload data contains no object IDs (OBIDs) and is therefore completely portable. The data may be loaded into a corresponding table at any DB2 installation. Figure 9–8 shows an example of the JCL and DSN RUN subcommand requirements.

The LOAD utility control statement will be written to the SYSPUNCH DD dataset, and the SYSREC00 DD will receive the sequential file. The SYSIN control card specifies the <u>table</u> <u>or</u> <u>view</u> to be unloaded and an optional WHERE predicate. Note that continuations are not permitted and that the WHERE predicate must fit on one line. If extensive conditional requirements must be met, create a VIEW that contains the necessary predicates.

The unload and reload process can be automated through the use of CLISTs. Figure 9–9 and Figure 9–10 exhibit a DSNTIAUL unload (MGRTUNLD) and the applicable LOAD (MGRTRELD), respectively. Both CLISTs edit their respective keyword and positional parameters and then submit batch jobs. Note that the reload CLIST (MGRTRELD) is invoked by the batch unload job after the unload has completed.

FIGURE 9–9
MIGRATE UNLOAD CLIST USING DSNTIAUL

```
     PROC 1 TAB APPL(ABL)  FMID(X012DBA) CLS(F) RCLS(G)
        /* FUNCTION:
        /*   USED TO UNLOAD DATA FROM PRODUCTION TABLES
        /*   ONLY USERID  X012JXC OR X012SYS MAY EXEC
5       /* PARAMETERS:
        /*   TAB - THREE LETTER TABLE ACRONYM
        /*   APPL - INDICATES WHICH APPLICATION   ABL OR LOC
        /*
     SET &UID = &SYSUID
10   IF &APPL NE ABL AND &APPL NE LOC   THEN +
        DO
              WRITE APPL = &APPL MUST BE LOC OR ABL, TERMINATING
              EXIT
        END
15   SET LEN = &LENGTH(&TAB)
```

FIGURE 9–9 *(continued)*

```
      IF &LEN > 4    THEN +
         DO
             WRITE &TAB    IS GREATER THAN 4 CHARACTERS, TERMINATING
             EXIT
20    END
      IF &LEN = 4 AND &SUBSTR(&LEN:&LEN,&TAB) = X THEN +
         SET MEM = &SUBSTR(1:3,&TAB)
      ELSE +
         SET MEM = &TAB
25    SET DSNTST = &SYSDSN('&UID..DB2.DDL(T&APPL.&MEM)')
      IF &DSNTST NE OK THEN +
         DO
             WRITE
             WRITE TABLE DEFINITION DOES NOT EXIST, TERMINATING
30           WRITE &DSNTST
             WRITE
             EXIT
         END
      PR:  WRITE BEGINNING JCL MODIFICATION AND SUBMISSION
35    SET CONT  = &STR(+)
      SET SLASH = &STR(/*)
      SUBMIT * END(@ @)
      //&UID.# JOB (  a c c t i n g  i n f o ),
      //   'MGRT &APPL &TAB TAB',
40    //   MSGCLASS=H,NOTIFY=&SYSUID,
      //   CLASS=&CLS
      &SLASH.JOBPARM SYSAFF=S3S3
      //DELT EXEC PGM=IEFBR14
      //SYSPUNCH DD DSN=&SYSUID..&TAB..CNTL,DISP=(MOD,DELETE),
45    //     UNIT=SYSDA,SPACE=(TRK,0)
      //SYSRECOO DD DSN=&SYSUID..&TAB..DATA,DISP=(MOD,DELETE),
      //     UNIT=SYSDA,SPACE=(TRK,0)
      //*************************************************************
      //*
50    //*            TMP BACKGROUND JOB
      //*
      //*************************************************************
      //TMP   EXEC PGM=IKJEFT01,DYNAMNBR=60,REGION=4096K
      //ISPPROF  DD  DSN=X012JXC.ISPF.PROFILE,DISP=SHR
```

FIGURE 9–9 (*continued*)

```
55   //SYSPROC   DD   DSN=DB2P.DSN130.DSNCLIST,DISP=SHR
     //               DCB=BLKSIZE=6233
     //          DD   DSN=SYSP.PROD.LOCAL.ISRCLIB,DISP=SHR
     //          DD   DSN=SYSP.ISRCLIB,DISP=SHR
     //          DD   DSN=SYSP.PROD.IBM.ISRCLIB,DISP=SHR
60   //          DD   DSN=X012JXC.CLIST,DISP=SHR
     //SYSTSPRT  DD   SYSOUT=*
     //SYSPRINT  DD   SYSOUT=*
     //SYSTSIN   DD   *
        DSN SYSTEM(DBP)
65        RUN PROGRAM(DSNTIAUL) PLAN(DSNTIB13) &CONT
             LIB('DB2P.DSN130.RUNLIB.LOAD')
          END
        MGRTRELD &TAB APPL(&APPL) FMID(&FMID) CLS(&RCLS)
     //SYSPUNCH DD DSN=&SYSUID..&TAB..CNTL,
70   //        DISP=(,CATLG,DELETE),
     //        UNIT=SYSDA,SPACE=(CYL,1),
     //        DCB=(LRECL=80,BLKSIZE=6160,RECFM=FB)
     //SYSRECOO DD DSN=&SYSUID..&TAB..DATA,
     //        DISP=(,CATLG,DELETE),
75   //        UNIT=(SYSDA,2),
     //        SPACE=(CYL,(25,20),RLSE,CONTIG)
     //SYSIN    DD *
     &FMID..T&APPL._&TAB
     @ @
80   WRAPUP:  WRITE END OF CLIST
```

Lines 1 through 33 edit the CLIST parameters. Line 37 submits the unload and resolves the substitutions within the JCL during the submit process. Lines 64 through 67 contain the DSN RUN subcommand that executes DSNTIAUL. Line 68,

```
MGRTRELD &TAB APPL(&APPL) FMID(&FMID) CLS(&RCLS)
```

invokes the reload CLIST illustrated in Figure 9–10.

The migrate unload CLIST may be invoked in foreground or, as in this example, by the migrate unload CLIST. In some cases, you may want to edit the utility control statements by adding LOG NO, removing a column reference, or modifying a column's input location or DEFAULTIF parameter.

FIGURE 9–10
MIGRATE LOAD CLIST USING LOAD UTILITY

```
      PROC 1 TAB APPL(ABL)  FMID() CLS(F)
       /* FUNCTION:
       /*   LOAD A TABLE FROM DATA CREATED BY ABLMUNLD
       /* TABLE SELECTION IS CONTROLLED BY THE ''TAB'' PARM
   5   /* PARAMETERS:
       /*   TAB - THREE LETTER TABLE ACRONYM
       /*   APPL - INDICATES WHICH APPLICATION   ABL OR LOC
       /*   FMID - OWNER OF TABLE WHERE DATA ORIGINATED
       /*

  10   IF &FMID = &STR()     THEN +
          DO
              WRITE FMID IS MISSING, TERMINATING
              EXIT
          END
  15   IF &APPL NE ABL AND &APPL NE LOC   THEN +
          DO
              WRITE APPL = &APPL MUST BE LOC OR ABL, TERMINATING
              EXIT
          END
  20   SET LEN = &LENGTH(&TAB)
       IF &LEN > 4 THEN +
          DO
            WRITE TABLE NAME GREATER THAN 4 CHAR   TAB = &TAB
            WRITE TERMINATING . . . . . . .
  25      EXIT
          END
       IF &LEN = 4 THEN +
          SET &TSNAME = &STR(&STR(T$)&TAB&STR(01))
       ELSE +
  30      SET &TSNAME = &STR(&STR(T$)&TAB&STR(001))
       SET &DB = NONE
       IF   &SYSUID = X012SYS THEN +
            SET &DB = AU&APPL.51
       IF   &SYSUID = X012JXC THEN +
  35        SET &DB = AU&APPL.01
```

FIGURE 9–10 (continued)

```
        IF &DB NE NONE        THEN +
             GOTO PR
        WRITE ONLY X012JXC OR X012SYS MAY EX THIS CLIST
        GOTO WRAPUP
   40   PR: +
        EDIT '&SYSUID..&TAB..CNTL'OLD DAT NONUM
        F 'INTO'
        C 'INTO' 'REPLACE LOG NO INTO'
        F '&FMID'
   45   C '&FMID..'  '
        END SAVE
         WRITE BEGINNING JCL MODIFICATION AND SUBMISSION
        SET SLASH = &STR(/*)
        SUBMIT * END(@ @)
   50   //&SYSUID.@ JOB ( a c c t i n g   i n f o),
        //          'LOAD &APPL &TAB TAB',
        //   MSGCLASS=H,NOTIFY=&SYSUID,
        //   CLASS=&CLS
        &SLASH.JOBPARM SYSAFF=s3s3
   55 //***********************************
      //*
      //*          DB2 UTIL
      //*
      //***********************************
   60 //UTIL EXEC D13UPROC,SYSTEM=DB2,UID='L#&APPL&TAB',
      //          UTPROC=''
      //*
      //D13UPROC.SYSUT1   DD SPACE=(CYL,(5,5)),UNIT=SYSDA
      //D13UPROC.SORTWK01 DD SPACE=(CYL,(5,5)),UNIT=SYSDA
   65 //D13UPROC.SORTWK02 DD SPACE=(CYL,(5,5)),UNIT=SYSDA
      //D13UPROC.SORTWK03 DD SPACE=(CYL,(5,5)),UNIT=SYSDA
      //D13UPROC.SORTWK04 DD SPACE=(CYL,(5,5)),UNIT=SYSDA
      //D13UPROC.SYSRECOO DD DSN=&SYSUID..&TAB..DATA,DISP=SHR
      //D13UPROC.SYSIN DD DSN=&SYSUID..&TAB..CNTL,DISP=SHR
   70 //*
      //***********************************
      //*
```

FIGURE 9–10 (*continued*)

```
     //*           DB2 REPAIR AND RUNSTATS
     //*
  75 //**************************************
     //UTIL EXEC D13UPROC,SYSTEM=DB2,UID='R#&APPL&TAB',
     //           UTPROC='',COND=(5,LT)
     //*
     //D13UPROC.SYSUT1   DD SPACE=(CYL,(5,5)),UNIT=SYSDA
  80 //D13UPROC.SORTWK01 DD SPACE=(CYL,(5,5)),UNIT=SYSDA
     //D13UPROC.SORTWK02 DD SPACE=(CYL,(5,5)),UNIT=SYSDA
     //D13UPROC.SORTWK03 DD SPACE=(CYL,(5,5)),UNIT=SYSDA
     //D13UPROC.SORTWK04 DD SPACE=(CYL,(5,5)),UNIT=SYSDA
     //D13UPROC.SYSIN DD *
  85   REPAIR LOG NO SET TABLESPACE &DB..&TSNAME NOCOPYPEND
       RUNSTATS TABLESPACE &DB..&TSNAME INDEX(ALL) SHRLEVEL CHANGE
     @@
     WRAPUP: WRITE END OF CLIST
```

Lines 1 through 39 edit the CLIST parameters. Since the example requires migration from a production to a system test environment, it is necessary to edit the utility control statements. Lines 41 through 46 add "REPLACE LOG NO" and remove the AUTHID (&FMID) from the production table name. The initial job was submitted by the AUTHID (TSOID) of the system test table owner. Therefore, it was necessary to qualify the SELECT for the unload used by DSNTIAUL.

By entering as a TSO command,

```
MGRTUNLD CLM
MGRTUNLD BAL
```

FIGURE 9–11
AUTOMATED MIGRATION BATCH JOB

```
//TMP EXEC PGM=IKJEFT01,DYNAMNBR=20
//SYSTSPRT DD SYSOUT=*
//SYSPRINT DD SYSOUT=*
//SYSTSIN DD *
       MGRTUNLD CLM
       MGRTUNLD BAL
```

two entire tables will be copied from a production to a system test environment. To automate the process further, create a background job that will invoke the CLIST for you, as in Figure 9–11.

If such a job exists and it contains a migrate unload CLIST for every table in your system, then your entire system could be copied with the execution of one SUBMIT. Note that each MGRTUNLD will cause two jobs to be executed.

CHAPTER 10

UTILITIES

D B2 utilities run as batch jobs in an MVS environment. Most of these utilities require DB2 to be running for the duration of their execution. They may be invoked through use of JCL catalogued procedures supplied with DB2, through the DB2 Interactive facility (DB2I, utilities panel), or through JCL streams that are either user-written, or created through the DSNU CLIST. DB2 utilities provide their own call attach facilities (CAF) as required.

Each utility to be discussed in this chapter will be designated as falling into one of three categories: standard utility, independent utility, and service utility.

To simplify the impact of DB2 Version 2, the utilities will first be presented as they functioned under Version 1.3. Then Version 2.1 differences and enhancements will be discussed. If you feel comfortable with your knowledge of Version 1.3 utilities, proceed to the "Generating Utility Control Statements" section in this chapter.

■ STANDARD UTILITIES

Standard utilities require DB2 to be running for the duration of their execution and may be invoked by any of the methods previously mentioned (supplied JCL catalogued procedures, DB2I, user-written JCL streams, or JCL generated by the DSNU CLIST).

Some of the standard utilities may be executed without the logging facility, by specifying LOG NO as a parameter. Eliminating log I/O is usually more efficient. Elimination of log I/O, however, will cause the *copy pending* flag in the SYSIBM.SYSCOPY DB2 catalog table to be set for the tablespace currently being manipulated. There are three ways to turn off this flag.

1. Execute the COPY utility
2. Execute the REPAIR utility to set the *copy pending* flag to "NO"
3. Issue a START DATABASE command

```
-START DB(dbname) SPACENAM(tsname) ACCESS(RW)
-START DB(dbname) SPACENAM(tsname) ACCESS(FORCE)
```

The COPY and REPAIR utilities are discussed within the next few pages and the START DATABASE commands have been presented in the **DB2 Commands** chapter.

A brief description of the standard utilities follows in alphabetical order.

- CHECK — may be used to verify the integrity of indices against the data they are supposed to index. Warning messages document integrity exceptions such as duplicate keys on a unique index, data without a corresponding index record (and vice versa), index entries which indicate a different table, or an out of sequence condition in the index. DB2 version 2 augments this utility to perform referential integrity verification. This utility is not restartable. The issuer must possess SYSADM authority; DBADM, DBCTRL, or DBMAINT authority for the data base; or have the STATS privilege for the data base that contains the tablespace in question. The authors recommend use of this utility when an index is suspected of being corrupted, but not after every LOAD, REORG, or RECOVER INDEX execution. See Figure 10–1 for CHECK format.

- COPY — produces an image copy of a complete tablespace, or dataset within the tablespace, on a full or incremental basis. A full image copy represents the entire tablespace or dataset as specified, and will successfully reset the *copy pending* flags for the dataset. The *copy pending* status may have been outstanding from LOAD or REORG execution with the LOG NO option specified, from RECOVER execution, or from a prior COPY utility failure.[1] An incremental copy represents only the data pages within the tablespace or dataset which have been changed since the last full image copy was produced with this utility. To execute this utility successfully, the issuer must possess SYSADM authority; DBADM, DBMAINT, or DBCTRL authority for the data base; or possess the IMAGCOPY privilege for the data base containing the tablespace in question.

FIGURE 10–1
CHECK UTILITY BASIC FORMAT

```
CHECK INDEX NAME(idx_name,...)
    TABLESPACE dbname.tsname
        or
CHECK INDEX TABLESPACE dbname.tsname
```

---

[1] This is DB2's way of preventing any subsequent incremental image copies from occuring until a new full image copy has been taken.

Recovery-related information for the full or incremental image copy is stored in the SYSIBM.SYSCOPY catalog table. This includes the dataset name, date, time, log, Relative Byte Address (RBA), device type, up to 297 volume serial numbers, and file sequence numbers for tapes or cartridges on which the image copy is stored. Recovery details are stored independently of any Tape Management System (TMS). If the installed TMS deletes a needed dataset, DB2 will not be aware of the deletion, and subsequent recoveries will fail. See the MODIFY utility to remove expired or unnecessary information from the SYSIBM.SYSCOPY catalog.

Note that you may not use the same tape volume (if tape is the image storage medium) to store multiple incremental copies, or one incremental and one full image copy for the same tablespace. Such a condition will cause a subsequent recovery attempt to fail because the same volume cannot be concurrently mounted on two units. Furthermore, image copy dataset names may not duplicate the dataset name of a previously catalogued copy. If the image copy dataset name was never catalogued, a duplicate DSN is allowed if the volume serial or the file sequence number of the latter image copy is unique. To DB2, uncatalogued image copy dataset names are qualified with dataset name, volume serial number, and volume sequence number. Generation datasets may be used.

A recovery effort will also fail if the image copy datasets available were produced prior to a reorganization of data and the recovery is supposed to restore the data to its reorganized form. During a REORG, DB2 will flag all prior image copies as invalid for recovery to the current state. Therefore, be careful to recreate image copies subsequent to a reorganization of data.

The decision to take a full or incremental copy should be based on the percentage of the data pages and not solely on the number of changed rows that have been modified. Specifically, if one row occupies 5 percent of a page and 5 percent or more of a tablespace is modified, then it is likely that most pages will contain at least one updated row. A full image copy is definitely in order.

Keep in mind that most utilities make full use of sequential pre-fetch to retrieve up to 64 pages for every I/O request. For this reason, if 50 percent of the pages are modified (e.g., 2.5 percent of the total rows in our 20 rows-per-page example), a full image copy is still more efficient than an incremental copy. Fact: a tablespace that consumes an entire 3380 can be image copied in less than 15 minutes! Also, full image copies will facilitate operational recovery requirements by minimizing the scheduling of merges (MERGECOPY) of incremental image copies. See Figure 10–2 for COPY format.

- LOAD — causes data to be loaded into a single table in a tablespace, partition, or one part of a partition; or into multiple tables in the same tablespace. The LOAD utility may replace data or add to data in a partition or table. The issuer of this request must have SYSADM authority;

FIGURE 10–2
COPY UTILITY BASIC FORMAT

```
COPY TABLESPACE dbname.tsname
    DEVT jcl-spec
    [DSNUM ALL | n]
    [COPYDDN SYSCOPY | ddname]
    [FULL YES | NO]
    [SHRLEVEL REFERENCE | CHANGE]
```

DBCTRL or higher authority for the data base; or possess the LOAD privilege for the data base containing the tablespace in question.

Data to be loaded is described by the LOAD DATA statement. Input records may be combined and an elementary selection criterion is available. Numeric data conversion is permitted. Any validation or edit procedures defined for the table, or field procedures defined for a column of the table, will apply during processing of the LOAD utility.

Load utilities should be executed serially by data base.[2] We have found that two or more LOADs may be in UTILINIT phase, but only one will be in the RELOAD phase. This is probably due to DB2 catalog contention, specifically involving the SYSIBM.SYSCOPY catalog table.

Note that use of LOG NO as an option will force *copy pending* status on the target object(s); this condition can be resolved by one of the three methods presented in the introduction to this chapter.

Unfortunately, duplicate keys are identified during the BUILD phase of a load and not during the RELOAD phase. You receive the following message when you attempt to create a duplicate index entry.

```
DSNU340I DSNURXBA - ERROR ....., DUPLICATE KEY
            INDEX =
            TABLE =
            RID OF INDEXED ROW = xxxxxxxx
            RID OF NON-INDEXED ROW = xxxxxxx
```

To avoid having to reload the table(s), execute the REPAIR utility specifying the RID(s) provided in the above message to delete the duplicate row(s).

As a performance consideration, the RUNSTATS utility should be run to analyze the new data for access path selection. Also, programs

---

[2] At this writing, contention is anticipated to remain a problem in DB2 Version 2.

FIGURE 10–3
LOAD UTILITY BASIC FORMAT

```
LOAD[DATA][INDDN SYSREC | ddname]
    [REPLACE | RESUME YES]
    [LOG YES | NO]
    [CONTINUEIF (field-condition)]
INTO TABLE table-name
    WHEN field-select-criteria
    (field-spec-1...
    ,field-spec-n
    )
```

accessing the LOADed data should be rebound to incorporate the newly chosen access paths, if any.[3]

The authors recommend that the load be run with LOG NO to reduce overhead. The related table(s) will then have a status of READ ONLY (RO) to reflect the *copy pending* flag set in SYSIBM.SYSCOPY. If the table is to be modified, execute the COPY utility immediately after the load completes. See Figure 10–3 for LOAD format.

- MERGECOPY — optionally produces either a new full image copy or a single incremental image copy from multiple incremental image copies created by prior executions of the COPY utility. The invoker of the MERGECOPY request must have the SYSADM authority; DBADM, DBMAINT, or DBCTRL authority for the data base; or possess the IMAGCOPY privilege for the data base containing the tablespace in question.

    Note that the frequency with which this utility is executed should be determined by your recovery requirements: You must decide if, in your environment, the time required to execute this utility on a timely basis is less costly than the extra time required to perform a recovery from multiple incremental copies.

    This utility is restartable from any phase which has completed successfully if an abnormal termination occurs subsequently.

    The authors do not recommend use of this utility unless table updates are both unevenly distributed and concentrated around contiguous data pages. See Figure 10–4 for MERGECOPY format.

- MODIFY — deletes image copies, catalog table entries and corresponding log records from the SYSIBM.SYSCOPY catalog table and the SYSIBM.SYSLGRNG directory table, respectively. Deletion criteria may

---

[3] Refer to the **DB2 Commands** chapter for a discussion of the -TERM UTILITY command with respect to the actions which should occur prior to restart of the LOAD utility.

FIGURE 10–4
MERGECOPY UTILITY BASIC FORMAT

```
MERGECOPY TABLESPACE dbname.tsname
    DEVT jcl-spec
    DSNUM ALL | n
    NEWCOPY NO | YES
    COPYDDN SYSCOPY | ddname
```

be based on date or age specifications. Execution of this utility will enhance DB2 performance by reducing the number of rows in the preceding two catalog tables. The issuer of this utility request must have the SYSADM authority; DBADM, DBMAINT, or DBCTRL authority for the data base; or possess the IMAGCOPY privilege for the data base containing the tablespace in question.

   The running of this utility must be synchronized with the retention periods specified during corresponding image copy dataset creation. If your installation Tape Management System deletes datasets in 15 days, then the DB2 catalog table entries must also be removed 15 days after their creation. Care must be exercised to retain the entry for the last image copy created for any table. Failure to do so will set the *copy pending* flag for the tablespace, forcing the tablespace to have READ ONLY status. See Figure 10–5 for MODIFY format.

● RECOVER — recovers data to either its current state or to a point in time determined by either the time of a prior image copy dataset or a specific log RBA. The data to be recovered may consist of one page, pages with reported I/O errors, or an entire tablespace. Image copy data for the tablespace and log change records are combined as input to the recovery process. The invoker of this utility request must have the SYSADM authority; DBADM or DBCTRL authority for the data base; or possess the RECOVERDB privilege for the data base containing the tablespace in question.

FIGURE 10–5
MODIFY UTILITY BASIC FORMAT

```
MODIFY RECOVERY TABLESPACE dbname.tsname
    [DSNUM ALL | n]
    DELETE
    AGE n or (*) | DATE n or (*)
```

This utility is also capable of recovery, with a single invocation, of all or selected indices for tables in the same tablespace.

If a particular image copy cannot be used, for reasons such as an I/O error or its deletion by a Tape Management System, RECOVER (without any options specified) will attempt to locate either a previous image copy or the log records from the last running of the REORG utility that was invoked with LOG YES specified. However, RECOVER cannot, under any circumstances, use the *log* to restore the data to the status it had prior to the last reorganization. Also recall that image copies taken prior to a REORG are marked as invalid by the REORG utility, and may be used only in conjunction with the TOCOPY or TORBA options. Additionally, RECOVER will fail if a target dataset still has the *copy pending* status from a utility execution where LOG NO was specified.

Therefore, to support fallback (prior point in time) recovery, <u>two image</u> copies must be made when any operation specifies LOG NO: one copy must be created before the operation and one copy must be taken after it. This requirement is particularly applicable to reorganizations.

When LOG YES is specified with a REORG request, only one image copy (taken prior to the REORG) is required to support fallback recovery.

Similarly, a partial recovery also requires that a full image copy be taken prior to any update attempts, since it is assumed that some log records have been lost and there is otherwise no means of restoring data to its partially-recovered state. Also, indices may require rebuilding because they may no longer be consistent with the partially recovered data.[4] See Figure 10–6 for RECOVER format.

FIGURE 10–6
RECOVERY UTILITY BASIC FORMATS

```
RECOVER TABLESPACE dbname.tsname
    [DSNUM ALL | n]
    [ERROR RANGE | TORBA string |
        TOCOPY dsname-info]
RECOVER TABLESPACE dbname.tsname
    PAGE n
    [CONTINUE]
RECOVER INDEX
    ALL | (idx_name1,...idx_name)
    [TABLESPACE dbname.tsname]
```

---

[4] Refer to the **DB2 Commands** chapter for a discussion of the -TERM UTILITY command with respect to the actions which should occur prior to restart of the RECOVER utility.

● REORG — enhances performance by reorganizing a tablespace and restoring the clustering sequences of all related tables. An alternative use for this utility is the unloading of data into a dataset that can then be used as input to the DB2 LOAD utility; use the REORG UNLOAD ONLY option to accomplish this. The issuer of this utility request must have the SYSADM authority; DBCTRL or higher authority for the data base; or possess the REORG privilege for the data base containing the tablespace in question.

Note that use of LOG NO as an option will force the target object(s) to have *copy pending* status, which can be resolved by execution of the COPY utility as previously described. As a performance consideration, the RUNSTATS utility should be run to analyze the new data for access path selection. Also, programs accessing the REORGed data should be rebound to incorporate the newly chosen access paths, if any.[5]

As with the LOAD utility, only one tablespace per data base may be reorganized at a time; this prevents conflicts of concurrent access of the DB2 catalogs. See Figure 10–7 for REORG format.

FIGURE 10–7
REORG UTILITY BASIC FORMATS

```
REORG TABLESPACE dbname.tsname
    [PART n]
    [LOG |YES | NO]
    [UNLDDN SYSREC | ddname]
    [UNLOAD CONTINUE | PAUSE | ONLY]
REORG INDEX idx_name
    [PART n]
    [UNLDDN SYSREC | ddname]
    [UNLOAD CONTINUE | PAUSE | ONLY]
```

● REPAIR — literally removes or replaces invalid data or index entries as specified by the user. For example, this utility may be invoked to delete the rows of a table that caused a LOAD utility to fail during its BUILD phase due to duplicate index entries:

```
REPAIR LOCATE TABLESPACE dbname.tsname
    RID X'42F0A'    DELETE
```

Deletions are always logged. Therefore, the LOG parameter may not be

---

[5] Refer to the DB2 Commands chapter for a discussion of the TERM UTILITY command with respect to the actions that should occur prior to restart of the REORG utility.

used in conjunction with the DELETE parameter. Furthermore, REPAIR may be used to reset *copy pending* flags or to print (dump) physical page images:

```
REPAIR LOG NO
    SET TABLESPACE dbname.tsname
    NOCOPYPEND
```

The invoker of this utility request must have the SYSADM authority; DBADM or DBCTRL authority for the data base; or possess the REPAIR privilege for the data base containing the tablespace in question.

This utility should be executed with extreme caution, due to the obvious potential for further corruption of data and indices. This utility is not restartable. See Figure 10–8 for REPAIR format.

FIGURE 10–8
REPAIR UTILITY BASIC FORMATS

```
REPAIR [LOG YES | NO]
 SET TABLESPACE dbname.tsname
        [PART n]
        NOCOPYEND
REPAIR [LOG YES | NO]
 LOCATE TABLESPACE dbname.tsname
        PAGE page # |
        RID rid # |
        KEY lit INDEX idx_name
     {DELETE
     DUMP  ······
     VERIFY ········
     REPLACE ··········}
REPAIR [LOG YES | NO]
 LOCATE INDEX idx_name PAGE page #
     {DELETE
     DUMP  ······
     VERIFY ········
     REPLACE ··········}
```

● RUNSTATS — records information in the DB2 catalog pertinent to access selection, space utilization, and index efficiency. The information stored in the DB2 catalog is referred to by the optimizer in selecting access path strategies during the bind process. Subsequent queries of the columns in the DB2 catalogs that are updated by this utility can be used for diagnostic purposes such as gauging table and index design, and scheduling of reorganizations. The invoker of this request must have SYSADM authority; DBADM, DBMAINT, or DBCTRL authority for the data base; or possess the STATS privilege for the data base containing the tablespace in question.

Access path information is stored in four DB2 catalog tables: SYSIBM.SYSCOLUMNS, SYSIBM.SYSINDEXES, SYSIBM.SYSTABLES, and SYSIBM.SYSTABLESPACE. Information available for evaluation by data base administrators is stored in the SYSIBM.SYSTABLEPART and SYSIBM.SYSINDEXPART DB2 catalog tables.

Note that whenever statistics are not available for determining access path strategy (e.g., the relative statistical columns are set to -1), the SQL optimizer will make its own evaluation of an access path strategy by default. Therefore, this utility should be invoked following a reorganization of a tablespace (or an increase in the volume of activity against a tablespace sufficient to necessitate a reorganization), a table load, or on index creation. Furthermore, application plans utilizing the data in question must be rebound prior to their execution in order to reflect the new access path strategy, if any. See Figure 10–9 for RUNSTATS format.

FIGURE 10–9
RUNSTATS UTILITY BASIC FORMATS

```
RUNSTATS TABLESPACE dbname.tsname
   [INDEX (ALL | idx_name1, idx_nameN)]
   [SHRLEVEL REFERENCE | CHANGE]
RUNSTATS INDEX
   idx_name1,...idx_nameN
   [SHRLEVEL REFERENCE | CHANGE]
```

- STOSPACE — refreshes the information stored in the DB2 catalog concerning the current allocation of space for stogroups, tablespaces, and indices. Authorization for execution of this utility includes the SYSADM authority or the STOSPACE privilege. This utility is not phase-restartable.

  Note that space statistics reflect total space allocations, even if some volumes are no longer in the stogroup. Recall that this is possible because volumes removed from a stogroup are ineligible only for future allocation; the datasets resident on them at the time of the removal will remain on these volumes. Also, the tablespaces and indices involved in the utility execution need not be available to DB2; only catalog information is required. See Figure 10–10 for STOSPACE format.

FIGURE 10–10
STOSPACE UTILITY BASIC FORMAT

```
STOSPACE STOGROUP (*) | (stogrp_name1...
                                  ,stogrp_nameN)
```

■ INDEPENDENT UTILITIES

Independent utilities do not require DB2 to be running for the duration of their execution, and may only be invoked through MVS JCL. These utilities include the Change Log Inventory and the Print Log Map programs.

● Change Log Inventory (DSNJU003) — can be used to modify the boot-strap datasets (BSDSs) to add or delete archive log datasets; it can also be used to control the next startup of DB2 by creating or deleting a conditional restart control record. This utility may be executed, for obvious reasons, only when DB2 is not running. See Figure 10–11 for format.

● Print Log Map (DSNJU004) — prints the name and related RBA for both copies of the active and archive log datasets. Other available information includes the names of active log datasets awaiting new log data, log dataset passwords, and status of conditional restart control records in the BSDS, as well as queue contents in checkpoint records in the BSDS. To execute this utility, the issuer must have the appropriate RACF authority or knowledge of the BSDS's VSAM password if the BSDS is protected. See Figure 10–12 for Print Log Map format.

FIGURE 10–11
CHANGE LOG MAP JCL

```
//EXEC PGM=DSNJU003
//SYSUT1  (primary BSDS)
//SYSUT2  (secondary BSDS)
//SYSPRINT DD SYSOUT=*
//SYSIN DD *
```

FIGURE 10–12
PRINT LOG MAP JCL

```
//EXEC PGM=DSNJU004
//SYSUT1  (BSDS allocation)
//SYSPRINT DD SYSOUT=*
```

■ **SERVICE UTILITIES**

Service utilities similarly do not require DB2 to be running during execution. They are also invoked only through MVS JCL. These utilities include DSN1COPY, DSN1LOGP, and DSN1PRNT. Since these utilities will most likely be active while DB2 is executing, it is strongly recommended that the applicable objects be either stopped or placed in read only (RO) status, depending on the type of operation. Use either the STOP or START command as follows to accomplish this.

```
STOP DATABASE(dbname) SPACENAM(tsname)
START DATABASE(dbname) SPACENAM(tsname) ACCESS(RO)
```

For more information on commands see the **DB2 Commands** chapter.

● DSN1COPY — can produce copies or listings of VSAM datasets that contain tablespaces or indexspaces; or it can copy a VSAM dataset to a VSAM or sequential dataset; or it can copy a sequential dataset to a

FIGURE 10–13
DSN1COPY UTILITY BASIC FORMAT

```
//EXEC PGM=DSN1COPY,PARM=
//SYSUT1   input dataset
//SYSUT2   output dataset
//SYSXLAT DD *
 DBID translate
 PSID translate
 OBID translate
//SYSPRINT DD SYSOUT=*
```

FIGURE 10–14
DSN1COPY OBID TRANSLATE EXAMPLE

```
//      JOB
//DS01 EXEC PGM=DSN1COPY,PARM='OBIDXLAT,FULLCOPY'
//STEPLIB  DD DSN=P070.DB23.DSN130.DSNLOAD,DISP=SHR
//SYSPRINT DD SYSOUT=*
//SYSUT1 DD DSN=  image copy dataset
//SYSUT2 DD DSN=vcat.DSNDBC.dbname.tsname.I0001.A001,
//       DISP=SHR
//SYSXLAT DD *
0266,0266       DBID
0027,0010       PSID
0028,0011       OBID
    ↑    ↑
    |    |_____      target
    |_____      source
```

VSAM or sequential dataset. It may also be invoked to copy hex dumps of DB2 data, to accomplish OBID translation of data for system migration or recovery, or to perform validity checking of data and index pages. Finally, DSN1COPY is the only utility that may be employed to recover a dropped tablespace.

The SYSXLAT DD statement is required only if the PARM = 'OBIDXLAT,......' is specified. See Figure 10–13 for DSN1COPY format. Figure 10–14 shows tablespaces being restored from an image copy where the tablespace was dropped and then recreated. This situation will occur when a tablespace must be extended or moved to another volume. At this point a common question may arise, "If a tablespace is inadvertently dropped, how do you obtain old OBIDs?" The solution is to use either DSN1COPY or DSN1PRNT to list the first three pages of the image copy dataset. DSN1COPY will print an unformatted listing, while DSN1PRNT will generate a formatted listing complete with labels.

- DSN1LOGP — displays the contents of the recovery log in one of two formats: detail reporting of individual log records, or summary reporting to assist in a conditional restart. This information is used to locate the relative byte addresses (RBAs) for recovery purposes. This utility may not read the log that is actively in use by DB2.

- DSN1PRNT — prints the contents of DB2 tablespace and indexspace VSAM datasets. It may be employed to print either hex or formatted dumps of DB2 data bases and datasets, image copy datasets, or sequential

FIGURE 10–15
DSN1PRINT JCL EXAMPLE

```
//  JOB
//DS01 EXEC PGM=DSN1PRNT,PARM='FORMAT,PRINT(000,002)'
//SYSPRINT DD SYSOUT=*
//SYSUT1 DD DSN= image copy dataset
//  DISP=SHR
```

datasets. Since it is a print-only utility, its printing capabilities are more
efficient than those of DSN1COPY, making it preferable for printing
purposes. This utility has no input control statements and is controlled
via PARM fields.

In Figure 10–15, the FORMAT parameter requests a formatted
dump, and PRINT(000,002) specifies pages 000 through 002. The 000
page (*header page*) contains the field HPGOBID, which is/was the DBID
and PSID of this tablespace. The OBID(s) will be found with the label of
"PGSOBD" in the data pages.

■ UTILITY IDs

Standard utilities have a 16-byte utility identifier (UID) assigned to them.
Requests to display utility status using the DISPLAY UTILITY command may
specify all of a UID or just the leading characters of a UID for a generic
request. Restart or termination of specific utility executions must include the
UID. Furthermore, UIDs must be unique for every currently executing utility.

Some care must be taken to establish a UID naming convention that can
identify a utility, identify an object (e.g., table), and maintain uniqueness
among TSOIDs or job names of the utility. For an image copy of the DDA
tablespace that was submitted by TSOID X1206, consider the following UID:

X1206.DDA.IC

In addition to ensuring uniqueness, careful assignment of UIDs will mean
that output from a DISPLAY UTILITY command will be ordered in a more
useful sequence.

■ GENERATING UTILITY CONTROL STATEMENTS

The preceding sections described the capabilities of Version 1.3 DB2 utilities,
processing considerations, and some potential problems. Beyond external
problems related to the actual execution of DB2 utilities, additional potential

for problems exists in the encoding of the individual utility control statements and the coordination of object names.

To make sure that no control statements were missed, you could query the system catalogs and use the results as a checklist. Better still, why not trap the output from the query and use it as the control statement input to a utility?

A query customarily returns columns from a table. Data base names and tablespace names are available as columns in the system catalogs. However, a utility will also require keywords and other parameters in its control statement input. The solution is to enter these keywords and parameters as literals in the query.

The best approach is to use SPUFI, changing the SPUFI list dataset record length to 80 (or a length divisible by 80), which may be edited by TSO. This must be done prior to entering a query. Recall that the SPUFI input dataset must be 79 or 80 characters in length. If the record length was originally 240, an IDCAMS REPRO could be used to reblock the input data set to 80 characters. Finally, the list dataset must be edited to remove messages and page header output.

The example in Figure 10–16 will create one COPY utility statement for every tablespace in data bases prefixed with "AUDDA" that was created by '*authid5*'.

FIGURE 10–16
COPY STATEMENT GENERATION

```
  --
  --CC CREATE COPY UTIL STATEMENTS
  --
    SELECT 'COPY TABLESPACE'
    ,SUBSTR(DBNAME,1,7)||'.'||NAME,
    'COPYDDN', NAME
    FROM SYSIBM.SYSTABLESPACE
    WHERE CREATOR = 'authid5'
    AND DBNAME LIKE 'AUDDA%';
```

The statement

```
SUBSTR(DBNAME,1,7)||'.'||NAME.
```

generates a fully qualified tablespace name such as

```
AUDDA01.T$DDA001
```

The SUBSTR is necessary because all data base names in this example are seven characters long. If naming conventions did not dictate a specific data base naming convention, it would be necessary to edit each COPY statement.

Additional utility statement generation examples follow in Figures 10–17 through 10–21.

FIGURE 10–17
MODIFY STATEMENT GENERATION

```
--
-- CREATE MODIFY STATEMENTS FOR ALL TS
-- IN DATA BASES AU%
--
    SELECT DISTINCT
     'MODIFY RECOVERY TABLESPACE'
     ,DBNAME||'.'||TSNAME,
     'DELETE AGE(2)'
       FROM SYSIBM.SYSCOPY
       WHERE DBNAME LIKE 'AU%';
```

The primary benefit of generating utility statements from the DB2 catalogs is the certainty that no object will be missed. At worst, there may be too many objects selected and you will have to delete a few of the generated statements. Similar queries could be used to generate JCL DD statements.

FIGURE 10–18
RUNSTATS STATEMENT GENERATION

```
--
--CC CREATE RUNSTATS CONTROL STATEMENTS
--
    SELECT 'RUNSTATS TABLESPACE'
     ,SUBSTR(DBNAME,1,7)||'.'||NAME
     ,'INDEX(ALL) SHRLEVEL CHANGE'
     FROM SYSIBM.SYSTABLESPACE
     WHERE CREATOR = 'authid1';
```

FIGURE 10–19
REORG STATEMENT GENERATION

```
   --
   -- CREATE REORG (UNLOAD ONLY)
   --
      SELECT 'REORG TABLESPACE'
       ,DBNAME||'.'||NAME,
       'LOG NO UNLDDN',NAME,'UNLOAD ONLY'
       FROM SYSIBM.SYSTABLESPACE
       WHERE CREATOR = 'authid1';
```

FIGURE 10–20
LOAD STATEMENT GENERATION

```
   --
   --CC CREATE LOAD CONTROL STATEMENTS
   --CC   (FOR REORG UNLOAD)
   --
      SELECT 'LOAD INDDN',TSNAME
      ,'REPLACE LOG NO FORMAT'
      ,'UNLOAD INTO TABLE'
      ,NAME
       FROM SYSIBM.SYSTABLES
       WHERE CREATOR = 'authid1';
```

FIGURE 10–21
REPAIR STATEMENT GENERATION

```
   --
   -- CREATE REPAIR STATEMENTS
   -- TO TURN OFF COPY PENDING FLAG
   --
      SELECT 'REPAIR SET TABLESPACE'
      ,SUBSTR(DBNAME,1,7)||'.'||NAME
      ,'NOCOPYEND'
       FROM SYSIBM.SYSTABLESPACE
       WHERE CREATOR = 'authid8';
```

■ UTILITY CONTENTION

There is very little documentation available on DB2 utility contention. Throughout the preceding chapters the authors have touched upon resource contention problems encountered during the execution of various utilities. The main concern for such resource contention is not the actual table/ tablespace being manipulated, but rather the rows and pages within the DB2 catalogs that must be read or modified as the result of a specific utility's execution. Table 10–1 relates utilities to DB2 catalog tables. Tables read for authority checking are not shown because they are not ordinarily modified during the execution of standard utilities. Although not a utility, the bind process is included so its impact on the utility runtime environment can be visualized. Also, DDL CREATEs and DROPs of TABLESPACEs/TABLEs would modify, at a minimum, the SYSCOLUMNS through SYSTABLESPACE tables in the following chart.

It would appear that RUNSTATS cannot concurrently run with any utility (including another RUNSTATS), any bind process, or during most DDL execution. Fortunately, this is not the case, as utilities use page locks when modifying data within the DB2 catalogs. To further reduce catalog table contention, row location within data pages is controlled with *strict clustering*. The intent of strict clustering usage is to relieve contention by segregating

TABLE 10–1
UTILITY CONTENTION WITH DB2 CATALOG TABLES

	VER 2.1 CHECK	COPY	LOAD	MERGECOPY	MODIFY	RECOVER	REORG	REPAIR	RUNSTATS	BIND
SYSCOPY	M	M	M	M	M	M	M			
SYSCOLUMNS	R		R			R	R		M	R
SYSINDEXES	R		R			R	R		M	R
SYSINDEXPART	R		R			R	R		M	
SYSTABLES	R		R			R	R		M	R
SYSTABLEPART	R	R	R			R	R		M	
SYSTABLESPACE	R	R	R			R	R		M	R

Legend: R = Read access; M = Insert, Delete, or Update access.
Note: All utilities update SYSIBM.SYSUTIL at each utility phase

rows in a catalog page by data base or CREATOR. Therefore, a given page within a catalog table (e.g., SYSTABLES) may only contain rows that have the same DBNAME (data base) or CREATOR (owner). Thus, a worst case of two concurrent RUNSTATS would suffer no contention if the respective tablespaces were defined within different data bases.

The SYSCOPY table is modified at least three times by most utilities during their execution. It is not the number of updates and related locks; rather it is the lock duration on SYSCOPY that may prevent utilities from completing. Lock duration by utilities on SYSCOPY was greatly reduced in Version 1.3, and we anticipate that Version 2.1 will further lessen this contention impact.

To minimize DB2 catalog contention, define one tablespace per data base and/or schedule utilities to eliminate conflicts.

■ APPENDIX 10A — DB2 VERSION 2: UTILITY IMPACT

The major impact on existing DB2 utilities results from the support of referential integrity introduced with Version 2. Two new tablespace statuses, CHECK PENDING and RECOVER PENDING, indicate the *potential*, respectively, for violation of referential integrity constraints and for invalid data or indices.

Recover pending was added to address the potential exposure of invalid data or indices. This status is set when either the REORG, LOAD, or RECOVER utilities is stopped by a DB2 TERM command. Recover pending may also be set when fewer than all the parts of a partitioned tablespace are recovered. Depending on which phase was terminated, the recover pending status will be set on either the tablespace or the indexspace. The best way to reset this status is to restart the utility and recover the indices.

CHECK PENDING status may only be designated for tablespaces that contain dependent tables, and varies in impact from a partial partition to an entire tablespace. With respect to concurrency, however, the status is considered to apply to the entire tablespace.

A parent table's status is considered incomplete, and therefore unusable, if its primary (unique) index is not defined. Furthermore, all rows that contain duplicates for any unique indices must be removed prior to successful completion of a LOAD (Ver 2.1) utility. Therefore, primary index entity integrity is enforced with unique index constraints — not with referential integrity constraints.

Constraint Violations

The potential for referential integrity constraint violations exists when:

1. A table is altered to introduce a new foreign key for a table considered to be populated. A table in a non-segmented tablespace is considered to be populated if it ever contained data, regardless of its current state. A

table in a segmented tablespace is considered to be populated only if it currently contains data.

2. A LOAD utility execution for a dependent table specified ENFORCE NO, indicating that referential integrity constraints should be ignored (i.e., not "enforced").

3. A LOAD utility execution replaced a table in the parent tablespace of a relationship, thus forcing the CHECK PENDING status assignment for all dependent tables.

4. A RECOVER utility was executed to restore data to a point in time other than that designated as a quiesce point.[6] Dependent tablespaces recovered, as well as any descendant tablespaces, will be assigned the CHECK PENDING status.

5. A RECOVER utility execution restored a <u>partial</u> <u>tablespace</u> <u>set</u>. A **tablespace set** is the collection of all tablespaces that are related on the basis of referential constraints. To state that a partial tablespace set has been restored implies that some components of a referential structure may be in an inconsistent state. Dependent tablespaces recovered, as well as descendant tablespaces, will be assigned the CHECK PENDING status. The RECOVER of only a parent table will place all its dependents in CHECK PENDING status.

6. A RECOVER utility execution restores a complete tablespace set, but one table of a tablespace contains a referential integrity constraint that did not exist at the time the quiesce point (used for recovery) was taken. The <u>entire</u> <u>tablespace</u> containing the table will be assigned the CHECK PENDING status, although the actual scope of the status will be at the table level only.

7. A CHECK DATA utility is executed with the DELETE NO option for a dependent tablespace that has referential integrity constraint violations detected. Since the violations are not automatically deleted through execution of CHECK DATA, the tablespace is designated in a CHECK PENDING state. This situation could occur when the REPAIR utility is incorrectly used to "fix" violations.

Information regarding the CHECK PENDING status itself is stored in DB2 catalog tables SYSIBM.SYSTABLES, SYSIBM.SYSTABLEPART, and SYSIBM.SYSTABLESPACE. Related information pertaining to quiesce utility execution may be found in catalog tables SYSIBM.SYSRELS and SYSIBM.SYSCOPY.

The CHECK PENDING status is removed from a tablespace when:

1. A CHECK DATA utility is executed with the DELETE NO option for a dependent tablespace that does not contain (or no longer contains) referential integrity constraint violations (e.g., the REPAIR utility was successful).

---

[6] Refer to the QUIESCE utility presentation to follow in this appendix.

2. A CHECK DATA utility is executed with the DELETE YES option for the tablespace in question.

3. A LOAD REPLACE utility is executed with the ENFORCE YES option for the tablespace in question.

4. A RECOVER utility is executed for an entire tablespace set to restore all tables to the same quiesce point. All tablespace tables that previously were designated in the CHECK PENDING state will no longer reflect that status.

5. A DROP of a table occurs that removes all previously existing constraint violations from the tablespace in question.

6. The foreign key causing the referential constraint violation for one or more tables is removed as a constraint via the ALTER command.

7. The CHECK PENDING status may be forcibly removed by execution of the REPAIR utility with the NOCHECKPEND option specified.

8. The CHECK PENDING status may be forcibly removed by execution of the START DATABASE(–) SPACENAM(–) command with ACCESS(FORCE) specified. Note that execution of this alternative will remove all restrictive statuses against the tablespace (e.g., COPY PENDING, RECOVER PENDING).

Implications of the CHECK PENDING status follow:

1. The CHECK PENDING status inhibits the execution of <u>any</u> <u>DML</u> <u>requests</u> for any tables within that tablespace. This restriction is extended to tables in non-restricted tablespaces that must access tables in restricted tablespaces due to referential relationships (e.g., A parent table in a non-restricted tablespace may insert but not delete or update its primary key if a dependent table is in a restricted tablespace. Also, a dependent table in a nonrestricted tablespace may delete but not insert or update foreign keys to a parent table that resides in a restricted tablespace).

2. The CHECK PENDING status inhibits execution of all but the ALTER and DROP DDL requests.

3. Most utilities will function concurrently with the CHECK PENDING status. Exceptions for COPY and REORG utility execution will be stated in the specific utility presentation to follow.

Specific utility impact is presented in alphabetical order in the next section of this appendix. Please crossreference the individual discussions as appropriate. Redundant information has been minimized.

CHECK

DB2 Version 2 augments this utility with the DATA parameter to perform referential integrity verification (i.e., foreign key equal to a primary key) and produce error messages as appropriate for the errors detected. Optionally, detected errors and related descendant rows may be copied to a user-defined exception table and then deleted from their respective tables.

The exception table must exactly copy the format of the target table, with the addition of two columns: the Row ID (RID) of the errant row (required), and (optionally) the timestamp reflecting when the CHECK DATA utility was initiated. The LIKE DDL (Ver. 2.1) function may be specified to accomplish the exception table format copy. The exception table should not be defined with any constraints that could cause an error situation upon insert (e.g., unique index). It is the user's responsibility to ensure that the exception table is empty prior to execution of the CHECK DATA function. The invoker of the CHECK utility must also hold insert privileges for the exception table. An example of exception table creation using the LIKE DDL statement is shown in Figure 10–23.

The deletion of rows in error is independent of their insertion into an exception table. Deletion, if specified, will occur without regard to delete rules established with referential integrity constraint definition. Furthermore, the DELETE YES specification will clear the check pending status of a tablespace and cause a report of deletions to be generated.

Regardless of any option specified, error messages are always produced for all foreign keys that do not have matching primary keys. See Figure 10–22 for CHECK utility format.

In the syntax presentation in Figure 10–22, SCOPE ALL indicates that the utility should be run for all tablespaces indicated; SCOPE PENDING (the default) indicates that the utility should execute only for those rows added by a LOAD utility execution since the last CHECK function was run.

The FOR EXCEPTION IN clause refers to the target table and corresponding exception table to be associated through error detection and copy, as previously mentioned. The integer specified in the EXCEPTION clause will

FIGURE 10–22
CHECK UTILITY FORMAT (V2.1)

```
CHECK DATA
     TABLESPACE ts_name1...ts_nameN
     SCOPE PENDING | ALL
     [FOR EXCEPTION
          IN tname1
               USE excpt_tb_name1
          IN tnameN
               USE excpt_tb_nameN]
     DELETE YES | NO
     EXCEPTIONS integer
```

FIGURE 10–23
CHECK UTILITY EXCEPTION TABLE

```
CREATE TABLE excpt_tname1
    LIKE tname1
    ;
ALTER TABLE excpt_tname1
    ADD rid_col CHAR(4)
    ;
ALTER TABLE excpt_tname1
    ADD time_col TIMESTAMP
    ;
```

cause processing to be terminated when the number of errors detected (not including descendant rows) exceeds the value of *integer*.

Primary and foreign key indices should be checked with CHECK INDEX(ix_name) prior to execution with the CHECK DATA option. Use of SCOPE PENDING rather than SCOPE ALL will significantly improve performance for any table where LOAD RESUME is utilized. Also, the SCANTAB and SORT phases will be skipped if related foreign keys are indexed.

COPY

For DB2 Version 2 installations, this utility will fail when invoked for a tablespace currently reflecting a status of *check pending*. Recall that if one table in either a simple or segmented tablespace is flagged, then all tables within that tablespace are considered in check pending status. There are no new COPY utility parameters or keywords for Version 2.

LOAD

DB2 Version 2 modifies three former utility phases (RELOAD, SORT, and BUILD) and introduces four new phases (INDEXVAL, ENFORCE, DISCARD, and REPORT) to support referential integrity checking. The SORTOUT DD statement is required when loading either an indexed table or a table with foreign keys (with or without an index). To facilitate error processing, optional SYSERR and SYSMAP DD statements have been added. SYSERR is required for discard processing and stores all errors detected during LOAD execution. SYSMAP is used to save RIDs for referential integrity checking and possible deletion of violations. SYSMAP is required for discard processing or if ENFORCE CONSTRAINTS is specified.

Discard processing is still controlled by the DISCARDS *integer* parameter and/or lack of SYSDISC DD statement.

The changes to the existing three phases follow:

1. RELOAD remains as the phase responsible for table loading—an error is issued if a LOAD statement references a table that does not have a complete definition (i.e., no primary index exists). However, the table is populated and data conversion errors will be detected. If discard processing is requested, all errors are written to the SYSERR dataset.
2. SORT utilizes the SYSUT1 dataset to write all indices and nonindexed foreign keys.
3. BUILD creates all indexes. Unique index violations are eliminated in this phase and written to SYSERR (discard processing) or the SYSUT1 dataset.

Constraint checking

Constraints introduced with referential integrity implementation (Version 2) are verified. Constraint violations (such as a foreign key without a primary key match) are detected and, optionally, enforced (i.e., eliminated through deletion if ENFORCE CONSTRAINTS is specified). Constraint violations that are not enforced by the LOAD execution will cause a dependent tablespace to be placed in CHECK PENDING status. Note that the primary key may exist in the current load input for the parent table when it exists in the same tablespace.

Specifically, four steps are included in the optional processing of LOAD utility constraint checking:

1. INDEXVAL, as its name implies, validates all unique indices and deletes duplicate target rows, if any. Rows will be removed with or without discard processing.
2. ENFORCE includes the verification and optional deletion of rows which cause referential integrity constraint violation errors. This checking requires READ (SHARE TABLE or TS LOCK) access of the parent table's primary index. Because multiple tables of a relationship may be loaded by the same LOAD utility execution, enforcement of constraints will *cascade* to other dependants and descendents in the same execution.
3. DISCARD processing produces a copy of rows in error (as defined in the ENFORCE discussion) to a DISCARD file. These rows are returned as they were presented for input to the LOAD utility.
4. REPORT processing returns the location of rows in error (as defined in the ENFORCE discussion) in both the discard and input datasets, as well as the target names of the input rows and constraint violations, as appropriate. Note that the discard dataset includes descendant row deletions. Also returned is the delete count and commit action of load processing when the count (exclusive of descendant deletion) exceeds 500.

Load processing in Version 2 differs from that of Version 1.3 (and prior) in that Version 2 creates a usable index and table with no duplicate records. Discarded errant rows need be corrected and reloaded only if appropriate on a case by case basis. In contrast, LOAD execution using prior versions of DB2 results in an unusable index which forces a tablespace scan—of a tablespace that retains access to the duplicate rows in error. The only way to correct the detected errors is to drop and recreate the table with a nonunique index, or to delete the duplicates by running the REPAIR utility against the rows in error.

The LOAD utility impacts check pending status as follows:

1. Initial or replace load processing with constraints enforced will clear a check pending status; whereas, the status will be set if constraints are not enforced.

2. Resume load processing with constraint enforcement will maintain the status of the original load effort, while unenforced constraint processing will set the status on only those rows added during resume processing.

LOAD enforcement of referential constraint violations is recommended over the facilities of CHECK DATA processing for reasons of efficiency. It is

FIGURE 10–24
LOAD UTILITY BASIC FORMAT (V2.1)

```
LOAD DATA INDDN SYSREC | ddname
        REPLACE | RESUME YES
        LOG YES | NO
        [CONTINUEIF (field-condition)]
    INTO TABLE table-name-1
        WHEN field-select-criteria
        (field-spec-1...
        ,field-spec-n
        )
    ENFORCE CONSTRAINTS                          (V2.1)
    INTO TABLE table-name_n
        WHEN field-select-criteria
        (field-spec-1...
        ,field-spec-n
        )
    ENFORCE NO                                   (V2.1)
```

more efficient to sort foreign keys during LOAD processing than to scan an entire tablespace or indexspace during execution of the CHECK utility.

Minimization of error processing during LOAD execution will be achieved when input rows are screened for unique index violations and data conversion errors prior to input to the LOAD. Furthermore, sequence of LOAD processing is significant: parent rows of a relationship should be loaded and corrected, if necessary, prior to LOAD attempts for dependent tables—if dependent tables to be loaded exist in a different tablespace. See Figure 10–24 for LOAD utility format.

MODIFY

The authors were unable to obtain any specific information about this utility for DB2 Version 2. We suspect, however, that it will also be able to remove QUIESCE type rows from SYSIBM.SYSCOPY. If subsequent utilities attempt to process any tablespaces that have had their respective rows deleted from this DB2 catalog table, a check pending and/or copy pending status will be set.

QUIESCE

QUIESCE establishes a point in time, designated by the Relative Byte Address (RBA), when all tablespaces in a tablespace set of a referential structure are consistent for the purposes of subsequent recovery efforts. This RBA and other recovery data is then stored in the DB2 catalog table, SYSIBM.SYSCOPY. To minimize the number of changes that must be reapplied during a point-in-time recovery, it is recommended that the QUIESCE utility be run close in time to the interval when image copies are taken for the tablespaces. To further ensure consistency of data, all related tablespaces should be started for either utility (UT) or read only (RO) access until all image copies have completed.

The QUIESCE function could have been partially achieved prior to Version 2 through the use of the START DATABASE command. However, determining an RBA for point-in-time recovery would have been a bit more complicated.

QUIESCE functions to effectively stop changes to related data by acquiring S-locks on the data. A timeout condition will occur if the S-locks cannot be obtained for all tablespaces. The short running time of this utility and the timeout feature enable it to run concurrently with other share-level processing.

QUIESCE will exclude data that reflects a pending status (i.e., CHECK, COPY, or RECOVERY), and it will terminate with a return-code of 8 ("resource not available") error message. Consequently, objects should be verified prior to execution to ensure that no outstanding pending status exists.

FIGURE 10–25
QUISCE UTILITY FORMAT (V2.1)

```
QUIESCE  TABLESPACE  dbname.tsname1...
                     dbname.tsnameN
```

QUIESCE also flushes all data buffers of tablespaces (specified in the utility control statements) to DASD and examines the data to anticipate potential problems in subsequent image copy execution (e.g., write error ranges or I/O errors). By flushing the buffers to DASD, QUIESCE enables the use of faster recovery techniques (e.g., such as recovery from volume dumps or image copies) than might otherwise have been possible. Additionally, it minimizes the failure rate of subsequent image copy efforts. Detection of such errors will produce a return-code of 4: Although the tablespaces are considered to be at a quiesce point, they will not be capable of being image copied—not all related table data is externalized.

The log RBA of the tablespace set is recorded in the DB2 catalog table, SYSIBM.SYSCOPY, as ICTYPE "Q" with a timestamp and RBA. One row is inserted for each tablespace. All rows related to the same QUIESCE execution will contain identical timestamp and RBA values. With QUIESCE, it is only necessary to query SYSIBM.SYSCOPY to determine the correct log RBA.

Figure 10–25 shows the syntax of the QUIESCE utility. Note that the tablespace set is indicated by the user and <u>not</u> <u>controlled</u> <u>by</u> <u>DB2</u>. This provides leeway to include tablespaces that are application related but not part of the same referential structure. See the REPORT utility in this section to determine which tablespaces and tables are part of a tablespace set.

RECOVER

In DB2 Version 2, RECOVER will finally allow recovery datasets to be allocated with JCL DD statements. Thus, retention will be possible for multiple dataset tape volumes.

RECOVER may be executed in conjunction with QUIESCE and REPORT to restore an entire tablespace set to a *point of consistency* or **quiesce point**. The quiesce point is designated by an RBA for each tablespace in the tablespace set to be recovered. The RBA is determined and logged by the QUIESCE utility and reported by the REPORT utility. (Presentation of both utilities is included in this chapter.)

The quiesce point holds special significance because it indicates a point in the data where referential integrity constraints were consistent among all related tablespaces (i.e., tablespace sets)—something never ensured by an

FIGURE 10–26
RECOVER TO QUIESCE POINT (v2.1)

```
RECOVER TABLESPACE dbname.tsname1...
    TABLESPACE dbname.tsnameN
    TORBA   X'string'
RECOVER
   INDEX(ALL) TABLESPACE dbname.tsname1
       ...
   INDEX(ALL) TABLESPACE dbname.tsnameN
```

image copy alone. Dubbed a **point in time recovery**, recovery to prior image copies is extended to include all changes up to the RBA in the log where data was considered consistent (i.e., the quiesce point).

Syntax for the recovery facility in DB2 Version 2 is illustrated in Figure 10–26.

Note that indices are included in the preceding syntax presentation because execution of the RECOVER utility for a quiesce point in a tablespace set will automatically place all related indices in a *recover pending* state. Also, all dependent tablespaces will be placed in a *check pending* state.

Furthermore, any non-quiesce recovery (i.e., RBA was not the quiesce point RBA, or not all of a tablespace set was recovered) will place all dependents of the tablespace set not in the recovery set in a *check pending* state. If a parent tablespace is not included in the recovery set, all dependent tablespaces (whether specifically recovered or not) will be placed in a *check pending* state. In this sense, it may be concluded that the RECOVER utility functions to set the *check pending* status on tablespaces.

RECOVER Version 2.1 also introduces the PART keyword. Recovery for index parts of a partitioned index may now be accomplished. Only a partitioned clustering index may be specified and not a simple tablespace that has gone into multiply data sets (see Figure 10–27).

FIGURE 10–27
RECOVER INDEX PART (V2.1)

```
INDEX(part_index_name)
PART integer
```

REORG

For DB2 Version 2 installations, this utility provides support for segmented tablespaces. Tables will be unloaded segment by segment, in clustering sequence or physical sequence, and appended to the unload data set. Thus, during reload, tables will be placed in contiguous segments.

This utility will fail when invoked for a tablespace currently reflecting a status of *check pending*.

REPAIR

In DB2 Version 2, REPAIR may be used to ignore constraint rules and turn off the check pending status assigned to a tablespace. No referential integrity constraint violations will be detected or corrected, making the user responsible for such considerations. The format of the request follows:

```
REPAIR
    SET TABLESPACE dbname.tsname1
    NOCHECKPEND
```

REPAIR may also be used to delete or replace a specified row with no effect on dependent rows. Additionally, primary, foreign, or independent keys may be updated with no impact on index entries. Again, the user is responsible for the ramifications of such intervention. The format of the request follows:

```
REPAIR
    LOCATE TABLESPACE dbname.tsname1
    [KEY literal | RID X'string' |
        PAGE X'string' ]
    [DELETE | REPLACE]
    REPORT
```

REPORT is a new utility, long overdue, which may be executed in two modes: TABLESPACESET or RECOVERY. This utility provides information from the hitherto inaccessible directory table, SYSIBM.SYSLGRNG.

TABLESPACESET identifies all tablespaces related to a specified tablespace with respect to referential integrity constraints. An obvious application of this utility would be the examination of relationships which could be associated with referential integrity constraint violations. Output includes the names of all tables in the tablespaces and dependents of the tables, as well as the quiesce points determined through execution of the QUIESCE utility.

The RECOVERY function of the utility returns recovery information for a specified tablespace and greatly facilitates control of point-in-time recovery. This report includes SYSIBM.SYSCOPY related information (i.e., timestamp, RBA) from the execution of COPY, LOAD, REORG, etc., utilities,

FIGURE 10–28
REPORT UTILITY FORMATS (V2.1)

```
REPORT TABLESPACESET TABLESPACE
        dbname.tsname1
        [DSNUM int | no spec]
        [CURRENT | no spec]
        [SUMMARY]
REPORT RECOVERY TABLESPACE dbname.tsname1
```

as well as other recovery information available in the SYSIBM.SYSLGRNG directory. BSDS information is also included in the output when available. REPORT also marks the ICTYPE field of nonCOPY operations with asterisks. SYSIBM.SYSCOPY records tablespace utility activity; SYSIBM.SYSLGRNG entries will list the RBAs for when a tablespace was opened for any access (e.g., START DATABASE, first SQL statement).

The syntax for the REPORT utility is given in Figure 10–28.

CHAPTER 11

SECURITY OVERVIEW

■ DB2 SECURITY ENVIRONMENT

The implementation of a security mechanism within any environment is intended to restrict access of system data to only those users having legitimate requirements for access. There is nothing controversial about this objective. The controversies arise with the attempt to balance desired restrictions with the costs incurred to achieve them—costs both financial and environmental.

The DB2 security mechanism meets two objectives: control that is effectively exercised on objects/resources at any required level (i.e., from one field in a row to a collection of TABLESPACEs) and control that is distributed on a centralized or decentralized basis.[1]

DB2 **resources** that may become the object of control include any DB2 **object** as defined in the DB2 catalog tables[2] such as data bases, tables, views, indexes, tablespaces, buffer pools, and storage groups; the invocation of most **utilities**; and the creation, modification, and invocation of **application plans**.

Every **user** of DB2 must have an authorization ID (AUTHID) provided by the subsystem connecting to it.[3] This authorization ID may be a TSO logon userid, a CICS SNT entry, an IMS signon ID, or some other ID as provided by the attaching subsystem.

Resources as they relate to users are controlled by DB2 security through issuance of authorization. **Authorization** may explicitly or implicitly

---

[1] However, the spirit of DB2 security is such that everyone and everything is guilty until proven innocent.

[2] Please refer to the introductory chapter for more detail on DB2 objects.

[3] Throughout this chapter we will use the terms AUTHID, user, and USERID interchangeably to refer to the DB2 authorization ID.

establish <u>privileges</u> (or capabilities) over DB2 resources.[4] <u>Explicit</u> authorization for use of DB2 resources is established by using two SQL statements, GRANT and REVOKE. **GRANT** provides a privilege to a user, while **REVOKE** takes it away.[5]

Privileges are categorized as single or grouped capabilities. **Single capabilities** pertain to one user and may be general or resource specific. <u>General</u> <u>capabilities</u> provide the ability to execute an action not directly tied to a specific resource. Display of data base status using the **DB2 DISPLAY** command is an example of a general capability. <u>Resource</u> <u>specific</u> <u>capabilities</u> provide access to only the resource specified in the authorization request. They include the ability of a user to GRANT the SELECT privilege over his own table to other users, or to delete rows from that table.

Grouped capabilities, in contrast, establish administrative authorities;

FIGURE 11–1
AUTHORIZATION FLOW

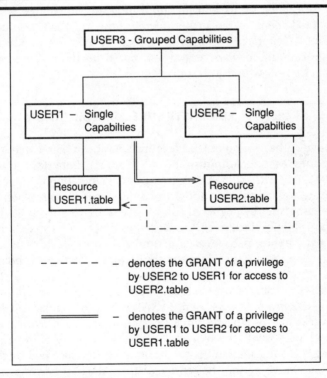

denotes the GRANT of a privilege
by USER2 to USER1 for access to
USER2.table

denotes the GRANT of a privilege
by USER1 to USER2 for access to
USER1.table

---

4 However the resources to which the authorization applies must exist before either type of authorization request may be satisfied.

5 These SQL commands are discussed in more detail within the "Data Control Language" section of this chapter.

they allow the holder to exercise a range of access requests over a pool of related resources which may have been created by more than one user. These administrative authorities include SYSADM, DBADM, DBCTRL, DBMAINT, and SYSOPR.[6]

DB2 security, therefore, establishes a connection between resources and the capabilities required to use those resources—the objective of any security implementation, as stated at the outset of this discussion.

Furthermore, DB2 security qualifies the connection between resources and capabilities with the concept of ownership. **Ownership**, in the context of security, serves to provide implicit authorization to a user. As the creator of a resource (e.g., a table), a user is automatically authorized for all privileges relating to that resource, including the extension of those privileges to other users.[7]

Authorization is automatically monitored by DB2 during several phases of user access to DB2. Examples of such phases include program preparation (e.g., DCLGEN), bind, and execution. Authorization is heavily dependent upon the DB2 catalog for its information during this function.

Figure 11–1 demonstrates the overall flow of DB2 resources and authorization. To reiterate, DB2 provides a security mechanism which allows control to be centralized or decentralized, based on the resource and user requirements for access to that resource.

■ GROUP CAPABILITIES: ADMINISTRATIVE AUTHORIZATION

Administrative authorization of DB2 resources has been segregated into three major categories: System Administration (SYSADM), Data Base Administration (DBADM, DBCTRL, DBMAINT), and System Operation (SYSOPR). Each category of authorization is composed of single user functions which have been grouped together by degree of control over DB2 resources. Such grouping of responsibilities facilitates the decentralization of capabilities while maintaining the appropriate level of centralized control of the overall DB2 environment. Recall that these are the two major objectives to be achieved by the DB2 security mechanism.

System Administration (SYSADM) provides a user with ultimate control over all DB2 resources. As such, SYSADM has the power to GRANT or REVOKE access to any DB2 resource to or from any user (with the exception of a user who owns the object). SYSADM authority is initially designated during DB2 installation. The authorization ID specified at this time (the install SYSADM) cannot be removed; that AUTHID becomes the peak

---

[6] This topic is more extensively presented in the "Administrative Authority" section of this chapter.

[7] Interestingly, such an extension of privileges demonstrates a transition from implicit to explicit authorization. The owner with implicit authorization must employ explicit authorization techniques to achieve the desired result.

of the security pyramid. Under this authority, DB2 resources are established and their use and privileges granted. Only one install SYSADM designation will exist at any time.

Once designated, the initial SYSADM user may specify additional authorization IDs as SYSADM via the GRANT command. Records of authorization granted to users are stored in one of the security tables of the catalog. The administrative authority and associated capabilities for the two types of SYSADM users are identical with one exception. Should a critical catalog table (e.g., the security table) become unavailable, the initial SYSADM user is the only SYSADM authorized to repair it. This distinction is necessary because, for the duration of such a situation, the authorization IDs of the additional SYSADM users will not be available to DB2.

Given the all-encompassing nature of SYSADM authority, the designation of candidate users with the SYSADM level of authority has great consequence for a DB2 installation. Such responsibilities are analogous to conventional definitions of data base administration, security administration, and system programming combined. Although the obvious implications point to rigid limitation of SYSADM designation, emergency authorization (i.e., alternate SYSADM users) must be considered.

The next layer of control over DB2 resources is specific to data bases. It is composed of three levels of administrative authorization: DBADM, DBCTRL, and DBMAINT. There is no limit to the number of users who may be designated at one of these three levels of control.

DBADM is the authorization level assigned to the data base adminstrator for all data bases specified in the authorization designation. This user is responsible for and has total control over these data bases and any of their dependent objects (e.g., related tables). DBADM may be implicitly obtained when creating a data base or explicitly granted by an AUTHID that holds the authority to do so. DBADM authorizations include table creation, modification of table definition and the data within the table itself, and execution of utilities such as LOAD or COPY against tables and table spaces in a DBADM authorized data base.

A **DBCTRL** user is authorized for all control given a DBADM user with two exceptions: neither a table definition nor the data within a table may be modified, unless the table in question belongs to the DBCTRL user; DBCTRL is not authorized to DROP the data base. Utilities pertaining to any tables within a data base for which DBCTRL is authorized are permissible at all levels.

Similarly, a **DBMAINT** user is authorized for all capabilities of a DBCTRL user with the exclusion of utility execution that updates tables within the data base. For our purposes, the COPY and RUNSTATS utilities are not considered to be update utilities.

Designation of DBADM, DBCTRL, and DBMAINT authorization should correspond to the level of update privileges deemed appropriate for specific data base administration functions. Production environments are apt to be more restrictive than test environments, although the level of restriction is purely installation dependent.

SYSOPR authority, as the name expresses, has operational control over DB2. The user having this level of authority, usually an MVS console operator, may issue DB2 commands such as STOP DB2, RECOVER INDOUBT, TERM UTILITY, DISPLAY, and may also start the TRACE facility. The START DB2 command has no authorization requirements, but must be entered from an MVS console. Since DB2 is not active when this command is executed, authorization cannot be verified.

The grouped capabilities of administrative authorization as presented in this section are not equivalent to the sum of the single capabilities that they represent. The ability to create and modify objects on behalf of another user, or to access tables created by another user in a data base for which a grouped capability has been established are both examples of this distinction.

Implicit Authorization Mechanism

The creation of an object implicitly establishes privileges related to it, based on the ownership concept of DB2 security. At the same time, the ability to create a DB2 object is itself a privilege that must be authorized for a user. The extent to which a user will automatically (implicitly) obtain privileges related to the DB2 object is directly dependent upon the type of authorization the user possessed for creation. To clarify, a user may receive full or partial implicit authorization as follows:

1. A user receives full implicit authorization for access of a DB2 object with the GRANT option if he or she is the original creator of the object and was not limited in authorization over the object at the time of creation. For example, a user who creates a base table qualified by the user's authorization ID has full access to that base table including update, modification of table definition, and the ability to GRANT privileges over that table to other users.

2. A user receives partial implicit authorization for a DB2 object if the user did not have full access to the object involved in the creation event.

In the previous example, our user might have granted read-only (SELECT) authority to a second user for the base table just created. Although the second user may create a view of the base table, he or she will not be authorized to update the view (assuming the second user has no other source of privileges against the base table). This restriction exists because the view object is dependent on the table object.

Other than from ownership based on creation, a user may receive implicit authorization if the user has SYSADM or DBADM administrative capabilities. Recall that these are group capabilities which extend to groups of DB2 resources.

As the peak of the security pyramid, SYSADM has total control over all DB2 resources without explicitly being granted privileges for them. The assignment of the authorization ID accomplishes the implicit authorization. The only limitation on this type of implicit authorization is the inability to revoke access to a DB2 object from the creator of the object. **SYSADM may never REVOKE object access from its creator.**

DBADM receives implicit authorization for access to tables within a data base by virtue of the fact that this level has been specifically designated to have administrative authority over the data base.

Some examples of implied privileges are: the bindor of a plan obtains execute authority for that plan; the creator of a tablespace may create tables within that tablespace and may also execute most utilities for both the tablespace and its table(s); and the creator of a data base, or a person with DBADM authority for that data base, has full authority for all the objects within that data base (he/she may even create a table for a different AUTHID).

Explicit Authorization Mechanism: Data Control Language

Authorization of privileges for a resource may be issued explicitly through the DB2 authorization mechanism of Data Control Language. As with the other components of SQL, Data Control Language (DCL) will always have an action and an object. Fortunately, there are only two actions, GRANT and REVOKE. **GRANT** provides an authority from one user to another, while **REVOKE** takes it away. Execution of the REVOKE request has a cascading effect on the resource in question—any users who explicitly derived their privileges solely from the user whose authorization is being revoked will, in turn, lose all privileges to the resource.

These statements may be issued at any time, as long as DB2 is active. Furthermore, two physical constraints impact the timing of an authorization request. The GRANT request requires that the resource for which privileges will be granted has been allocated. Similarly, all authorizations obtained for an object which has been dropped are automatically revoked by DB2. The requested actions become effective immediately after execution has completed.

In order to execute a GRANT request, you must be the creator of the object (implicit authorization), have a grouped capability (SYSADM, DBADM, etc.) with the implied authority, or have had the authority explicitly granted to you. Execution of the REVOKE request requires that the requester be either the original grantor of that privilege or a SYSADM user.

The privileges that may be assigned through GRANT and REVOKE fall into five classes: DATABASE, PLAN, SYSTEM, TABLE and USE.

The **DATABASE** class will permit the invocation of the START or STOP data base command, execution of data base related utilities, the creation of tablespaces and tables, and the granting of data base administration privileges (i.e., DBADM, DBCTRL, DBMAINT).

PLAN privileges are BIND and EXECUTE. (Please note that BINDADD is not included as a PLAN privilege; it is actually a SYSTEM privilege.)

The **SYSTEM** related privileges are administrative authorities (i.e., SYSADM, SYSOPR), authority to execute the RECOVER commands for either DB2 or BSDS (Boot Strap Data Set), the authority to create data bases and storage groups, and the ability to add new PLANs, and other system privileges.

TABLE privileges allow for the modification of a table definition—not table creation. They include ALTER, SELECT, INSERT, UPDATE, DELETE, INDEX and ALL. The ALL privilege includes INDEX, the creation of new indexes. Also, UPDATE may be column specific.

The **USE** class grants authority to use buffer pools, storage groups, and tablespaces. Note that if you are the creator of the tablespace or hold DBADM or DBCTRL authority, then you hold an implicit privilege for use of the tablespace. Of the five, USE has a unique format.

Examples of explicit authorization requests follow. The syntax of each explicit authorization example precedes the example as specified.

FIGURE 11–2
GRANT PRIVILEGE FORMAT

```
        GRANT privilege ON object/resource
                TO authorization-ID I PUBLIC
                [WITH GRANT OPTION];
example:
                GRANT SELECT ON TABLE TEST_TABLE_33
                    TO TSOID02;
```

The example in Figure 11–2 grants a table class privilege. The SELECT authority on table TEST_TABLE_33 is being given to TSOID02. The table name is unqualified and must therefore exist under the AUTHID of the person executing this statement.

FIGURE 11–3
GRANT USE FORMAT

```
        GRANT USE OF object/resource
                TO authorization-ID I PUBLIC
                [WITH GRANT OPTION];
example:
                GRANT USE OF BUFFERPOOL BPO
                    TO PUBLIC;
```

The example in Figure 11–3 grants the use of BUFFERPOOL BP0 to everyone (PUBLIC). It may be executed by a user holding SYSADM authority or by a user who received this privilege with the WITH GRANT OPTION.

FIGURE 11–4
REVOKE PRIVILEGE FORMAT

```
       REVOKE  privilege ON object/resource
               FROM authorization-ID I PUBLIC
               [BY  authorization-ID I ALL];
example:
               REVOKE DBADM ON DATABASE BUCFH01
                  FROM AUTHID1
                  BY AUTHIDA;
```

The DATABASE example in Figure 11–4 revokes the DBADM privilege from user AUTHID1. For this request to succeed, user (AUTHIDA) must hold the SYSADM privilege.

FIGURE 11–5
REVOKE USE FORMAT

```
       REVOKE USE OF object/resource
               FROM authorization-ID I PUBLIC
               [BY  authorization-ID I ALL];
example:
               REVOKE USE OF STOGROUP TSTSG01
                  FROM PUBLIC;
```

The USE example in Figure 11–5 revokes from PUBLIC the authorization to use the named STOGROUP. The AUTHID executing this statement must have either created the STOGROUP or received the authority with the WITH GRANT OPTION.

■ APPLICATION ENVIRONMENT CREATION SCENARIO

The easiest way to understand the relationships between these classes is to walk through a typical application development environment creation scenario. We first define the five requirements for the environment.

1. Control must be decentralized to the project level.
2. Table privileges may be granted by the owner or the local administrator.
3. Each user must be isolated.
4. Any table may be read by any team member.
5. Tables may only be modified by their owners.

Initially, one candidate (AUTHID) is chosen as the local DBA for the application. In our example, this AUTHID will be PRJDBA1. A person with total control over the DB2 environment (i.e., SYSADM authority) would execute the DCL illustrated in Figure 11–6.

FIGURE 11–6
APPLICATION ENVIRONMENT CREATION SCENARIO

```
#1   GRANT USE OF BUFFERPOOL BP0 TO PUBLIC;
#2   GRANT USE OF STOGROUP APPLST1 TO PRJDBA1
        WITH GRANT OPTION;
#3   GRANT CREATDBA TO PRJDBA1;
#4   GRANT BINDADD TO PRJDBA1
        WITH GRANT OPTION;
#5   GRANT SELECT ON TABLE    SYSIBM.xxxxxxxxxx
                             ,SYSIBM.xxxxxxxxxx
                             ,..........
        TO PRJDBA1;
```

Statements (1) and (2) grant USE class privileges, statements (3) and (4) grant SYSTEM privileges, and statement (5) grants a TABLE privilege.

Statement (1) is one of the few times you will see anything granted to PUBLIC. Before a user may execute any SQL statements, he must be authorized for use of a bufferpool. This grant to PUBLIC will reduce administrative bottlenecks by allowing current and future users to utilize BP0 without having to re execute this statement. Remember, even if bufferpool use is granted to PUBLIC, other resources will be required before a query, for example, may be executed.

Statement (2) will allow the local DBA use of the specified STOGROUP. Of course, the STOGROUP had to exist prior to invocation of this statement. The WITH GRANT OPTION delegates further authorization of its use to the same local DBA. Thus, the applications staff will be limited to creating tablespaces within this STOGROUP. This, in turn, will facilitate space management.

Statement (3) will allow the local DBA to create data bases! The first concerns of the DBA may well be, "Where may these data bases be created and how many may be created?" With respect to the first half of the question, recall that data bases are not physical objects, but merely entries in a DB2 catalog.[8] To answer the second part of the question, as many data bases as are required may be created—at least one per application team member. Note that all TABLESPACEs must be created in the APPLST1 STOGROUP. Again, control is decentralized to the project level.

Statement (4) will allow PLANs to be added. The WITH GRANT OPTION delegates control of application PLANs to the project level.

Statement (5) will allow the local DBA to SELECT information from the DB2 catalogs. In short, environmental control cannot be decentralized without all the required tools. Our project DBA must query the DB2 catalogs to monitor space utilization, PLAN use and age, or other catalog abuses. The GRANT option is not specified; its omission serves to reduce catalog lock contention by limiting the number of reads that may be executed. A page held with a share lock (SELECT) and its related indexes cannot be updated for table/tablespace creation, RUNSTATS, and the like until the share lock is released. Recall that an exclusive lock, required for update operations, may not be obtained when a share lock is in effect.

As our scenario progresses, recall that as far as the DB2 security mechanism is concerned, no action against system data will be allowed unless the user has explicitly or implicitly been granted authorization to do so.

At this point, the system administrator has delegated all control of the application environment to the local DBA. He, in turn, will delegate application specific control to individual users. In other words, actual tablespace, table, and index creation may be performed by each team member. Our resident DBA would then execute the DDL and DCL shown in Figure 11–7.

FIGURE 11–7
APPLICATION ENVIRONMENT CREATION SCENARIO

```
#1   CREATE DATABASE DBAPPL01
            STOGROUP APPLST1
            BUFFERPOOL BPO;
#2   GRANT DBADM ON DBAPPL01
            TO TSOIDxx;
#3   GRANT BINDADD TO TSOIDxx;
```

Statement (1) is DDL and does not grant a privilege; statement (2) grants a DATABASE privilege; and statement (3) grants a SYSTEM privilege.

Statement (1) creates a data base and assigns it a default STOGROUP and

[8] Refer to the **Data Definition Language** chapter for presentation of this concept.

BUFFERPOOL. At least one data base will be created for each team member. The executing AUTHID must hold the CREATEDBA privilege, which was issued to the PRJDBA1 ID in the prior example.

Statement (2) gives the individual (TSOIDxx) complete control of the data base and all resources that will be created within it. In this manner, the local DBA avoids personally having to create tablespaces and having to grant their use. For a medium size project (five people with 15 tables each), this will alleviate many administrative headaches for the local DBA. Having created the data base, the local DBA holds DBADM authority WITH GRANT OPTION for the data base. **Caution:** the user who received the DBADM authority may also DROP the data base. The extension of DBADM authority may therefore require more consideration. An alternative solution may be to grant DBCTRL authorization for a data base rather than risk the excesses of DBADM authority.

Statement (3) will allow the team member (TSOIDxx) to add new PLANs. WITH GRANT OPTION was not specified so that plan additions can be controlled.

Some overall comments:

1. Each data base has 2 users with DBADM authority. PRJDBA1 obtained DBADM while creating the data base. TSOIDxx was explicitly granted DBADM by PRJDBA1.

2. DBADM authority over a data base permits dependent object creation, utility execution, and DB2 commands.

3. In order to DROP (delete) all of one user's tablespaces, tables, and views, merely DROP the data base. DB2 will remove all objects of that data base. This is great for cleanup.

4. Both PRJDBA1 and TSOIDxx may grant table class privileges to others on tables within data base DBAPPL01.

5. Both PRJDBA1 and TSOIDxx may create tables within the related data base for themselves or any other users (implied tablespace use).

6. When a PLAN is added, only the creator of the PLAN, an AUTHID holding BIND authority, or SYSADM may FREE (delete) it.

The application is now established. All stated environmental requirements have been met, except the fourth, "Any table may be read by any team member." There are two ways to accomplish this (see Figure 11–8).

Both statements in Figure 11–8 grant TABLE class privileges.

Statement (1) requires that each team member maintain a current list of project AUTHIDs and that the SELECT privilege be granted for every new person. However, statement (2) need be executed only once. In a development climate, where security is not an issue, the choice is clear. GRANT SELECT AUTHORITY TO PUBLIC.

Finally, our application is complete and all requirements have been met.

FIGURE 11–8
APPLICATION ENVIRONMENT CREATION SCENARIO

```
#1  GRANT SELECT ON TABLE    SOME_TABLE_1
                           , SOME_TABLE_2
                           , . . . . . . .
         TO TSOID1, TSOID2, TSOIDn;
#2  GRANT SELECT ON TABLE    SOME_TABLE_1
                           , SOME_TABLE_2
                           , . . . . . . .
         TO PUBLIC;
```

Control has been decentralized, yet each team member is restricted to a specific STOGROUP and is isolated to a unique data base for his or her own tablespaces and tables.

In a much tighter environment, tablespaces may be created and controlled by users with SYSADM authority, who will then have to grant their use to individual AUTHIDs explicitly. The resulting delay may be unacceptable in most situations.

■ GRANT AND REVOKE EXAMPLES

The following illustrations will show how the results of a REVOKE statement are dependent on either the AUTHID of the issuer of the GRANT request or the time when it was executed. Additionally, all GRANT requests have to include the WITH GRANT OPTION. All object names (e.g., tables) must be qualified if the person invoking the DCL is not the object creator."

EXAMPLE 11–1
MULTIPLE GRANTS BY SAME USER

Time		Action
11:00	usr1	GRANT SELECT ON TABLE T_PROJ TO usra
11:08	usr1	GRANT SELECT ON TABLE T_PROJ TO usra
11:15	usr1	REVOKE SELECT ON TABLE T_PROJ FROM usra

usra receives the same privilege from **usr1** twice. At a later time the privilege is REVOKEd by **usr1**.

Result: The privilege is revoked because the last chronological action was the REVOKE.

EXAMPLE 11–2
MULTIPLE GRANTS BY DIFFERENT USERS

Time		Action
12:00	usr1	GRANT SELECT ON TABLE T_PROJ TO usra
12:05	usr2	GRANT SELECT ON TABLE T_PROJ TO usra
13:10	usr1	REVOKE SELECT ON TABLE T_PROJ FROM usra

usra receives the same privilege from **usr1** and **usr2**. At a later time the privilege is revoked by **usr1**. Both **usr1** and **usr2** obtained the privilege from another AUTHID (creator?).
Result: The privilege is not revoked because the privilege is still in effect from **usr2**.

EXAMPLE 11–3
CASCADING REVOKE DEPENDENCY

Time		Action
12:00	usr1	GRANT SELECT ON TABLE T_PROJ TO usra
12:05	usra	GRANT SELECT ON TABLE T_PROJ TO usrx
13:10	usr1	REVOKE SELECT ON TABLE T_PROJ FROM usra

usra receives a privilege from **usr1**, and then **usra** GRANTs the identical privilege to **usrx**. Later **usr1** revokes the privilege that was originally given to **usra**.

Result: The privilege is revoked from both **usra** and **usrx** because the principle of a REVOKE is to reset authorities to what they were prior to the related GRANT.

EXAMPLE 11–4
GRANT AND REVOKE TIME DEPENDENCY WITHOUT LOSS

Time		Action
10:00	usr1	GRANT SELECT ON TABLE T_PROJ TO usra
10:20	usra	GRANT SELECT ON TABLE T_PROJ TO usrb
11:00	usrx	GRANT SELECT ON TABLE T_PROJ TO usra
13:10	usrx	REVOKE SELECT ON TABLE T_PROJ FROM usra

usra receives a privilege from **usr1**, then **usra** gives the same privilege to **usrb**. Later, **usrx** GRANTs the same select privilege to **usra**. Finally, **usrx** revokes the select privilege.

Result: The privilege is not revoked from either **usra** and **usrb** because **usra** received the select from **usr1** prior to the GRANT executed by **usrx**.

EXAMPLE 11–5
GRANT AND REVOKE TIME DEPENDENCY WITH LOSS

Time		Action
15:00	usr1	GRANT SELECT ON TABLE T_PROJ TO usra
16:20	usra	GRANT SELECT ON TABLE T_PROJ TO usrb
17:00	usrx	GRANT SELECT ON TABLE T_PROJ TO usra
17:10	usr1	REVOKE SELECT ON TABLE T_PROJ FROM usra

usra receives a privilege from **usr1**; then **usra** gives the same privilege to **usrb**. Later, **usrx** grants the same select privilege to **usra**. Now for the difference from example 4: **usr1** revokes the select privilege.

Result: The privilege is revoked from **usrb** and not **usra** because **usra** received the select principle from **usrx** subsequent to the initial extension of the privilege form **usr1**. The REVOKE removed the path through which **usrb** received the privilege. However, **usra** retains the select privilege through a second path established by **usrx**.

By now you have a healthy respect for the potential impact of multiple levels of privileges. The previous examples, by no means a worst case scenario, were intended to give you a flavor of DB2 security.

■ PLAN PRIVILEGES

To review, a plan entry must exist in the DB2 catalog tables in order to execute any program which contains SQL statements. An existing plan must be replaced (updated) whenever the SQL statements in its respective program have been modified.[9] A plan must be rebound to reflect authorization changes, table additions, index additions or deletions—in general, any events that have rendered the previous plan invalid without modification of SQL statements. (REBIND is not an option for plans that must reflect changes to SQL statements, as the modified DBRMs reflecting the SQL changes will not be incorporated into a plan that is rebound).[10] Additionally, a plan may be deleted and all associated execute authority over it eliminated.

Certain privileges are required for execution of the commands which accomplish the DB2 catalog updates for the plan; specifically, the system privilege of BINDADD and the plan privileges of BIND (REPLACE) and EXECUTE.

---

[9] Of course we are using the term *modification* to encompass additions and deletions in this discussion.

[10] This topic is presented in detail in the "Typical BIND Scenario" example in this Chapter.

As mentioned earlier, the system privilege of BINDADD must be held by an AUTHID prior to adding any new plans. The addition of a new plan becomes the <u>initial</u> <u>point</u> <u>of</u> <u>ownership</u> of that plan. A user with SYSADM authority has implicit BINDADD authority. All other users must receive this authority explicitly.

PLAN privileges are required to modify, delete, or execute the plan subsequently. Plan privileges include BIND (REPLACE) and EXECUTE. The **BIND** privilege over a plan enables a user to execute the BIND, REBIND, and FREE DSN subcommands. The **EXECUTE** privilege permits the use of the RUN DSN subcommand. Of course, a SYSADM user always holds both PLAN privileges over all plans. The creator of a plan always has BIND and EXECUTE authority with the GRANT OPTION.[11]

Some overall comments:

1. GRANT of the BIND privilege does not by itself enable execution.
2. EXECUTE authority is implicitly obtained by binding a plan, but must be explicitly granted to AUTHIDs that have not executed a BIND of that plan.
3. Any user with the BIND privilege may also FREE (delete) a plan.
4. To save prior EXECUTE privileges, RETAIN must be specified at bind time.
5. REBIND may be executed to pick up the latest RUNSTATS statistics and/or Index access.

The typical bind scenario shown in Table 11–1 illustrates the implications of plan privileges and binding, both with and without the RETAIN parameter. We now discuss this scenario in the AUTHID action sequence. Actions will be identified by the bracketed numbers in Table 11–1.

TABLE 11–1
TYPICAL BIND SCENARIO

AUTHID	Action
AUTHaa	[1] BIND PLAN(TSTPLAN) ACTION(ADD)
	[2] GRANT BIND, EXECUTE ON PLAN TSTPLAN TO AUTHbb, AUTHcc
AUTHbb	[3] BIND PLAN(TSTPLAN) ACTION(REPLACE)
	[4] GRANT BIND ON PLAN TSTPLAN TO AUTHmm, AUTHpp
AUTHmm	[5] BIND PLAN(TSTPLAN) ACTION(REPLACE) RETAIN

---

[11] The last bindor of a plan (i.e., the creator) becomes the owner of the plan.

AUTHaa   [1] User AUTHaa creates a new plan ACTION(ADD). Only AUTHaa may bind or execute the PLAN.

[2] BIND and EXECUTE authority are given to AUTHbb and AUTHcc. All three users may now bind, free, or execute the plan.

AUTHbb   [3] User AUTHbb does a BIND(REPLACE). Since AUTHbb did not specify RETAIN, only he may execute the plan. All other execute privileges have been lost! However, as of VER 1.3, bind privileges are still held. Recall that the bind privilege also includes the ability to free a plan!

[4] BIND authority is given to AUTHmm and AUTHpp.

At this point, AUTHaa, AUTHbb, AUTHcc, AUTHmm, and AUTHpp may bind or free the plan, but only AUTHbb may execute the plan.

AUTHmm   [5] User AUTHmm performs a BIND (REPLACE) with RETAIN. All AUTHIDs may BIND or FREE, but only AUTHmm and AUTHbb may EXECUTE the PLAN.

The preceding scenario was only an example, but it should serve as motivation to keep things simple.[12]

■ GENERIC AUTHORIZATION IDS

At this point, let's reinforce a concept inferable from prior discussion of security issues: Authorization IDs (AUTHIDs) are very tightly coupled to TSO userIDs (TSOIDs). As demonstrated by the preceding scenarios, an AUTHID/TSOID combination is responsible for the installation of DB2, the establishment of an application environment, and the granting of plan privileges.

Administrative concerns arise with respect to the assignments of authorization IDs and consequently, TSO userIDs within the DB2 security environment. Consider the impact of a shift in responsibility, or worse still, termination of the individual(s) whose AUTHIDs were designated for administrative security privileges. Given the significance of administrative authorization over DB2 resources,[13] the individual possessing the administrative capabilities probably had been responsible for several DB2 objects, and may have represented the starting point for many privileges. The dropping of any

---

12 Note that we did not discuss the ramifications of unqualified tables within the related program. Please refer to the "Plan Considerations" section of the **Practical Procedures** chapter for more discussion of this issue.

13 Please refer to a preceding section of this chapter, "Group Capabilities: Administrative Authorization," for a review of this topic.

of the objects controlled by the user's auhorization ID would result in the loss of all related privileges extended to other users.

Typically, organizations have assigned a new individual to the vacated position, and allowed him or her use of the existing TSOID. In light of the current trend toward single corporate IDs (i.e., where TSO userIDs are related to a person and not a position), this procedure becomes administratively impossible. The solution: Generic authorization-IDs.

A **Generic authorization ID** (AUTHID) remains with the position, not with any one individual. When the individual assigned the generic AUTHID no longer serves in the intended security capacity for any reason, his personal USERID goes with him. However, the generic AUTHID is passed to the person who will take over the position. Both people will still own the TSO userids originally issued to them (i.e., assuming, of course, that a termination is not involved), but administrative capabilities will have been shifted to represent the change in individual reponsibility. In this manner, administrative and internal auditing requirements can be satisfied.

There are two methods available for implementation of generic AUTHIDs:

1. An installation written DB2 authorization exit.
2. The creation of additional TSO userIDs for each position.

The authorization exit alternative will require more work to set up, but less effort to maintain, than the additional TSOIDs. For every TSOID established, access rules must be defined and maintained. Further, consider that a unique AUTHID may have simultaneous connections with DB2, but a TSOID may be logged on only once. Thus, multiple TSO userID assignments may allow multiple users to maintain the same environment simultaneously. Figure 11–9 shows two different TSOIDs being changed to the same AUTHID by the authorization exit.

There are two major functions of an AUTHID exit program: (1) intercepting the TSO userID supplied by MVS and substituting a specified DB2 generic ID in its place, and (2) verifying that the substitution is permitted. A user may request that a substitution take place, but it may not be allowed within the context of security administration.

Typically an authorization exit may be invoked with a TSO CLIST or automatically during CONNECT processing. The substitution verification may be controlled by tables within the CLIST. But the actual substitution must be performed by an assembler language program that is reentrant, has been MVS authorized for protect key 7 storage, has a CSECT name of DSN3@ATH, has addressing mode 31, and has residency mode ANY.[14] A CLIST will allow one TSOID to substitute different generic IDs.

---

[14] Please refer to the IBM *System Planning and Administration Guide* manual for an itemization of current requirements.

FIGURE 11–9
AUTHORIZATION EXIT EXAMPLE

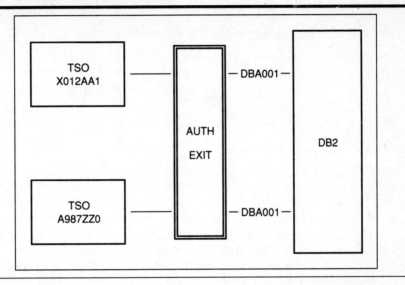

When DB2 is installed, an IBM supplied default authorization exit (DSN3@ATH) is included. Its purpose is to provide an AUTHID for TSO foreground and background applications. Its code may be found within the sample source library provided by IBM.

In conclusion, the authors recommend the use of AUTHID exits over creation of additional TSO IDs.

■ DB2 SECURITY ENVIRONMENT: MVS CONSIDERATIONS

Overview

Since DB2 is not isolated from the effects of other security facilities, the subject of this section is to introduce some environmental considerations as they apply to the DB2 security mechanism. DB2 normally coexists in an MVS installation with several other components to make up the overall security environment.

Other components include, but are not limited to MVS Resource Access Control Facility (RACF), CICS Sign-on Names Table (SNT), the IMS security generation process, and even the Subsystem Vector Table (SVT) (Figure 11–10).

Our discussion will begin with the SVT. Simply stated, one subsystem (TSO) cannot communicate with another subsystem (DB2) unless the subsystems are known to one another. In this case, TSO must know the correct Subsystem ID (SSID) for DB2; and that SSID must have been entered

FIGURE 11-10
MVS SUBSYSTEMS

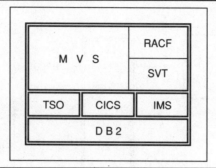

in the SVT. This SVT protocol is the method through which most subsystems communicate. Moreover, the same technique is used by IMS dependent regions to communicate with their related control regions.

Within TSO, the Subsystem ID for DB2 is specified on the DB2I defaults panel. During an initial session of DB2I/SPUFI, it is not uncommon for a user to stumble across the defaults panel and unknowingly change the SSID to DB2. To further confuse the issue, the following message is generated by DB2I/SPUFI: "XXXX is not active", where "XXXX" is the SSID specified on the default panel. The baffled new DB2 user will likely contact the DBA to inform him that "DB2 is not active". After confirming that this isn't the case, the DBA should politely request that the user correct his defaults panel!

The remainder of this general security discussion will deal with individual USERIDs and their use with subsystems. Be aware that there is currently a move under way nationally to establish one CORPORATE ID per user within a company. This means that one ID will be used to gain access to CICS, IMS, TSO, etc.

The CICS Sign-on Names Table (SNT)

The CICS Sign-on Names Table (SNT) is composed of a list of USERIDs and their related transactions. In order to process transactions, an entry must exist that ties a USERID to a specific transaction code. Additionally, terminals may be limited to specific transactions. Of course, when an operator signs on to CICS, the appropriate Subsystem ID must be known.

IMS Sign-on Facility

IMS also has a sign-on facility that functions much like the CICS Sign-on Names Table. Like CICS, this facility may also restrict terminals to specific transactions.

TSO Considerations

In order to use TSO, the USERID must exist in the User Attribute Dataset (UADS). Additionally, the TSO user may be functionally restricted by his respective logon PROC.

Furthermore, each of the above subsystems will most likely require its own password from the same physical user. However, if corporatewide passwords are in effect, the same USERID/password combination may be used across all MVS environments and all subsystems. If a password is changed while logging on to TSO, then the password change will be reflected for all other subsystem accesses.

■ DB2 SECURITY MECHANISM

Version 2.1 Considerations

With DB2 Version 2.1, grouped AUTHIDs will facilitate plan execute authority maintenance and implementation. New security features of this release will allow a user to perform the functions of a different AUTHID, thus separating the owner from the creator of a DB2 object. This feature allows AUTHIDs to be function-oriented and less user specific.

New Authorization Exits

DB2 Version 2 utilizes the existing group RACF authorization facility as well as two exit routines invoked during **IDENTIFY** and **SIGNON** to establish a **composite AUTHID** available to TSO, IMS, and CICS sessions.[15] This composite AUTHID is simply the user's **primary AUTHID** (the default) plus any **secondary AUTHID(s)** included in the security exit routines. A maximum of 245 secondary AUTHIDs may be specified. (See Figure 11–11.)

Composite AUTHID

Consequently, an administrative composite AUTHID may be tailored to the specific functional requirements for a group of DB2 users, distinct from the privileges associated with one user. Functional composite AUTHIDs will thus minimize the number of GRANT requests and rows required within the DB2 security catalog table; any authorization associated with one AUTHID in the security exit routine will then apply to the composite AUTHID itself, essentially making it the union of all individual privileges (i.e., **composite privileges**—see Figure 11–12).

---

[15] The IMS component of the SIGNON authorization exit was not functional within DB2 Version 2.1 at this writing.

FIGURE 11–11
BASIC AUTHID RELATIONSHIPS V2.1

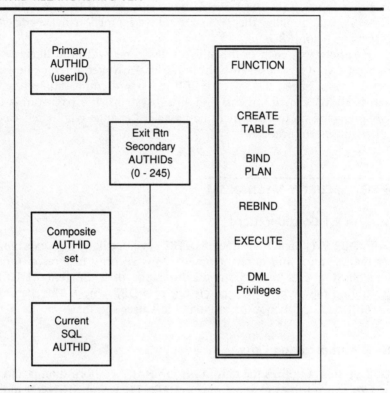

FIGURE 11–12
COMPOSITE PRIVILEGES V2.1

UserID	Secondary AUTHID	Composite Privilege
UserIDA	HUMRES MKTG ACCTG PROJST	Human Resources Marketing Accounting Project Status UserID A
UserIDB	HUMRES	Human Resources UserID B
UserIDC	HUMRES PROJST	Human Resources Project Status UserID C

- UserIDA — is a director requiring access to human resources information, accounting data, marketing data, and project status information.
- UserIDB — is a personnel employee requiring access to human resources information only.
- UserIDC — is a project manager requiring access to human resources information and project status information.

SQL AUTHID

For functions requiring that a specific AUTHID be identified (i.e., Dynamic SQL such as CREATE, GRANT, or REVOKE functions, as well as unqualified SELECT requests), the SQL AUTHID[16] may be (re)set by executing a user-written authorization exit routine or the following new SQL statement:

```
SET CURRENT SQLID = 'compid';
```

The SQL AUTHID, *compid*, may be any one of the individual AUTHIDs which make up the composite AUTHID. It may be supplied as a string constant or as a host variable. DB2 will default to the primary AUTHID in effect as the SQL AUTHID. The SQL AUTHID will remain in effect until

1. A new primary ID is established (i.e., new SIGNON)
2. A new SET statement is executed
3. The end of the DB2 session occurs.

DB2 Object Creation

In prior releases of DB2, creation of DB2 objects was performed by the AUTHID, who was also destined to become the owner of the object. The only exception was for special privileges assigned to administrative AUTHIDs (e.g., SYSADM, DBADM).

With DB2 Version 2.1, one AUTHID may create DB2 objects for another AUTHID to be known as the **owner** as long as (1) both AUTHIDS exist in the same composite set, and (2) the would-be owner AUTHID possesses the create privileges exercised on his or her behalf. The AUTHID to become the owner of the DB2 object(s) must be designated as the current SQLID at the time of the create request. From the point of creation forward, the owner will be designated as **CREATOR** in DB2 catalog tables and will have full ownership privileges and the GRANT option. The original AUTHID exercising the create function will be designated as the **CREATEDBY (BOUNDBY)** AUTHID in DB2 catalog tables, and will not have explicit ownership privileges.

DB2 objects subject to extended create capabilities include tables, views, synonyms, tablespaces, data bases, and stogroups. Corresponding DB2 catalog tables containing the new columns, CREATEDBY/CREATOR are

---

[16] Note that the SQL AUTHID applies to dynamic SQL only, and may not be used within QMF.

SYSIBM.SYSDATABASE

SYSIBM.SYSINDEXES

SYSIBM.SYSSYNONYMS

SYSIBM.SYSTABLES

SYSIBM.SYSTABLESPACE

SYSIBM.SYSTOGROUP

SYSIBM.SYSPLAN contains the column BOUNDBY, rather than CREATED-BY, although CREATOR does exist to store the ownership AUTHID (see Figure 11–13).

FIGURE 11–13
COMPOSITE PRIVILEGE CREATE

UserID	Action Requested	Accept/Reject
UserIDA	CREATE TABLE ACCTG_TABL	Accept
UserIDB	CREATE TABLE USERIDB_TABL	Accept
UserIDC	CREATE TABLE MKTG_TABL	Reject

- UserIDA — derives the create privilege from the ACCTG secondary AUTHID supplied via the security exit routine.
- UserIDB — derives the create privilege implicitly from his or her userid. Even if the security exit routine did not supply any secondary AUTHIDs, this implicit privilege would remain.
- UserIDC — does not derive the create privilege for MKTG from the secondary AUTHID security exit routine or from his or her userid. Therefore, create privileges for MKTG do not exist for this user.

PLAN

Specific to BIND authorization requirements, DB2 Version 2.1 has introduced the concept of plan ownership as distinct from that of plan bindor. The primary (LOGON) AUTHID invoking the BIND process has the capability to assign all privileges to another AUTHID by designating the second AUTHID as the OWNER/CREATOR of the plan.

If the OWNER is specified during the bind process, the designated AUTHID must be one AUTHID from the composite AUTHID list. Furthermore, the designated OWNER of the plan must be authorized for all SQL in the DBRM, as well as for the bind function itself. Let us be very clear on this point: The AUTHID designated as owner may not derive any authorizations for BIND or DBRM requirements from the composite privilege set;

the OWNER AUTHID must be totally self-sufficient for all authorizations required for the plan in question. In contrast, the primary AUTHID invoking the bind process need not hold any authorizations specific to the plan being created; the primary AUTHID need only be associated with the designated OWNER through the same composite AUTHID set. The primary AUTHID will be identified as the CREATEDBY or BOUNDBY AUTHID in the DB2 catalog tables SYSIBM.SYSTABLES and SYSIBM.SYSPLAN, respectively. The OWNER AUTHID will be identified as the CREATOR in the same catalog tables and will hold all privileges afforded the CREATOR of a plan in prior versions of DB2. All AUTHIDs in the composite set will hold EXECUTE privilege for the plan.

If the OWNER is not specified during the bind process, the primary AUTHID must be authorized for all SQL in the DBRM as well as the bind function itself. In this case, composite privileges do not come into play for bind processing at all. The primary AUTHID will be identified as the CREATEDBY or BOUNDBY AUTHID in the DB2 catalog tables SYSIBM.SYS-TABLES and SYSIBM.SYSPLAN, respectively, and the primary AUTHID will be identified as the CREATOR in both catalog tables.

For REBIND or FREE processing, the same conditions as those detailed for BIND apply when OWNER is specified for the request. In addition, the old owner retains BIND and EXECUTE privileges with GRANT OPTION for the plan. However, a difference in impact is felt in cases where no OWNER is specified. In the latter case, the primary AUTHID, rather than requiring all authorizations for the DBRM and BIND request, need only derive such authorization from the composite privilege set. In other words, no self-sufficiency of authorizations applies in this instance. Care must be exercised in REBIND processing, since the former owner of the plan (according to the SYSIBM.SYSPLAN catalog table) retains ownership by default, but may not be appropriate as the qualification for DB2 table, view, and synonym names. Recall that holders of the BIND privilege also hold the FREE (implied) privilege (See Figure 11–14).

FIGURE 11–14
COMPOSITE PRIVILEGE BIND V2.1

UserID	Action Requested	Accept/Reject
UserIDA	BIND PLAN (ACCTGPL) OWNER (ACCTG)	Reject
UserIDB	BIND PLAN (HUMRESPL) OWNER (HUMRES)	Accept
UserIDC	BIND PLAN (HUMRESPL)	Reject

- UseridC — does not derive the BIND privilege for ACCTG from his or her composite privilege set. Therefore, BIND privileges to establish ACCTG as the owner of the plan do not exist for this user.
- UserIDC — does derive the BIND privilege for HUMRES from his or her composite privilege set. Therefore, BIND privileges to establish HUMRES as the owner of the plan do exist for this user. Furthermore, HUMRES, as one of the composite set, is self-sufficient for all BIND and EXECUTE privileges for this plan. The BIND requrest will be accepted.
- UserIDC — does derive the BIND privilege for HUMRES from his or her composite privilege set. However, HUMRES is not designated as the owner of this plan. Since UserIDC is not self-sufficient for all BIND and EXECUTE privileges for this plan, the BIND request will be rejected.

Authorization Exit Routines

Authorization exit routines are invoked at two different points of authorization processing: connection (DSN3@ATH) and sign-on (DSN3@SGN). Connection is the actual process of establishing a DB2 session prior to issuing any other requests of DB2. Sign-on processing, in contrast, occurs subsequent to connection processing. It establishes AUTHIDs and the authority necessary for IMS and CICS users to access plans via the AUTHIDs.

Both authorization exit routines function to restrict access to DB2, as well as to define primary, secondary, and current SQL AUTHIDs. UserIDs default to primary AUTHIDs unless explicitly replaced by exit routine processing. Similarly, secondary AUTHIDs are optional within the exit routines, although the routines themselves are invoked without option.

As in the prior version of DB2, RACF (or other security processors) may be integrated into connection evaluation. If integrated, RACF receives control before the connection exit routine. Once invoked, the connection exit routine evaluates the request made of the appropriate CALL ATTACH facility (i.e., TSO, CICS, IMS). If the connection request succeeds, further access capabilities will be determined based on the user's authorization for application execution.

If sign-on to IMS or CICS is requested, resource access control processing will pass control to the IMS or CICS attach facility. At this point, the CICS sign-on exit routine will be invoked.[17] Again, further application access evaluation will occur beyond this point.

Note that different transactions can execute the same plan by invoking sign-on with another primary AUTHID. The same transaction may request a different plan by invoking sign-on processing with the same primary AUTHID.

Both authorization exit routines receive input through two parameter lists: the Exit Parameter List (EXPL) and the Authorization ID List (AIDL).

---

[17] IMS attach support for the sign-on exit routine is not available at this writing.

The Exit Parameter List indicates items such as the subsystem name and the user connection name and type. The Authorization Id List provides the primary AUTHID, current SQL AUTHID, and the number of secondary AUTHIDs, as well as addressability to them. The primary AUTHID of the AIDL parameter list is defaulted to a resource access control value if active (or to IMS or CICS value, if during sign-on); otherwise, the primary AUTHID is set to blanks. Both the current SQL AUTHID and secondary AUTHID fields are set to blanks.

Default exit routines may be replaced by versions modified as appropriate for the installation. IBM supplies sample source code for the same.

Summary

In summary, DB2 Version 2.1 differentiates between creator and owner on a dynamic and static SQL basis. The owner in dynamic SQL situations is either the current SQL AUTHID by default or an explicit qualifier chosen from the composite AUTHID set. For static SQL creation, the plan owner retains object ownership by default unless an explicit qualifier is designated and the plan owner is authorized to create the DB2 objects on behalf of the owner candidate. The current SQL AUTHID is not a consideration for plan creation, since the BIND command is executed outside the realm of SQL and obviously could not be set.

In both dynamic and static SQL, the CREATOR is recorded as the primary AUTHID. Qualification only applies to tables, views, and indices.

Performance considerations dictate that the actual number of secondary AUTHIDs be kept to a minimum and that exit routine processing avoid logic that could potentially degrade transaction throughput. Furthermore, catalog contention may become more of an issue as object qualifiers become less unique (i.e., as secondary AUTHIDs become more popular to express functional requirements).

AUTHORIZATION CHARTS

While the authors were finishing this book, one of their clients asked, "What authority do you need to execute a COMMENT ON statement?" We were not sure of all possible authorities, so we opened the correct manual and read the answer aloud. The client responded, "There ought to be a quick reference chart for required authorities." We decided that a quick reference table was such a great idea that we have added the charts here. We hope you appreciate it as much as our other clients have.

The tables are broken out into five diagrams, one for each of the major groups: ALTER (Table A–1), CREATE (Table A–2), the two documentation statements COMMENT ON and LABEL ON (Table A–3), DROP (Table A–4), and DML Privileges (Table A–5). The upper left-hand corner of each table will identify the major group. The actual statements are listed down the left side and the possible authorities are listed across the top. Exclusive authorities are indicated with an OR between their headings, while inclusive authorities are specified with an AND between their headings. A blank box at the intersection of a statement and an authority indicates that no authority is required.

In DB2 Version 2.1 a new column, CREATEDBY, is added to

```
SYSIBM.SYSDATABASES
SYSIBM.SYSINDEXES
SYSIBM.SYSSYNONYMS
SYSIBM.SYSTABLES
SYSIBM.SYSTABLESPACE
SYSIBM.SYSSTOGROUP
```

Which allows one AUTHID to create objects for a different AUTHID. This is accomplished with the use of the new

```
SET CURRENT SQLID = xxxxxxxx
```

statement. Therefore, the existing CREATOR column in the previously listed catalog tables implies ownership, and the new CREATEDBY column implies the AUTHID that executed the DDL statement.

In the following tables, the heading for CREATOR also implies that the CURRENT SQLID may be substituted, provided it is still one of the valid secondary composite AUTHIDs. For more information on composite AUTHIDs, please refer to the "DB2 Object Creation" section of the **Security Overview Chapter.** Note that DBADM, SYSADM, and so on, may still create, alter, and drop objects for other AUTHIDs.

TABLE A–1
DATA DEFINITION LANGUAGE ALTER AUTHORIZATION

To ALTER:	you must be the CREATOR	OR hold DATABASE privilege	OR hold SYSTEM privilege	OR hold TABLE privilege	AND hold USE privilege
INDEX	Y	DBADM	SYSADM		BUFFERPOOL
STOGROUP	Y		SYSADM		
TABLE	Y	DBADM	SYSADM	ALTER ALL	
TABLESPACE	Y	DBADM	SYSADM		BUFFERPOOL

If an index was created by an AUTHID different from the creator of its related table, then that table's creator may also alter that index.

TABLE A–2
DATA DEFINITION LANGUAGE CREATE AUTHORIZATION

To CREATE:	you must be the CREATOR	AND hold DATABASE privilege	OR hold SYSTEM privilege	OR hold TABLE privilege	AND hold USE privilege
DATABASE	Y	CREATEDBA CREATEDBC	SYSADM		BUFFERPOOL (stogroup)
INDEX		DBADM DBCTRL	SYSADM	INDEX ALL	BUFFERPOOL (stogroup)
STOGROUP	Y		SYSADM CREATESG		
SYNONYM	Y				
TABLE		CREATETAB	SYSADM		
(any AUTH)		DBADM	SYSADM		
(any AUTH)		DBCTRL			
(any AUTH)		DBMAINT			
TABLESPACE	Y	CREATETS DBADM DBCTRL DBMAINT	SYSADM		BUFFERPOOL (stogroup)
VIEW (any AUTH)	table		SYSADM	SELECT	

There is no special privilege required to create a SYNONYM. Also, only the CREATOR (OWNER) or CREATEDBY (CURRENT SQLID) AUTHID of a SYNONYM (not even SYSADM) may DROP it.

Before an INDEX or TABLESPACE name may be reused, a COMMIT, either explicit or implicit, must occur.

Prior to DB2 Version 2.1 indices, tables and views could be created by explicitly specifying the AUTHID of another user as the qualifier of the object. In Version 2.1 this explicit qualifying AUTHID becomes the CREATOR, and the AUTHID executing the statement becomes the CREATEDBY value. The same thing could be accomplished by setting the CURRENT SQLID and executing the DDL with an unqualified object name.

TABLE A–3
DATA DEFINITION LANGUAGE DOCUMENTATION STATEMENT AUTHORIZATION

| To execute: | OR | OR | OR | AND |
	you must be the CREATOR	hold DATABASE privilege	hold SYSTEM privilege	hold TABLE privilege	hold USE privilege
COMMENT ON	Y	DBADM	SYSADM		
LABEL ON	Y	DBADM	SYSADM		

No TABLE or USE privileges are required to execute a COMMENT ON or LABEL ON DDL statement. Note that both statements may be used with either a TABLE or a VIEW.

TABLE A–4
DATA DEFINITION LANGUAGE DROP AUTHORIZATION

| To DROP: | OR | OR | OR | AND |
	you must be the CREATOR	hold DATABASE privilege	hold SYSTEM privilege	hold TABLE privilege	hold USE privilege
DATABASE	Y	DBADM DBCTRL DROP	SYSADM		
INDEX	Y	DBADM	SYSADM		
STOGROUP	Y		SYSADM		
SYNONYM	Y				
TABLE	Y	DBADM	SYSADM		
TABLESPACE	Y	DBADM	SYSADM		
VIEW	Y		SYSADM		

In an application development environment it is very common to provide one data base per developer and grant DBADM to that person. Even though that person is not the creator of the data base, he or she may still drop it.

TABLE A–5
DATA MANIPULATION LANGUAGE PRIVILEGES TABLE

To execute:	OR you must be the CREATOR	OR hold DATABASE privilege	OR hold SYSTEM privilege	AND hold TABLE privilege	hold USE privilege
SELECT	Y	DBADM	SYSADM	ALL SELECT	BUFFERPOOL
UPDATE	Y	DBADM	SYSADM	ALL UPDATE	BUFFERPOOL
DELETE	Y	DBADM	SYSADM	ALL DELETE	BUFFERPOOL
INSERT	Y	DBADM	SYSADM	ALL INSERT	BUFFERPOOL
LOCK	Y	DBADM	SYSADM	ALL SELECT	

Note that an AUTHID holding DBADM authority over a data base may grant the SELECT privilege on any of its TABLEs or VIEWs, no matter who created the TABLE or VIEW.

INDEX